WHITBY
LIFEBOATS

WHITBY LIFEBOATS

AN ILLUSTRATED HISTORY

NICHOLAS LEACH

To Sarah

Front cover: Whitby lifeboat George and Mary Webb powers her way out of harbour. (Nicholas Leach)

Page 2: George and Mary Webb on exercise. (Nicholas Leach)

Published by
Landmark Publishing Ltd
The Oaks
Moor Farm Road West
Ashbourne
Derbyshire DE6 1HD
England
Tel (01335) 347349 Fax (01335) 347303
landmark@clara.net
www.landmarkpublishing.co.uk

British Library Cataloguing in Publication Data.
A catalogue record for this book is available from the British Library.

ISBN 9781843064244

Layout and design by Nicholas Leach
Printed by Cromwell Press, Trowbridge

Contents

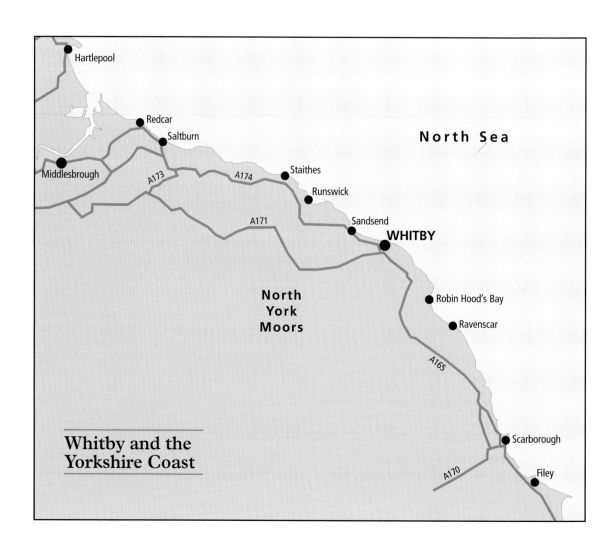

Whitby and the
Yorkshire Coast

Introduction

The port of Whitby, on the North Yorkshire heritage coast, stands astride the estuary of the river Esk, which effectively divides it in two. St Mary's Church and Whitby Abbey are on the eastern headland, visible from miles around, while Cook's statue and the famous whale bones sit atop the West Cliff. The Abbey dates back to AD675, when St Hilda founded a monastery, but it is now a ruin as a result of the actions of the Vikings and, latterly, Henry VIII. But Whitby not only has a long and proud history as a port and a town, a ruined abbey, a working harbour, and a claim to the country's best fish and chip shops, it also boasts one of the Royal National Lifeboat Institution's most famous lifeboat stations.

The Whitby lifeboat station has an unusual history because not until 1861 did it come under the auspices of the RNLI having operated independently for more than half a century. The lifeboat crews have endured their fair share of tragedy, but also been involved in many daring rescues, some of which have entered the annals of the RNLI as the most outstanding ever performed. The station is now one of the most modern, having been upgraded in 2006-7 so that the facilities for the volunteer crew are second to none.

This book provides, for the first time in one volume, a complete and detailed history of the Whitby lifeboat station, including details of all the lifeboats that have served and encompassing all the major and many of the minor rescues that have been undertaken.

Whitby's maritime past

The background to Whitby's lifeboat operations is the town's links to the sea. Up to the sixteenth century, Whitby was basically a small fishing village with a small population. However, in the early seventeenth century it expanded to transport alum produced at Sandsend, extending its shipping activities.

Its maritime importance was enhanced when it became a centre for whaling,

Approaching Whitby harbour in heavy weather, taken from on board the 47ft Tyne City of Sheffield. This gives an idea of the difficulties faced by vessels trying to enter the port. (By courtesy of Whitby RNLI)

with the first whaling ship leaving for Greenland in 1753. This initiated a new phase in the town's development, and by 1795 Whitby was a major centre for the whaling industry. Between 1753 and 1833 more than 2,500 whales were brought back to Whitby, and their blubber was boiled on the quaysides to make oil. The explorer Captain James Cook, who was apprenticed to a Whitby shipowner in 1746, also helped to elevate Whitby's status and expand its seafaring base.

During the industrial expansion that took place between 1750 and 1850, trade was dominated by the movement of coal from the ports of Newcastle and Sunderland to London, passing Whitby on its way and the coal trade was the largest single activity of coastal shipping for much of the nineteenth century. A variety of other commodities were also carried, and vessels crowded the North Sea shipping lanes and passed the Yorkshire coast.

The nationwide expansion of shipping and trade was reflected in Whitby, where the harbour expanded during the seventeenth century in response to the burgeoning coal trade. The tonnage of shipping registered in Whitby during the eighteenth century grew as well, almost sixfold, from 8,300 tons in 1702 to 47,900 tons in 1788. At the same time, tonnage registered in London went from 140,000 to 315,300 and in Newcastle from 11,000 to an incredible 106,100. Whitby was, in 1788, the seventh largest port in terms of registered tonnage, and it grew to accommodate the trade, with quays and wharves developed to facilitate shipping, all of which led to an increase in prosperity for Whitby's merchants.

Whitby was also a centre of shipbuilding and at one time the town boasted of being the country's second biggest shipbuilding location, with eleven yards along the estuary of the Esk constructing vessels of various sizes. Fishing was also an important occupation for many in the town, although it was overshadowed by the growth of whaling. Until the late twentieth century many in the town were employed in fishing and the fishing fleet was quite large. The port continued to receive large commercial vessels until the 1990s, but now the majority of craft using the quays do so only for pleasure.

Acknowledgements

I am grateful to many people at Whitby lifeboat station who have assisted with the compilation of this book. Peter Thomson, Curator of the Lifeboat Museum, got the project under way by expressing his desire to have Whitby's long and complicated lifeboat history contained within a single volume; Coxswain Mike Russell, Mechanic Glenn Goodberry, Lifeboat Operations Manager Roy Weatherill and former Coxswain Keith Stuart have all answered many questions. Jeff Morris provided a selection of excellent photos, and kindly supplied extra information about photos. Des Sythes, Curator of Photographs, and Mark Edwards, at Whitby Museum, provided access to numerous historic images of the town's lifeboats, and their cooperation and assistance are most appreciated. At the RNLI, Brian Wead in the Rescue Records Section provided informaton to fill various gaps, as did Barry Cox, the Honorary Librarian, and I am grateful to them both. Arnold Taylor, Tony Denton, John Harrop and Dave Charlton also provided illustrations for possible use. Finally, my gratitude as always to Sarah for her help and support during my researches and writing, and for sharing many enjoyable visits to Whitby.

Nicholas Leach, Lichfield, September 2008

Bibliography

Barker, Malcolm: *Portrait of a Lifeboat Hero: The Story of Henry Freeman of Whitby* (Smith Settle Ltd, Otley, 2000).

Brittain, Colin: *Into the Maelstrom: The wreck of HMHS Rohilla* (Tempus Publishing Ltd, Stroud, Glos, 2002).

Davies, Joan: 'Whitby: The Lifeboat Station and her people' in *The Lifeboat* journal, Vol.XLVI, pp.162-65 (1979).

Humble, A. F.: *The Rowing Lifeboats of Whitby* (1974).

Lister, J. Robin: 'Hazards, Thrills and Tragedy', in *Country Life*, 31 March 1983.

Morris, Jeff: *The Story of the Whitby Lifeboats* (1982, 1989, and 1997).

Whitworth, Alan: *The Story of the Whitby Lifeboat Robert Whitworth* (Culva House Publications, 1999).

The First Lifeboats at Whitby

The establishment of lifeboats at Whitby came at a time when trade along the east coast was expanding and the necessary finance to pay for such a boat was available. The port had become an important harbour of refuge by the nineteenth century and was often used by vessels plying the increasingly busy North Sea shipping lanes which were populated by sailing vessels which, if caught in a sudden gale, particularly from the north or east, could be driven helplessly towards the shore. They would therefore make for a roadstead where the land might offer a little shelter and the seabed provide good ground for an anchor, enabling them to safely ride out the storm.

North of the Tees, Hartlepool Roads offered good shelter, as did the Roads of Bridlington south of Whitby, but, in between, the cliffs, headlands and reefs offered little in the way of safety. Whitby was situated in the middle of this dangerous coast and as a result proposals were made to turn it into a harbour of refuge. The entrance to the river Esk, however, was narrow, shallow and poorly marked, and only in the eighteenth century were attempts made to improve it.

The east coast coal trade provided a solution to the most difficult problem faced when building harbours of refuge, which was not a practical or technical one, but rather a financial one. Harbours built for ships engaged in the coal trade could be funded by levying a tax on ships entering port. In 1701 an Act of Parliament granted duties on all coal leaving the northern ports to be used for the maintenance of piers at Whitby and, as a result, two old piers were largely rebuilt. Further Acts in 1735 and 1750 provided funds for their improvement, and later Acts supported other works which made Whitby a crowded anchorage when storms forced ships to seek shelter.

But the harbour entrance was still dangerous with conditions on the bar frequently treacherous. To improve access

The entrance to Whitby harbour in a storm, with the piers being lashed by breaking seas. The slipway on the left down onto the West Beach was used by the lifeboats for many years, and the stone piers were built during the nineteenth century to create a harbour of refuge.

during the nineteenth century, two stone piers were built with a lighthouse on the end of each. The West Pier lighthouse of 1831, the first navigation aid to be built, was an 83ft stone column with a square base. The East Pier lighthouse, on the East Breakwater, was built in 1855 and was a smaller tower, at 55ft, with a round base. This light was discontinued when the pier extensions were built.

In 1914, the entrance channel was further improved when the pier extensions were constructed. Each was stone based with raised wooden sections, marked at their extremities by light beacons. The West Pier light consists of a 26ft green lantern showing a fixed green light visible for three miles. The East Pier light, which displayed a fixed red light visible for three miles, consisted of a red lantern mounted on a 45ft square wooden support.

The piers with their lights improved access to Whitby harbour, but a further aid to navigation was introduced in the mid-nineteenth century, in the form of a lighthouse two miles east of Whitby at Ling Hill. This made it easier for ships travelling down the east coast to navigate safely. The lighthouse, known as Whitby High, was constructed in 1858 by Trinity House to James Walker's design, and originally consisted of two towers aligned to mark Whitby Rock. The lower light, a 66ft white octagonal tower, was deactivated in 1890 and later demolished.

The High Light was refurbished and the 44ft octagonal tower equipped with a more effective light mounted in an octagonal lantern. The Whitby Rock was marked by a red sector and the electrically powered isophase white and red light now in use is visible for eighteen miles. Two single-storey keepers' dwellings were built on each side, and a fog signal station, now non-operational, was constructed.

The early lifeboats

But despite the improvements to harbours and the building of aids to navigation, ships continued to be wrecked. Safely navigating the entrance to harbours such as Whitby was often fraught with danger, and the solution to aiding vessels once they were in difficulty close to shore was the construction of a shore-based lifeboat. Vessels attempting to enter Whitby were faced with numerous dangers from reefs, sandbanks and the narrow harbour entrance itself. When they foundered or got into difficulty, they were in full view of the town's populace, who could usually only watch helplessly.

To remedy the situation, at the start of the nineteenth century a lifeboat was acquired. At this time, Britain's industrialisation was starting to take hold, and the country's expanding economy had a bearing on the establishment of the nation's first lifeboat stations. Indeed, the

The High Light, two miles east of Whitby, was built in 1858 by Trinity House and remains operational, although since 1992 it has not been manned. When first established, the station consisted of two towers to mark Whitby Rock but the lower light was deactivated in 1890 and subsequently demolished. (Nicholas Leach)

financing, building and manning of the first lifeboats should be seen in the context of the development of the industrial base. Whitby was one of a number of ports, the majority on the east coast, where, in the early 1800s, sufficient money was available to fund and operate a lifeboat.

The origins of Whitby's first lifeboat can be found on the Tyne, where the first boat designed specifically for life-saving was built. This boat, 28ft 6in in length and 9ft 6in in breadth with a curved or rockered keel, was constructed by boatbuilder Henry Greathead in 1790 at South Shields, and operated from there for several decades. A second boat was built by Greathead in 1798 and stationed at North Shields. This second boat was 2ft larger than the first boat with a greater beam, but was essentially the same. The design was double-ended so that it was unnecessary to turn the craft in heavy surf and bring it broadside to the seas, with Greathead describing its as follows:

> 'She requires twelve men to work her; five men on each side – with an oar slung over an iron thole with a grommet so as to enable the rower to pull either way, and one man at each end to steer her, and to be ready at the opposite end to take the steer-oar when wanted'.

Soon after completing his second boat, Greathead realised that by promoting his lifeboat design he could generate a demand and construct further such boats, thus benefiting financially. His motives seem to have been essentially financial, but he received support from an influential publication, the *Gentleman's Magazine*, which reported the work of those boats he had built and showed them to be of 'great humanitarian benefit'. Greathead mounted his own promotional campaign with the help of Sir John Edward Swinburne, an influential parliamentary figure.

As a result of this, Greathead came into contact with the London-based insurers Lloyd's, who, in May 1802, awarded him 'the sum of one hundred guineas . . . as an acknowledgement of his talents and exertions in inventing and building a Life Boat'. At the same time, the insurers realised that lifeboats could help to reduce ship losses, and thus reduce moneys paid out to shipowners. At a General Meeting of Lloyd's Subscribers on 20 May 1802, a resolution was passed which

> 'made available the sum of £2,000 from their fund . . . for the purpose of encouraging the building of Life Boats, on different parts of the coast . . . The Parties desirous of the undertaking . . . at the different ports or places are to engage Men and take care of the Boats at their own expense'.

It was agreed that each applicant should receive £50 towards the cost of the boat once it had been delivered to its station, but Lloyd's would play no part in the management, maintenance or upkeep of any boats. This fund, promoted by J. J. Angerstein, the Chairman of Lloyd's, provided a considerable impetus to early lifeboat building, and helped pay for almost thirty lifeboats down to the 1820s, including several on the east coast.

In 1802, Greathead built boats for, among other places, Redcar and Holy Island. Another lifeboat, built for Scarborough in 1801, was not constructed by Greathead but was built to his design, and the same was the case with the Hartlepool lifeboat built in 1802. Lloyd's contributed towards both the Hartlepool and Redcar boats, voting the standard £50 contribution to each on 28 July 1802. The Redcar boat, the eleventh built by Greathead, has an unusual history and enjoyed an impressively long life, surviving today to claim the title of the oldest lifeboat in existence. She performed her last service on 28 October 1880, and, although not in use, survived until eventually placed on display in Redcar.

Whitby's position at the heart of the east coast shipping highway, with vessels moving goods from the burgeoning ports of the north-east to the expanding capital straddling the bustling river Thames, made it a prime candidate for one of Greathead's lifeboats. The large number of vessels passing and often entering the port, and the expansion of wealth in the town,

combined to create conditions favourable for the establishment of a lifeboat. The need for such a boat at Whitby was evident when, on 1 January 1800, seventy-one laden colliers, which had sailed from Shields and Sunderland, were caught in a gale, and all but two were wrecked just off the port with considerable loss of life.

The ingredients for providing a lifeboat were present – the need was obvious; a suitable design of boat could be built at a port nearby; and Lloyd's would provide some of the funding. Francis Gibson, Collector of Customs at Whitby, began raising funds for the boat and enlisted a number of subscribers. Details of Gibson's work, how much money was raised and how the money was administered are not known. However, once sufficient finance was raised, he approached Lloyd's for a grant and a lifeboat was ordered from Greathead, with a low, four-wheeled transporting carriage, at a cost of £160.

The new boat arrived at Whitby on the evening of 15 September 1802. She was 30ft long, rowed ten oars and had the rockered keel typical of Greathead's design, which had become known as the North Country type. On 15 October 1802, Gibson notified Lloyd's of the acquisition for Whitby and, on 10 November 1802, the insurers voted their draft of £50. Gibson and his associates found extra money to build a boathouse and a site, close to the West Pier, was

The first lifeboat at Whitby was built by Henry Greathead of South Shields and was similar in appearance to this line drawing which was published in contemporary journals.

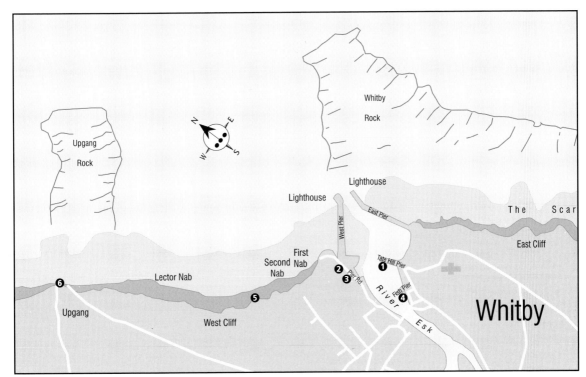

obtained from which the boat could be launched over the West Beach. This boathouse stood until 1847, at which time it was removed to make way for the Khyber Pass, a new road up the West Cliff.

The new lifeboat was launched for the first time in December 1802 when she saved the crew of the sloop *Edinburgh*. An account of the rescue appeared in the *Newcastle Chronicle* on 11 December 1802:

'At about eleven o'clock in the forenoon, nearly at low water, the wind blowing strong ENE, and the sea very high, the sloop Edinburgh, Joseph Poole, Master, coal laden from Sunderland, in attempting to enter the harbour grounded (as was expected) a considerable distance from the pier head. A coble, which had with some difficulty proceeded over the bar . . ., being struck by a heavy sea, was instantly overset, and the people, three in number, plunged into the water. Being excellent swimmers, they gained the shore, nearly exhausted by their efforts, and were conducted up the beach by some sailors who at the hazard of their lives had ventured among the breakers to receive them. While the poor men were struggling . . . the lifeboat (being the first time of its

being employed) was brought down and launched into the water, when a party of sailors . . . pushed her through the heavy surf, proceeded to the vessel, took out the crew and brought them to shore.'
This was the only rescue performed by the Greathead lifeboat of which details are known. If she carried out any further rescues, details are missing, and she subsequently became disliked by the local boatmen. After the death of Francis Gibson in 1805, enthusiasm for life-saving matters declined, and the boat deteriorated through neglect. It is possible that Gibson had the assistance of a committee when originally obtaining the lifeboat, but, if anyone else was involved (and no record exists of a committee), they made no efforts to ensure the lifeboat was properly maintained after Gibson had died.

George William Manby, a Norfolk resident with a military background who wrote extensively on a wide range of subjects including shipwreck, found the boat disliked when he visited the area, about a decade after the boat had been built. Manby is best known for his life-saving mortar, which he developed in 1807 and with which a shot with a line attached could be fired from the shore to a shipwrecked vessel. His invention was

Map of Whitby and the immediate coastline. The numbers indicate the various positions of the lifeboat stations around the harbour and at Upgang. They are as follows: (1) Tate Hill Pier (on davits) 1822–63, (2) Pier Road (two adjacent sites) 1802–63, 1863–94 and 1895–1957 (double boathouse), (3) Pier Road (south) 1847–95, (4) Fish Pier 1919-2005 (afloat since 1974 with ILB in boathouse) and 2007 onwards, (5) ILB house 1968–74, and (6) Upgang 1865–1919. See map on page 46 for more detail of the Pier Road boathouses. The Coates Marine site used from 2005 to 2007 is not marked.

quite widely used at various points along the east coast, and was generally successful in helping to save lives from shipwreck.

Manby also went on a tour of the coast and published, in 1813, a 'General Report on the Survey of the Eastern Coast of England for the purpose of carrying into effect and establishing the system for saving ship-wrecked persons'. In this Report, he described most of the ports along the east coast, assessing their dangers and indicating what kind of life-saving measures he believed were most suitable for each locality.

Manby described Whitby as presenting 'every feature of horror to a navigator's mind, from the broken water indicating sunken rocks, rugged cliffs, and extreme flat shores'. He recommended one of his own mortars, a six-pounder, which, 'from its portability can be used with great success'. He recommended a slightly smaller five-and-a-half inch mortar for use at Sandsend, and similar equipment for Runswick and Staithes. He also commented on the lifeboat at Whitby:

> 'For the sake of humanity, I had to regret . . . that the life-boat was in total disuse, from a general prejudice against it; although certainly the place offers advantages peculiar to a boat of this description, by having a harbour to go from, but they assured me its size and weight prevented a possibility of her being forced against a violent wind and over a high raging sea. To impel her by the power of oars, from a flat shore, in such weather as described, when the surfs are broken or white water, I admitted to be impossible, but urged the advantage here, of going out with the ebb tide. Finding the prejudice rooted, that nothing would induce them to use it again, I submitted the plan of a boat, . . . which was much approved, constructed by me in . . . 1808, for the use of the public, and sent to the Island of Anhalt for their benefit.'

What followed as a result of Manby's suggestions is not known, but it seems they were largely ignored. He never supplied a lifeboat to Whitby, or indeed to any other place in England, but his mortars were widely used. It seems that the 1802 lifeboat was, by the second decade of the century, completely out of use and seen by those who would man it as unsuitable. This is somewhat surprising given the success of similar boats elsewhere along the east coast, which had geographical features similar to Whitby, such as flat shores and sandy beaches.

By 1817, the boat was reported as being 'quite unserviceable' as Dr Young's *History of Whitby*, published in 1817, explained:

> 'Whitby is provided with a life-boat. . . It has saved several lives and some vessels, and would have saved many more had it been smaller; for being large and clumsy, it requires too much

The East Side lifeboat house on Tate Hill pier was used from 1822 until 1863. By the 1860s, both boathouses on the West Side were damp, and the one on Tate Hill Pier had almost reached the end of its useful life. The rope ladders, used to reach the crews of ships aground close to the East Cliff, also needed repair.

time to get it launched and manned. At present it is quite unserviceable.'

It is not clear whether the problems with the boat's size were the actual reason for its lack of use, or whether this explanation was just Dr Young speculating.

Although the initial enthusiasm to get the boat built and in operation ensured the boat's construction in 1802, maintaining and using the craft needed a degree of finance and organisation that was subsequently lacking. The soft sand at the foot of the slipway may have made launching difficult, but delays in getting the boat into the water were likely to have been caused as much by poor organisation as the clumsiness of the boat. The economic downturn of the second decade of the century would also have reduced finance available for lifeboat matters, and so Whitby's first lifeboat can be regarded as something of a failure.

A few years after Dr Young's book was published, the situation improved with the building of two new lifeboats and the formation of an organisation to manage them. The impetus for the construction of the new boats is unclear, but it may have been a storm on 4 November 1821. The *Yorkshire Gazette* described the events that day when a fierce gale hit the east coast, wrecking eight vessels at Scarborough, six at Redcar and fifteen at Hartlepool. This incident may have helped to stimulate a renewed bout of lifeboat building in the area for, although no mention was made of any shipwrecks at Whitby, the following year two new lifeboats were built for the town and in 1823 Seaton Carew (a small town south of Hartlepool), Scarborough and Filey each had new lifeboats built, and Bridlington followed suit in 1826.

Of the two new lifeboats for Whitby, one replaced Greathead's boat, which must have been completely unserviceable by this stage. The new boat, built by Wake, of Sunderland, at a cost of £100, was on the same lines as Greathead's and, like her predecessor, was housed in the lifeboat house of 1802 close to the West Pier. She was usually launched down the slipway and across the beach. Known as the 'Sunderland Boat' or the 'West Side Boat', she was 26ft 6in long, with a beam of 9ft 3in, and rowed ten oars. She lasted for more than half a century, and, although

condemned in 1860, she was then bought by a group of fishermen, rebuilt, renamed *Fishermen's Friend*, and used for harbour work for many years. There is no record of her after 1889, when she was advertised for sale, and she may have left the area.

The other boat, known as the 'East Side Boat', was similar to the Wake-built boat and was 26ft long, with a beam of 9ft 6in, pulling ten oars. She was built by local boatbuilder Christopher Gale, of Church Street, and was smaller and lighter than Wake's boat. She was intended for work inside the harbour and on the harbour bar. Variously known as 'Mr Gale's Boat', 'The Green Boat' or 'The East Side Boat', she was in later years named *Petrel*. This boat was suspended from two large stanchions built on the landward side of Tate Hill Pier, from which she was lowered into the water. She was protected by a wooden shed, standing partly on the pier and partly on heavy timbers projecting over the water, supported by wooden brackets. This unusual boathouse was constructed by the Piers and Harbour Board on behalf of the Whitby Lifeboat Association. The Board's accounts shows that Mr Campion, acting for the Association, paid the Board £30 for the work in 1823.

Precise details of services by these boats are lacking, although they seem to have been quite well used as vessels often got into difficulty near the port and needed assistance. Some notes published in the *Whitby Repository* for 1827 detailed wrecks that occurred and the rescues undertaken, but information about the involvement of the lifeboats was somewhat scant. On 29 January, the vessel *Active*, of Aberdeen, came ashore on Whitby Rock around midnight and soon started to sink, but her crew were saved. On 17 February, five vessels were stranded off Whitby during a severe storm; they were *Oak, Comet* and *Henry & Mary*, all of Whitby, *Traveller*, of Sunderland, and *Ann*, of Stockton. The crews of each vessel were saved by the lifeboats, and all the vessels later got off and were brought into harbour, except *Oak* which became a total wreck.

Other vessels got into difficulty during 1827. On 20 April, *Pedestrian*, of Shields, bound for London, was driven onto Whitby Rock in dense fog, but, after throwing out much of her cargo of coal, floated clear unaided. When the crew of a collier was forced to jettison their cargo, as in this instance, the fishermen would fill their cobles seeing that, as the coal was being discarded, it could be legitimately collected for their own use.

On 12 August 1827, during a north-easterly squall, the sixty-three-ton sloop *Comet* was driven ashore near Upgang, but was subsequently got off. This was the second time *Comet* had stranded near Whitby, but, like most of the other vessels at this time, she was fairly small and refloating her was quite straightforward. On 23 October, *Despatch*, in ballast, struck the West Pier while attempting to enter the harbour in an easterly gale and was damaged. Later in the year, the ship *Speedwell* struck the bar while entering harbour, but was refloated after she had discharged most of her cargo of coal.

In these accounts, the lifeboat is mentioned only once and, although its services were obviously needed, whether it was used is not recorded. A letter published in the *Whitby Repository* in December 1827 criticised the management of the lifeboats, suggesting that the boats were not used. Although the craft themselves were regarded as excellent, they were neglected and a regular crew was not formed. Comparisons were made to the lifeboat at Shields, where preparations were made for launching as soon as a storm broke out. In contrast at Whitby nothing was done, and delays in gathering men to form a crew, many of whom had never been in a lifeboat, meant the boats rarely went out. Payments were only occasionally made to the crew if sufficient funds were available and, even then, they were not paid promptly.

Reforms were needed and a properly constituted organisation, with a treasurer, secretary and committee of management, was needed. Regular annual subscriptions also needed to be paid to ensure the organisation could carry out its work. A levy on masters whose ships had been helped into harbour was advocated, providing funds with which to pay the lifeboat crew. The boats were to be taken out for practice once a quarter, so that the crews could be exercised.

The need for these reforms was tragically demonstrated the following year

in another incident which led to further criticism of the operation of the lifeboats. About 5am on 13 September 1828, a group of pilots and Preventive men (forerunners of the Coastguard) on the East Pier noticed a small collier, *Elizabeth* of Hull, approaching the harbour in a strong north-easterly gale. She appeared to be unmanageable and heading towards Whitby Rock. Lieut King, the Preventive Officer, suggested that the lifeboat should be launched, although a rescue would be extremely hazardous. The collier drifted onto the Rock about a quarter of a mile from the pier, and was soon on her beam ends. The three men and one woman on board got out their boat and tried to reach shore, but a few minutes later were thrown into the water and drowned. No bodies were recovered, but the collier was carried in by the tide and stranded on rocks just beyond the Spa Ladder, where it broke up.

Although the facts as stated here suggest that nothing could be done to aid the collier, an article published in the October 1828 edition of the *Whitby Repository*, signed 'ZZZ', painted a different picture and the author concluded that the lives were lost because the spectators displayed 'the most appalling apathy and recklessness'. This statement caused considerable resentment amongst the town's seafaring community, and a furious dispute ensued between 'ZZZ' and another writer, 'Amicus', whose views appeared in the *Panorama*, one of Whitby's three literary magazines.

Whatever the accuracy of the accounts or the correctness of the assertions on either side, concern was expressed about the inadequacies of the lifeboats. Attention was drawn to the fact that, although the town had two relatively new lifeboats, no attempt had been made to use them to help the collier. 'ZZZ' stated that there were 'no rules or regulations . . . [and] no plan' for getting the lifeboat to launch and another writer stated that, when a ship was in danger, long discussions were usually held as to whether the lifeboat should go out, resulting in an unnecessary delay.

These criticisms highlighted serious problems with the management of the lifeboats, one of which was the need for some kind of committee. When the two boats had been built in 1822, a committee

had been in place to collect subscriptions, draw up specifications and administer funds. Although this committee still existed six years later, little was known of its activities, and its members failed to offer any leadership when *Elizabeth* was lost. Two days after the wreck, the lifeboat was launched to save a man who had fallen from the West Pier, and it got to sea very quickly on this occasion. But, despite this, the criticism aroused by the boat's failure to attempt to rescue the crew of *Elizabeth* was not allayed. While public indignation was not directed at the lifeboat crew, several members of the committee resigned as a result of the criticism.

Although this is the first recorded reference to a lifeboat committee, undoubtedly one existed in 1822 when the two new boats were bought. Mr Campion's payment for the new boathouse on Tate Hill Pier suggests that, as a banker, he had been appointed Treasurer to the Committee. Indeed, he served the Lifeboat Association for more than twenty-five years, resigning the chairmanship in 1847 aged seventy-four. If Francis Gibson formed a committee in 1802, it is possible that Campion was a member then, for although he was only twenty-nine at the time, he was a wealthy and prominent man in the town, and his involvement in such matters is likely.

On 14 November 1828, two months after the *Elizabeth* wreck, a public meeting of subscribers to the Lifeboat Fund was held in the Town Hall, with Campion acting as Chairman. During the meeting, the subscribers re-elected eight members of the old committee, including Campion, Mr Yeomans and Mr Chapman, and appointed sixteen new members, all of whom were well known in the town. One of these was Francis Pickernell, the engineer to the Harbour Board, and another George Willis, the Harbour Master, both of whom served as Secretary in later years. The meeting passed a series of resolutions, which were published in summary form in the *Whitby Panorama*, providing the first definite information about the constitution and running of the Lifeboat Association.

Although the subscribers met only rarely, they held the power within the Association. In 1828 they appointed a committee and indicated the general lines of policy which they expected it to follow. At this time, each boat had a captain (rather than a coxswain, as the position was subsequently known), with the subscribers deciding that 'William Douglas and W. Wilson, who are captains of the boats, shall not deliver up the keys of the life-boat houses to any person unless a member of the Committee be present'. The subscribers wished to prevent 'improper persons getting into the boats and damaging them'. This implies that difficulty in finding keys and damage to equipment may have accounted for delays in launching. No other reference has ben

Model of the lifeboat Petrel. This lifeboat was built locally by Christopher Gale and was involved in the dramatic rescue from the barque Royal Rose. (Nicholas Leach, by courtesy of Whitby Museum)

A model of the East Side lifeboat at the Mystic Seaport Museum in Connecticut, USA. The lifeboat was built by Christopher Gale at Whitby, and is variously described as 28ft by 9ft with eight oars, and 26ft by 9ft 3in with ten oars. She was undoubtedly altered several times during her career, which lasted until well into the 1860s. In 1861 she was taken over by the RNLI and became the No.2 lifeboat, being renamed Petrel in 1863. She was broken up in 1872 after being replaced. (By courtesy of Whitby Museum)

found to either a captain or a coxswain of the lifeboats until the RNLI got involved.

Coastguard rescue work

The forerunners of the Coastguard, the Preventative Water Guard (PWG), played a prominent role in rescue work at Whitby during the first half of the nineteenth century. The Water Guard was established in 1809 to tackle smuggling in coastal waters, and seven years later was joined by a new service, the Coast Blockade, launched by the Admiralty to operate onshore. By 1831 both the Coast Blockade and Water Guard had been absorbed into the newly formed Coastguard.

At most Coastguard stations, the chief officer, chief boatman and boatman were usually experienced naval seamen and thus well suited to life-saving matters. During the 1820s and 1830s, many Coastguardsmen demonstrated considerable courage and bravery in rescue work and their efforts on many occasions were recognised by the Royal National Institution for the Preservation of Life from Shipwreck (RNIPLS).

The RNIPLS was founded in March 1824 with responsibility for 'the preservation of lives and property from shipwreck'. This encompassed the funding, building, operation, maintenance and organisation of lifeboats and lifeboat stations throughout the British Isles. The Institution also presented Gold and Silver medals to reward acts of exceptional bravery to anyone saving lives at sea. Several awards were made by the Institution to Whitby Coastguardsmen who, despite the problems with the management and operation of the lifeboats described above, used the lifeboats to carry out some fine rescues as well as undertaking rescue work independently.

A rescue took place off Whitby in September 1829 which the RNIPLS recorded in its Annual Report and which involved the Coastguard and fishermen cooperating closely. The brig *Aurora* got into difficulty and the lifeboat, manned by five Coastguard men lead by Lieut R. E. Pym, was used to rescue nine men and the master's wife from the brig. Pym was awarded the Institution's Gold medal for his efforts, and twenty-one others shared £13 from the Institution and a further £13 given by the Whitby Lifeboat Committee. Evidently a double crew was needed for this rescue, but further details of the exact course of events have not been found.

The next rescue involving both the lifeboat and Coastguard was to the 161-ton brig *Smales*, owned by local shipowner Gideon Smales, which stranded in bad weather. The brig arrived in Whitby Roads on 19 January 1830 and took a pilot on board. Shortly before midday the following day, in a north-easterly gale and constant snow showers, *Smales* attempted to enter the harbour. However, in the terrible conditions, she was driven on to the sands near the West Pier. Captain Morgan, RN, Inspector Commodore at Whitby, described what happened next:

> 'The crew had taken to the top, but were in great danger from the sea breaking over the mastheads, and in consequence of a strong flood tide the lifeboat could not make way against the violence of the elements, to their assistance. At this critical period, Lieut R. Jones, RN, Chief Officer of Coastguard, and four men, launched the four-oared gig, and at the imminent hazard of their lives, succeeded in reaching the wreck, when the gig was almost immediately swamped. The Lieutenant then secured the crew, several of whom must otherwise have been swept overboard, being completely exhausted from cold, wet and hunger when, the tide having changed, the lifeboat got off to their assistance and saved all hands, being ten of the crew and Lieut Jones and his four men'.

Although the report does not say which lifeboat carried out the rescue, an article in the *Whitby Repository* indicates it was that from the East Side. The newspaper states that no attempt was made to launch the West Side boat which, normally, would be taken down the slipway and launched from the beach.

When *Smales* was stranded, the state of the tide made conditions at the slipway impossible to launch through. The slipway itself was narrow, with the stone pier on one side and the stonework of the Battery Parade on the other. The descent to the beach was steep and, in rough weather,

the seas were funnelled between the pier and the stonework, creating strong cross currents which swept up the slipway, and producing a strong undertow. It was known that launching the West Side lifeboat at the height of a storm was impossible as the waves would just drive the boat ashore again, or more likely, smash the boat against the stonework on either side of the slipway.

The *Repository* stated that Lieut Jones launched his gig 'down the sandway', taking a considerable risk in so doing. Even when he reached *Smales*, all he could do was make sure that the crew did not get washed overboard before further help arrived. Two hours later, when the tide had fallen sufficiently to allow a boat to be launched, the East Side boat was launched but, when almost at the end of the East Pier, for some reason was ordered back by Gideon Smales. By the time the lifeboat had returned to her station, Captain Willis, the harbour master, who was in charge of the lifeboats, realised what had happened and immediately ordered the crew to launch the boat again, and subsequently the crew of *Smales*, together with Lieut Jones and his men, were landed on the beach.

It is not clear why Smales ordered the lifeboat to return, but his actions were not approved. The *Whitby Magazine*, always looking at ways to question the operation of the lifeboat, criticised the inactivity of the West Side boat, and suggested that in a storm it should be out of its shed, on its wheels, ready for launching.

Five days later, on 23 January 1830, two smacks from Dundee were wrecked on Whitby Rocks and Lieut Jones again went out in the small galley, this time with seven men, to help. At considerable risk, and after a long, hard struggle, they reached the vessels. However, the gale worsened, creating very heavy seas, and

The Bronze medal presented to Lieut George P. Brittain, RN, by the Corporation of Lloyd's on 12 December 1838 for saving nine of twelve crew from the brig Middlesbrough in December 1837. Brittain, a pilot, was described as 'Steersman of the Whitby Lifeboat', and received Gold and Silver medals from the RNIPLS for rescues in 1837 and 1838. The medal is on display in the Whitby Museum. (Nicholas Leach)

Lieut Jones had to call for assistance from the lifeboat. The East Side lifeboat was launched and managed to save the crews of both smacks, ten men in all, while Lieut Jones and his crew reached the shore safely unaided. The seven men who had gone out with Jones were awarded £1 each for their services and, for his fine seamanship and gallantry during this incident and that of five days earlier, Jones was awarded a Gold medal by the RNIPLS.

Less than a year later, Jones received the 'golden boat', the equivalent of a clasp or bar to his medal, for a rescue on 12 December 1830 when he swam from the beach to the stranded collier *Northfield*, which had been wrecked during a severe gale with heavy hail storms. After reaching the casualty, he returned to shore with a rope which was used to save the entire crew. To establish communication between shore and vessel was a hazardous undertaking and Jones was nearly swept away several times by the surf.

During the late 1830s, the lifeboat crews were kept fairly busy and, although no systematic records were kept, accounts of a number of rescues exist. The *Hull Advertiser* reported that, on 1 July 1835, the brig *Thales*, bound from Sierra Leone to Sunderland with teak, palm oil and pepper, was dismasted in Sandsend Roads, and driven ashore in a heavy north-easterly gale. The lifeboat, probably the West Side boat, was dragged several miles across the beach to Sandsend, as there was no road at that time, and saved the crew of ten as well as the pilots who were on board.

On 29 October 1837, during a severe north-westerly gale, the brig *Ivanhoe* ran aground half-a-mile north of the West Pier. In very heavy seas, the West Side lifeboat was launched under the command of Lieut George Brittain and saved the crew of eight. Two months later, on 21 December, Lieut Brittain and his crew went to the brig *Middlesborough*, of Stockton, laden with coal, which had been driven ashore in an easterly gale. Although a man and a boy had been swept overboard from the brig, the lifeboat succeeded in saving nine others from the vessel. For his gallantry on this service, Lieut Brittain was given the Honorary

Silver Medal by Lloyd's, awarded at the organisation's General Meeting of 14 March 1838, and, for both rescues, the RNIPLS awarded him its Silver medal.

At twilight on 29 October 1838, the brig *Jupiter* of Whitby, carrying coal, was wrecked between Upgang and Whitby. She lost a mast and her sails were torn to pieces. Lieut Brittain and ten men launched the lifeboat through mountainous seas, and, according to the RNIPLS report of the incident,

> 'With the greatest difficulty and at the risk of their lives, for the boat filled twice, reached the *Jupiter* and rescued the nine men who had been clinging to the rigging'.

Lieut Brittain was awarded a Gold medal by the Institution for this rescue, and the crew were given £5 for their part. *Jupiter* was refloated on 2 November 1838, when the storm had blown itself out, and sailed on for a number of years.

The Lifeboat Association

Since 1822, the Whitby Life-Boat Association had been responsible for the running of the lifeboats. The organisation had three tiers of operation: in overall charge were the subscribers, beneath whom was a committee whose members reported to the subscribers; and beneath the committee was the secretary who was responsible for the weekly running of the lifeboats. Captain George Willis was in the position in 1828, but resigned the post in October 1835, and in his place Francis Pickernell was appointed at a salary of £5 per annum. The committee had been elected at the meeting of the subscribers held in 1828, after the loss of *Elizabeth*, of Hull, described above, which had highlighted some inadequacies in the lifeboats' management.

Meetings of the committee were very rare and when the members did get together only routine business was dealt with. On average five members attended the meetings, on one occasion only three were present, and gradually numbers dwindled as members died or moved away from the area. On 20 February 1840, the subscribers met to fill fourteen vacancies on the Committee, to approve the accounts for the year 1839, and to amend

The stanchions on Tate Hill Pier (above) pictured in the 1960s before they were demolished, and Tate Hill Pier seen from the West Side of the harbour. The Pier has been little altered since, apart from the removal of the stanchions. (Photos by courtesy of Grahame Farr)

the rules. A published report of this meeting gives an insight into the operation of the Association.

The report, for circulation amongst the subscribers, stated that the Association had two functions: to provide a lifeboat at Whitby, and to insure subscribers against being called upon to pay lifeboat charges if one of the ships on the Association's register should be wrecked near the port. This register had been created in 1840, when eighty-three persons had listed 116 ships, and the register was printed in the report. The ships varied from the forty-two-ton smack *Duke of York* to the 399-ton whaling ship *Camden*. The shipowners paid the Association half-a-crown for each vessel registered.

The rules and the statement of accounts which accompanied the register provides

an indication of how the Association was organised. The lifeboats were manned by fishermen and practice launches were held, although a regular crew was not appointed. If the boat was launched on service but failed to save life, the crew received nothing, even though the risks might well have been considerable. A service to a Whitby fishing vessel was also unpaid, whether men were rescued or not, because it was supposed the fishermen would have helped each other in any circumstances without thinking of payment. If, however, men were saved from a wreck, the lifeboat's crew of twelve each received eleven shillings, unless the rescue involved no risk. This sometimes happened when a vessel ran on to Whitby Rock in fog, in a flat calm, in which cases each man received five shillings, although the full rate was usually paid. When a vessel belonging to a subscriber needed lifeboat service, the Association met all the expenses. Owners of non-registered vessels were required to pay the boatmen's fees, the cost of horses for launching and the cost of any repairs.

Raising the necessary funds to continue rescue work was always difficult, and, when owners of ships that had been wrecked failed to pay, the Association found itself in considerable financial difficulty. The Report of 1840 stated that, of the five ships which had been wrecked during 1839, the owners of two, *Brilliant* and *John and Anne*, had not yet paid for the use of the lifeboat. As the annual income from the subscribers amounted to approximately £15, the failure of these owners to pay the £9 15s due from them was a serious matter. Fortunately, incidents of this kind were uncommon as shipowners usually paid for the assistance of the lifeboat within a few days of a service to their vessels.

The summary of the year's accounts for 1839 shows that a loss of almost £9 came after expenditure of £39 2s. The two sources of income came from subscriptions and donations (£15 5s) and owners of wrecks (£14 18s), while, of the total expenditure, £26 5s 0d was paid to the men who crewed the lifeboats. Almost £3 was paid for the hire of horses and almost £2 for repairs to the boats. The Association was clearly in a precarious financial state, and funds did not exist to provide for extra items such as compensation for men incapacitated or lost on service, while major repairs to the boats or boathouses could not be undertaken. The subscribers did not meet again for over twenty years, although the committee held about forty meetings during that time to ensure the continued operation of the lifeboats.

Individual donations to further the work of the Association seem to have been few and far between, and subscriptions made up the bulk of the regular income. In 1847 Robert Lashley, under the title 'collector', asked for voluntary contributions round the town, but the revenue from such sources was small. By this time, income had dwindled and in 1859 the Association had roughly £90 left. Although it charged

owners of wrecked ships not on its register the full cost of the lifeboat, it was not always possible to recover these fees. Some owners were genuinely unable to pay, having been ruined by the loss of their ship, and others were more concerned with avoiding salvage charges than with preserving the lives of their own men.

In 1837, after the lifeboat had rescued the crew of the Leith schooner *Matilda*, the owner, David Jackson, asked for the remission of the fees for the use of the lifeboat, on the grounds that he had 'been at great expense in consequence of the vessel having come under salvage, from the crew having deserted her by the lifeboat'. The Committee replied that the charge was the usual one to non-subscribers, and insisted on payment.

The level of payment the lifeboat crew should receive for a rescue often caused difficulty, and depended on the dangers involved in putting out. In March 1851 a difference of opinion arose regarding the appropriate fee for going off to the vessel *Saxon Maid* and bringing in her crew. The vessel had grounded on Whitby Rock in 'a fair wind', and the crew were landed by the lifeboat while the master and crew were found to be intoxicated. The vessel, which was carrying coal, became a total wreck, and was not insured. The Committee, finding out that the service to *Saxon Maid* was not dangerous, offered 5s per man to the crew. However, a later meeting decided that, as the rescue might be considered dangerous, the twelve men were offered 10s each. Eventually, the Committee recovered £3 6s from the owner and the matter was resolved.

On 6 October 1841, in very rough seas and a strong south-easterly gale, two fishing yawls were unable to enter the harbour so the East Side lifeboat put out. With local pilot John Barrett at the helm, the lifeboat was struck by several very heavy seas and, as she crossed the bar, capsized and drifted to sea. The West Side boat was immediately launched and the men clinging to the upturned boat were saved, but five were trapped beneath her. A hole was cut through the bottom of the boat and one man, Gatenby, was freed. He survived being trapped for nearly two hours, but the other four men were not so fortunate. They were Ralph Storr, a youth

The lifeboat going to the brig Vine, of Bristol, on 14 June 1850. The vessel went aground on the sands as it tried to enter the harbour, and was watched by hundreds of spectators from the piers as it was smashed to pieces in a strong south-easterly gale. The lifeboat, probably the Sunderland-built boat of 1822, saved the crew but the master, Captain John Honey, refused to leave and remained with his vessel until the situation had got so bad that his life was in serious peril. The lifeboat, on its fourth trip to the brig, then took him off at about 5pm, by when he was 'in an exhausted and almost lifeless state'.

named Pattinson, ship master John Wilson, and fisherman Robert Walker, who left a widow and three children. The damaged boat drifted ashore at Sandsend.

Following this tragedy, the West Side boat's crew were remunerated according to the regulations, but payment to the other crew is not mentioned in the minutes, and nothing appears to have been done by the Association to assist the bereaved families. Meanwhile, two days after the accident, the Committee decided that both boats should be repaired by Christopher Gale, the local boatbuilder, although no details exist of any work that was undertaken. The East Side boat reportedly remained unused for many years after this, although over the next twenty years several bills for painting and repairing her were paid.

In December 1859 the West Side boat was condemned as unserviceable and sold a few weeks later. On 25 January 1860, the Committee wrote to Thomas Chapman, Vice-President of the RNLI and who was also from Whitby, explaining their intention to build a new boat locally and asking for advice. The Institution responded on 2 February 1860 by sending 'the usual preparatory Life-boat Papers . . . to the Local Committee'. However, the Whitby Committee seems to have ignored the Institution's advice, and decided instead to employ local boat-builder Francis Falkingbridge, son of the William Falkingbridge who had produced the best of the Whitby models for the Duke of Northumberland's prize model lifeboat competition of 1851 to find a new and better design of lifeboat.

Before starting work, Falkingbridge was sent to examine the lifeboats in use north of Whitby. He visited Cullercoats, Seaton Carew, Sunderland and Shields and found, at the first two stations, self-righting boats, with a North County type, similar to the 1822 boats, at the latter. The Committee did not like self-righting boats, mainly because they believed that the air cases at bow and stern hampered rescue work. They were not alone in their dislike of the design, and many lifeboat crews would not man the self-righters, and so the non-self-righting North Country type was chosen.

The plans and specifications for the new boat were approved at a Committee meeting held on 15 May 1860, four months after the old boat had been condemned. The new boat was 30ft long with a beam of 8ft 9in, but the crew, while approving her general abilities, complained

that she had 'not sufficient beam at the top, as there was no room to pull'. On the other hand, the *Whitby Gazette* stated that 'a handsome and most perfect boat had now been completed'. The boat was officially launched on 6 October 1860, although she had performed her first service on 3 October, when two men and a woman were rescued from the sloop *Keltie*, a Whitby vessel and owned by a subscriber to the Life-Boat Fund.

The officials were impressed by the performance of the lifeboat, which was also praised in the press, but the crews were less enthusiastic. One of the leading lifeboatmen of the time, John Storr, said of the new boat that 'it is all right but too narrow; there is not leverage to pull the oars. If we had to pull off with a heavy sea, it would tire any man to get her off.'

The cost of the boat, including expenses incurred by Falkingbridge during his visits to Northumberland and Durham, was £140. Although the Committee had decided as early as January 1860 that the new lifeboat should be built, and entered into a contract with Falkingbridge in May, raising funds was not undertaken with any great urgency. A payment of £50 was made in June, but not until August were the first subscriptions towards the cost of the boat received with a public appeal on 1 October bringing a generous response. On 7 October, the day after the boat's acceptance, Falkingbridge received his second instalment of £50, and on 17 November the remaining £40 was paid.

The subscription lists remained open until February 1860, by when £313 had been received, a considerable sum for the time. But nothing seems to have been done with the extra money that had been received, and a year after the subscription list closed events overtook the new lifeboat, the Life-Boat Association, and the Committee, completely changing the station's operation and management.

The RNLI takes over

During September 1859 the Whitby Committee considered a tentative proposal of merger with the RNLI, but the members rejected this and decided to carry on independently. However, less than two years later, events changed the Committee's attitude towards such a merger, and as a result the station was taken over and the way it was organised completely changed. The prelude to the takeover was the 'Great Storm' of February 1861, which wreaked havoc along the east coast. On 9 February 1861, shipping was driven south by the gale, which caught the collier fleets at sea, and a total of 210 ships were lost. At Hartlepool, more than fifty vessels were wrecked on the beach, and others were seen sinking while at sea.

At Whitby, the fierce north-easterly gale had been blowing for some days, churning up violent seas, and the lifeboat rescued a number of vessels. At daybreak on 9 February some fishermen were walking on the beach toward Sandsend when they saw a vessel, the Sunderland brig *John and Ann*, in distress. She had gone aground and was in considerable danger, so the fishermen immediately put out in a coble and saved the vessel's five crew, a rescue performed with great difficulty and at great risk to the fishermen.

After this first rescue, the fishermen went to the lifeboat house where they found the new West Side lifeboat being readied for service. One of the fishermen, John Storr, took charge of her on what was only the third time she had been at sea. In total twelve men crewed the boat, most experienced lifeboatmen. They launched through very heavy surf to another vessel, the schooner *Gamma*, which was carrying coal for London and had run aground about 400 yards from the pier. The lifeboat was brought out of the lifeboat house, and hauled on her carriage along Pier Road, down the slipway, and to the water's edge by a team of four horses, not far from the pier. The boat was then launched and the four crew on board the schooner rescued without incident, after which the lifeboat returned to the beach to be recovered on her carriage.

Shortly after landing the *Gamma's* crew at 11.30am, the lifeboatmen saw the barque *Clara*, of Sunderland, run aground some distance from *Gamma*. The lifeboat was brought down the beach and launched again. The crew had a hard pull to get alongside *Clara*, and were frequently driven back by the severe seas. Despite the heavy seas pounding the vessel and making the lifeboatmen's task difficult, the lifeboat lay alongside the casualty for a quarter of an hour, held by lines from the bows and amidships. All eleven members of the barque's crew were saved and, as soon as the rescuers and rescued were on the beach, the barque broke up.

At about 1pm, another vessel, the brig *Utility*, was driven ashore, to the north of the battery, followed a few minutes later by the Newcastle-bound schooner *Roe*, which was thrown on to the beach opposite the coastguard station. The lifeboat was launched for a third time, with a crew of thirteen, one more than her usual complement, because competition for places in the boat seems to have been fierce and one man, Robert Harland, got into the boat and refused to get out despite being told to do so. The lifeboat was safely launched and battled through mountainous seas to reach the two vessels and both crews were saved. After she returned to the beach, she was placed on her carriage ready for another launch.

At about 2pm, two more ships were seen approaching and, despite the risks, their only chance of safety was to run into the harbour. The first of the two vessels, the schooner *Flora* of London, got into the harbour safely, although she hit Tate Hill Pier on the way in. However, the other ship, the schooner *Merchant* of Maldon, was driven ashore and struck the beach close to the Battery, between *Utility* and *Roe*. The lifeboat was launched for the fourth time that day, but as the lifeboatmen struggled to reach the stricken vessel, two waves met beneath the lifeboat causing very confused seas which immediately capsized the boat. The account in the *Yorkshire Gazette* provided a vivid account of events:

> 'The lifeboat was soon launched, manned with the same crew. They had some difficulty in getting to the ship, as there was a very heavy sea running, and there was a schooner between the shore and the vessel they were going to. However, they succeeded in getting to the vessel once, but were driven back again by a nasty cross sea, which came around both ends of the vessel and drove them back several times. At length two waves meeting the wave rebounding from the ship on the beach, culminated in one point, and spurted up in . . . 'the knot all of the sea'.
>
> 'This spurting up of the waves immediately under the bottom of the boat threw her completely out of the water, and took the boat broadside on, and turned her right over. The sight, the shrieks, the moans, the anxiety of mind, will not readily be forgotten: to see the poor men floating about, and no assistance could be rendered them. Only one man was saved and this was entirely by the life-belts he had on.'

The survivor, Henry Freeman, on his first day as part of the lifeboat crew, later described how he had been trapped by the gunwale of the boat. When he was thrown free, the waves carried him towards the pier where he believed he would be crushed between that and one of the wrecked ships, but a big sea came and carried him safely between the ship and the pier side, towards the slipway. Twice he was carried to the top of the slipway by the waves, and twice dragged away by the backwash. The third time he was washed in, however, some men seized him and pulled him clear.

The overturned lifeboat was washed up on a narrow strip of sand between the north end of the battery wall and the cliffs, with two men under her. Rescuers risked their lives to free the men. Thomas Robinson tried to cut through the bottom of the boat, but the men were dead when they were reached. As soon as the lifeboat capsized, the coastguard had tried to fire a line over her using the mortar, but the rocket failed. However, the mortar was used to establish communication with *Merchant*, whose crew were successfully hauled to the pier one by one, after which the schooner broke up.

The storm raged on for the rest of the day, and two further ships were wrecked. At about 4pm, the brig *Urania*, of Sunderland, on the way to her home port, was driven ashore, stern first with her mainmast broken. The rocket party succeeded in getting a line to her from the West Cliff, but the crew remained in the rigging until the tide had fallen, when they were brought ashore. At 7pm, the ship *Tribune*, of Brixham, was wrecked near the entrance to the harbour and, after a long delay, the East Side lifeboat was brought across the harbour and placed on the carriage, which was pulled by horses along the beach to the wreck. A crew of six master mariners, a mate, three seamen, a fisherman and two jet ornament manufacturers took the boat out, launching at 10pm. An hour later, the crew of *Tribune* were brought ashore, apart from one man who had been missed as he had been unconscious from exposure.

Tribune was the eighth ship to run aground that day near Whitby, while a schooner had been lost with all hands off Sandsend, and a Dutch vessel off Ravenscar. Most of the stranded vessels

The scene on 9 February 1861 at the height of the storm with ships being blown onto the beach.

broke up during the night, and the only ones which were brought into harbour were *John and Ann*, *Gamma* and *Utility*. The following morning the beach was littered with wreckage and throughout the day crowds of people salvaged anything of value they could find. While the wreckage was being salvaged, another collier, the brig *Memnon* of Shields, was at anchor off Sandsend, leaking badly, with her crew making strenuous efforts to keep her afloat and ride out the gale. But when water was found in the hold, the cable was cut and the brig was allowed to run ashore at about 7pm. The East Side lifeboat was brought out again and, with William Walker (a namesake of one of the drowned lifeboatmen) in charge but with a different crew from that which had gone to *Tribune*, was pulled by horses on the carriage to the scene of the wreck. The boat was launched and *Memnon's* crew brought ashore without incident. This somewhat routine rescue was almost an anticlimax after the drama and tragedy of the previous day, and it also proved to be the last service undertaken by a lifeboat belonging to the independent Committee.

On 11 February 1861 an inquest was held into the events of two days previously to determine exactly what had happened. The question of the physical condition of the crew was discussed, as was the suitability of the life-belts, but neither factor had contributed to the loss of life.

The sole survivor, Henry Freeman, was wearing a different life-belt to the others, having found a cork belt sent to the station as a sample and which fitted over the shoulders. He wore this throughout the day, while the others had older designs of life-belt that fitted low on the body.

Freeman's life-belt impressed onlookers, and it was thought that if all the crew had worn such belts none would have been drowned, except the two trapped under the boat. But even if the best life-belts had been worn, conditions were so bad that the lifeboatmen would still have been swept out to sea, and most probably drowned. Only three bodies were washed far enough in to be recovered, and while better life-belts might have saved these three, the argument that life-belts would have saved

An old photo taken on 10 February 1861 showing local people surveying the damage of the storm the previous day with five ships wrecked on the beach.

Henry Freeman, only survivor of the 1861 disaster, went on to become Coxswain for more than twenty years. This portrait shows him wearing the cork life-jacket which saved his life and enabled him to become something of an iconic figure not just in his home town but nationwide as this image was and is often used as an example of a typical nineteenth century lifeboat man. (By courtesy of Whitby RNLI)

Drawing of the life-belt recommended by he RNLI similar to that which Henry Freeman was wearing when the lifeboat capsized leaving him as the sole survivor.

all the crew is based on conjecture. The capsizing of the boat, and subsequent loss of life, was caused by the severity of the seas rather than anything else, and trying to apportion blame was not a particularly productive move.

Five days after the accident, a public meeting sponsored by the Lifeboat Committee was held in St Hilda's Hall. After a resolution was passed expressing sympathy to the bereaved families, it was agreed that a subscription should be raised to assist the families and dependants of the lifeboatmen who had given their lives. A fund was then set up and a total of £5,200 was donated from all over the country. Meanwhile, for his gallantry, the survivor Henry Freeman was awarded a Silver medal by the RNLI and Thomas Robinson, who had displayed considerable bravery during the efforts to save the other lifeboatmen after the capsize, also received a Silver medal.

Of more significance to the future of the lifeboat operation was the decision by the Whitby Life-Boat Association to join with the RNLI. Two

days after the disaster, the Committee met and passed two resolutions: to call a public meeting to consider measures to help the widows and children of the men drowned in the lifeboat, and to purchase twenty-four Birt's Cork Life Belts. The latter resolution suggests that the Committee intended not only to continue with lifeboat operations but to maintain two boats, hence the provision of belts for two crews.

Four days later, on 19 February 1861, another meeting was called, this time for the subscribers to the Lifeboat Fund. This was organised by Francis Pickernell with the intention of determining 'the best course to be adopted under existing circumstances'. With John Chapman, brother of RNLI Vice-Chairman Thomas Chapman, in the chair, the Rev William Keane moved the following resolution:

'It is the opinion of this meeting that the utility of the Whitby Life-boat Association would be much increased by unity with the Royal National Lifeboat Institution, and that the Committee be requested to co-operate with it in the establishment of a branch in this Port.'

This was passed unanimously and the process of merger with the RNLI began. On 23 February 1861, the Committee met and read a letter from the RNLI's Inspector of Lifeboats, Captain J. R. Ward, RN, explaining the terms of merger. The proposal was discussed by the RNLI's Committee of Management at its London Headquarters on 7 March 1861, at which details of the disaster were also given and £50 was granted to the Whitby Widow and Orphan Fund. Captain Ward visited on the invitation of the local committee, and 'made arrangements for the complete reorganisation of the establishment.'

The RNLI decided to send a 32ft self-righting lifeboat, and the station's management was to be organised according to the Institution's rules. The Whitby Committee promised to pay the coxswain's salary and cover the cost of exercises. The boathouse was altered in accordance with the wishes of Captain Ward, and a crew found for the new lifeboat. Ward examined the damaged lifeboat, and as he approved of its design it was resolved that the Committee should have her hull repaired at Whitby, paying for this from existing funds, and then sending the boat to London for modifications specified by Captain Ward. After the payment of all accounts and outstanding debts, the surplus funds were handed over to the RNLI.

The last meeting of the Whitby Committee was held on 12 April 1861, when the medals described above were presented to Robinson and Freeman. Francis Pickernell resigned, and his place as Honorary Secretary was taken by Edward Chapman, while John Pickering was appointed Coxswain-Superintendent of the new boat. Meanwhile, the old 'West Side lifeboat', which had been withdrawn in 1859, was bought by some local fishermen, who had it repaired, renamed her *Fishermen's Friend* and used her for rescue work until the mid-1870s.

Following the Institution's takeover, expenditure on the station increased considerably. Previously, the Association had operated on essentially a year-by-year basis, using income from subscribers and ships that had been aided by the lifeboats. Funding new lifeboats and boathouses under these arrangements was not practical, and between 1850 and 1860 about £40 was spent on maintenance of boats and houses by the Association. The total cost of painting and repairing the boats, as well as replacement of lost or damaged equipment, was £16.

In contrast, during the five years from 1861 to 1865, the Institution spent £69 on renovating the West Side boathouse, £54

on a house near Khyber Pass to replace the old one on Tate Hill Pier, and £220 on a new boathouse at Upgang, where a completely new station was established. Maintaining the boats involved an outlay of £21 5s, with a further £32 15s on the repairs of *Petrel*, which was badly damaged on service in 1862. The RNLI also provided new lifeboats, one for Whitby and another for Upgang, and the station was considerably improved as a result of this extra investment.

Under the RNLI's management, the operation of the station changed

The memorial in St Hilda's Church on the West Cliff to those lost in the lifeboat disaster of 1861. The front panel is inscribed with a letter to The Times written by the Rev W. Keane on 9 February 1861 describing how the lifeboat was 'manned by the finest picked seamen in Whitby' but on its sixth launch of the day 'had gone fifty yards [when] a wave capsized the boat. Then was beheld by several thousand persons . . . unable to assist the fearful agonies of those powerful men buffeting with the fury of the breakers, till one by one twelve out of thirteen sank, and only one is saved.' (Nicholas Leach)

Henry Freeman is one of the most famous lifeboatmen in Whitby and he is well remembered in the town to this day. His grave can be seen in the Cemetery (left), and mounted on the west side of the new lifeboat station at Fish Pier is a bronze bust (far left) by sculptor Richard Sefton and officially unveiled on 7 September 2007. (Nicholas Leach)

A model of Fishermen's Friend after rebuilding, on her launching carriage. The accuracy of either boat or carriage is unknown, and the boat is facing the wrong way on the carriage. The model is on display in Whitby Museum. (Nicholas Leach)

considerably, with additional finance being met entirely by the national body. A permanent paid Coxswain was employed to be responsible for maintaining the boats and boathouses. Crews were paid for each service launch undertaken irrespective of whether or not lives had been saved, the factor under the Association which determined whether they were paid. Practice launches, hitherto unknown, were held quarterly and the crews were also paid for participating in them. As a result, enough volunteers were soon trained for an efficient crew to be quickly assembled when needed.

From the takeover in 1861 until well into the twentieth century, the RNLI supplied a series of pulling and sailing lifeboats to Whitby. The practice of operating two lifeboats was maintained throughout, and the two lifeboats often worked in tandem to effect a rescue. In order to simplify accounts of the rescue work, rather than describe services in strictly chronological order, mixing No.1 and No.2 lifeboats together, this chapter and the following one describe the work of the lifeboats at the West Side and East Side stations respectively.

Lucy
1861 – 1870

When the RNLI took over the station in 1861, they ordered a new lifeboat to replace the boat that had capsized during the Great Storm. Built by Forrestt at Limehouse at a cost of £195 14s 2d, she arrived on 12 April 1861 having been transported from London free of

charge by various railway companies. She was a 32ft self-righter, pulling ten oars double-banked, and a new launching carriage, which cost £72 18s 0d, was also supplied, while a further £69 was spent on renovating the West Side boathouse to house her. The lifeboat was funded by A. W. Jaffray, of London, at whose request she was christened *Lucy*. Self-righting lifeboats had a narrower beam than the non-self-righting North Country type boats, a feature that made them more liable to capsize, although in such an eventuality they would in theory right themselves with the large air boxes at bow and stern making them unstable in the overturned position.

Lucy, the first self-righting type lifeboat to serve the port, was quite different in design from the locally-run lifeboats used hitherto, and the local boatmen who were to form her crew were somewhat mistrustful of the new design. Dislike of the self-righter was not uncommon amongst lifeboat crews, particularly on the east coast, where the type was often regarded as being poorly suited for the seas with which it would have to contend.

However, as it was the RNLI's standard design from the 1850s onwards, its use became widespread and, at Whitby, the District Inspector had to promote the boat to ensure the crew would be willing to use her. As soon as *Lucy* and her carriage reached the railway station in April 1861, the Inspector had her brought down to the beach and organised an exercise launch. She performed well during this, impressed the crowds who had turned out to see her, and, according to local reports, 'the prejudice against the air-boxes at bow and stern began to die away'.

Regular practices were held and *Lucy* remained on station for nine years, during which time she was launched nine times on service and saved more than fifty lives. Despite receiving favourable reports initially, this first RNLI-funded lifeboat faced competition in life-saving matters from the other lifeboats in the town, notably the 1822-built lifeboat, which became known as the 'green boat'. A month after *Lucy* had been delivered, some fishermen got into trouble at the harbour entrance so the new boat was made ready. However, as the tide was too high for a launch from the slipway, the crew could only watch as the old 'green boat' completed the rescue.

As well as the 'green boat', the lifeboat built in 1822 by Wake, and which had been condemned in 1859, was acquired by a group of local fishermen, repaired, renamed *Fishermen's Friend* and operated as another lifeboat. The repairs were completed during the early months of 1862, and so Whitby had effectively three lifeboats. In the hands of experienced men such as Mark Winn and John Douglas, both of whom had served as steersmen, *Fishermen's Friend* proved to be a major rival to *Lucy*. On 13 March 1862, both boats were called into action after the steamship *Deptford* ran onto Whitby Rock in fog. Both boats were launched, but *Fishermen's Friend*, being lighter and faster, reached the casualty first and assisted

steam tugs in a rescue, after which the crews shared in the salvage award.

This incident did not help the standing of *Lucy* with those who were to operate her, and the next service in which she was involved hardly improved matters. During December 1862, a severe north-easterly gale blew for three days. At noon on 21 December, the height of the storm, the Whitby-owned barque *Royal Rose*, bound for Leith with a cargo of wheat, was seen struggling through the heavy seas and, just before high tide, she was driven on to the sands. *Lucy* was brought out, but conditions were too bad to launch from the beach. The Rocket Brigade succeeded in getting a line to the vessel, but it was out of reach of the crew, and fell into the sea. Further attempts also failed as the lines either broke or fell short.

With the vessel in danger of breaking up, the twelve men on *Royal Rose* were forced to take to the rigging. The only hope of saving them was the lifeboat, but in the heavy seas and at high tide it was impossible to launch it down the slipway. Some of the fishermen, led by boatbuilder Christopher Gale, thought it might be possible to drag a light boat down to the beach at the Caulkhills. *Lucy* was too heavy, but to get *Fishermen's Friend* out of the harbour in such a storm was impossible. However, some of the veteran lifeboatmen took *Petrel*, which had been left on her carriage in the Pier Yard, manhandled her up Khyber Pass to the cliff top, took her off her carriage

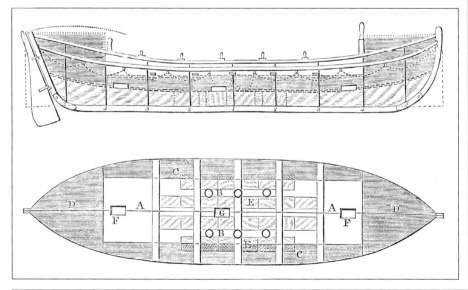

Line drawing showing the deck plan and sheer plan of the RNLI's self-righting lifeboats of the 1860s and 1870s. Although this was a generic drawing used throughout the RNLI's publications of the time, it shows a boat similar in appearance to Lucy, with high end boxes giving the boat its self-righting capability.

and lowered her down the cliffs to the north of the wreck. Although the cliff was not sheer, the descent was steep and the undertaking was dangerous. But the boat was got down to the beach and launched.

The crew, led by John Pickering as Coxswain, had a hard struggle to reach the wreck and then, once alongside, they were in great danger as the casualty rolled in the surf. However, despite the dangers, the lifeboatmen saved all twelve of the barque's crew, including one man who had broken his leg. Two of the barque's crew fell into the sea during the transfer, but they were hauled aboard the lifeboat. When all were rescued, the lifeboat made for the beach but, as the tide was up to the foot of the cliff, beaching her was almost impossible. As she approached the shoreline, an enormous wave carried her in, and a second hurled her against the cliff, damaging and almost wrecking her. With great difficulty, the rescued men and the lifeboat crew were helped up the cliff, with thousands of spectators cheering them on. A few minutes later, *Royal Rose* became a total wreck.

The lifeboat built forty years earlier had proved her worth in somewhat unusual circumstances and, although damaged against the foot of the cliffs, she was repaired for £32 15s 0d. She remained in service for another ten years, but this proved to be her last outstanding service (see chapter on East Side lifeboats). For the remainder of the decade, *Lucy* was used when a vessel was in difficulty and, presumably, her greater size made her more suitable than the other lifeboats. Indeed, the day after the *Royal Rose* rescue, 22 December 1862, she was called out and launched to the steamer *Alice*, which was assisted safely into harbour.

The next rescues took place during 1865 when *Lucy* was launched three times, making this her busiest year. On 19 April she put out through heavy surf to the screw-steamship *Ocean Queen*, of Newcastle, which was in difficulty off Whitby in a north-westerly wind. The lifeboat took fifteen people off, including the captain's wife, and brought them ashore. On 9 May, she went to another large vessel, the coal-carrying barque *Maria Somes*, of London, which had hit rocks off Whitby. Several cobles had

attempted to get to the vessel, but they had to abandon their attempts to help as the weather was worsening. The lifeboat managed to get off the crew of nineteen and landed them in the harbour. The final service of the year, on 19 October 1865, was to the schooner *Elizabeth*, of Goole, which was in difficulty in a north-easterly gale. The lifeboat launched and was able to render assistance, but she was not needed to take any of the crew off.

A few months later, on 2 January 1868, *Lucy* had her busiest day. At about 7pm, the steam tug *Swan* was towing the sloop *Industry* and the schooner *Mulgrave* into Whitby when a heavy sea on the bar pushed the tug against the pier, disabling it and causing the tow ropes to break. The vessels were driven ashore on the beach north of the West Pier, and *Industry* sank while *Mulgrave* was stranded. The lifeboat was quickly launched and took two men off each of the vessels with *Industry* full of water as her crew were saved. The tug's two crew were also saved by the lifeboat.

What proved to be the last service undertaken by *Lucy* took place on 27 December 1869 when, at dawn, the brigantine *Lutha*, of Leith, got into difficulty off Whitby and lost her masts and sails. *Lucy* was taken down to the beach on her carriage but, as she was launched, her rudder was damaged and she was thrown back on to the beach. The launchers struggled to haul the boat, then broadside on, clear of the surf, while the crew managed to scramble ashore. After the rudder had been replaced, a second launch was undertaken and the lifeboat was able to reach the casualty, saving the six men on board *Lutha*.

During this time, a couple of rescues were undertaken in which the lifeboat was not involved, but which were formally recognised by the RNLI. One took place on the evening of 23 February 1868 when the schooner *William Barker*, of Whitby, was driven ashore and wrecked near the East Pier during a fierce gale. The Chief Officer of Coastguard at Whitby, William Quigley, with ten men, managed to get down the cliffs and, at considerable personal risk, saved the crew of three by means of ropes. For his gallantry, Quigley was awarded a Silver medal by the RNLI. Just over five years later, on 16 October

1873, a young boy fell into the sea from the West Pier at Whitby and a youth who saw what had happened, William Moate, dived into the water and rescued him. For his bravery, William Moate was accorded the Thanks of the Institution on Vellum.

Robert Whitworth
1870 – 1881

A month before she had undertaken the service to *Lutha*, *Lucy* was found to be in rather poor condition: some of her planking was rotten and she was deemed beyond repair. So a new lifeboat, the second RNLI lifeboat supplied for the West Side, was immediately ordered from Forrestt. The new boat, a 32ft ten-oared self-righter similar to *Lucy*, arrived in January 1870 having been built at a cost of £248 7s 6d, with a new launching carriage costing an extra £100 10s 0d. This lifeboat undertook her first service on 26 July 1870 when she helped to save the brigantine *Mary and Jane*, of Sunderland, and her crew of four after they got into difficulty in dense fog. Although initially given the name *Lucy*, this lifeboat was renamed *Robert Whitworth*. The RNLI's Committee of Management decided, at a meeting on 22 February 1871, to rename her after the Honorary Treasurer of the

Manchester Branch in recognition of the outstanding fund-raising work that he had done for the Institution.

During her career at Whitby, *Robert Whitworth* served as the No.1 lifeboat on the West Side until 1881, launching twenty-two times on service and saving 130 lives. In 1881, she was transferred to the No.2 station where she served for a further six years. Her first service under her new name took place on 2 October 1871, when she went to the schooner *Dispatch*, which got into difficulty entering port. The lifeboatmen towed the schooner to safety and she was anchored, with the lifeboat landing the vessel's master and two crew. The next morning the vessel was still at anchor, so the lifeboat took the three men back out to her.

Many of the services performed by the lifeboats during the nineteenth century were to local fishing cobles, such as on 6 December 1871 when six local cobles got caught out in a strong gale and heavy seas. Both *Robert Whitworth* and the No.2 lifeboat *Harriott Forteath* were launched to their aid and *Robert Whitworth* saved twelve men from four of the cobles, while the other lifeboat saved the remaining crews. The six cobles, damaged in the heavy seas, were later washed onto the beach with their gear and catch lost. *Robert Whitworth*

Lifeboat regatta at Whitby in the late 1880s, entitled 'Finish of Lifeboat Race'. Taking part were both Whitby lifeboats, which were joined by the Upgang and Robin Hood's Bay boats. (By courtesy of Whitby Museum)

undertook another service to local fishing cobles on 24 May 1876 with similar results, assisted by the No.2 lifeboat. These cobles, caught out in a strong gale, were abandoned, their crews rescued by the lifeboats, and they were washed up on the beach, damaged but repairable.

During 1878, *Robert Whitworth* was called upon to perform several services and this proved to be her busiest year as No.1 lifeboat. On 5 January, she rescued the crew of the steamship *Oscar*, of Leith, which sunk after striking Whitby Rock in thick fog and heavy seas. On a voyage from Shields to Cadiz, the steamer became a wreck the next day, after the lifeboat had taken the captain out to her to save some papers and instruments. On 8 May, she assisted two fishing cobles, *Eliza* and *James & Sarah*, of Scarborough, after they had been caught out in a strong south-easterly breeze. One of the boats sank but the other was beached.

On 12 September, about fifty fishing vessels were lying at anchor in the roads when a northerly gale suddenly sprung up. As the crews had landed with their catch, and were unable to get back to their vessels, *Robert Whitworth* and the No.2 lifeboat *Harriott Forteath* were launched and reboarded some of the crews. By then, four of the craft had been driven ashore but their crews were saved, while the majority of the boats slipped their anchors and headed south. *Robert Whitworth* was out for about two hours, during which time she also saved two men from the Hartlepool fishing coble *Welcome*.

On 28 October 1880 *Robert Whitworth*

assisted no fewer than three different vessels during a severe east-north-easterly gale, with extremely heavy seas. The first vessel to need help was the schooner *Reaper*, of Douglas, which drifted towards Whitby Rocks at noon and, although the disabled vessel cleared the rocks, she was driven ashore. *Robert Whitworth* was immediately launched, under the command of Coxswain Henry Freeman, and with considerable difficulty, rescued the schooner's crew of four and landed them safely. At 1.30pm, the fishing yawl *Good Intent*, of Staithes, was seen in difficulty approaching the harbour, so *Robert Whitworth* was launched again and saved the yawl's eight-man crew.

The final service of the day took place after the Great Yarmouth schooner *John Snell*, bound to Newcastle with a cargo of wheat, went aground on the beach at 4.30pm. *Robert Whitworth*, after being pulled for some distance through a 'seething mass of broken water', reached the vessel and managed to land her crew of five. For his fine seamanship and outstanding courage during these services, during which twenty-two lives had been saved, Coxswain Henry Freeman was awarded his second Silver Medal.

In 1881, the Whitby No.1 lifeboat was involved in a service that brought recognition to the station and its lifeboat crews on a national level, and has become one of the most famous rescues in the history of the RNLI. The epic began on 16 January 1881 when, despite frost, snow showers and heavy seas, which had already wrecked the collier *Lumley* (see chapter on

Upgang), the brig *Visitor* sailed from the Tyne for London with a cargo of coal. The east coast coal trade was very competitive and the crews of colliers involved in it were prepared to take risks to get their cargo to market. *Visitor* was an old vessel, built at Sunderland in 1823, registered at Whitby, and owned at Robin Hood's Bay. She left the Tyne with a crew of six and soon afterwards the weather rapidly deteriorated with the whole country snowbound. At sea, the wind was rising, and the seas were getting rougher.

Late on the afternoon of 18 January, when *Visitor* was off Flamborough, the wind changed direction and increased to a full south-easterly gale, driving the brig northwards and destroying most of her sails. The master realised that his vessel was in danger of being blown ashore, so he anchored in the comparatively shallow waters of Robin Hood's Bay hoping to ride out the gale. But gradually the seas overwhelmed the vessel, and soon waves were breaking right over her deck. The crew put her boat over the side and five of them scrambled into it.

The last to leave, an apprentice, instead of getting into the boat, misheard instructions shouted to him and, in the confusion, cast off the boat before he could jump into her, and it drifted away from the brig. About an hour later, *Visitor* went down while still anchored. As she sank, the apprentice lashed himself to a lifebuoy, jumped into the sea, and swam to

the boat. The five men pulled him in, and there they remained waiting for daylight and knowing that only the slight shelter of the wrecked brig prevented them from being driven on to the rocks.

Ashore, nothing was known of *Visitor's* fate until her quarter-board was found on the beach but, as daylight broke, coastguards saw the wreck. She was too far out for the rocket apparatus to be of use and the lifeboat at Robin Hood's Bay was unusable, old and neglected; the local fishermen refused to launch her, and the coastguards were instructed that she was not to be used. But, in the bitter wind and snow showers, something had to be done and so the Vicar, the Rev J. Cooper and his son, sent a telegram stating: 'Vessel sunk, crew in open boat riding by the wreck, send Whitby life-boat if practicable'.

Whitby lifeboatmen, including Henry Freeman (second right) on hand at Shibden Park in Halifax to promote the work of the RNLI. (By courtesy of Whitby Lifeboat Museum)

Watched by a large crowd from the pier, the first Robert and Mary Ellis (ON.180) launching from the West Beach. (RNLI, by courtesy of Jeff Morris)

Painting of the heroic efforts of the Whitby lifeboatmen and townspeople struggling to get the No.1 lifeboat through the snow and across the moors to help the brig Visitor in January 1881. A plaque (right) to mark the famous rescue stands at the side of the road to Robin Hood's Bay.

along a road that climbed to a height of more than 500ft, and then dropped steeply down Bay Bank to the sea. The snow had drifted in places to seven or eight feet deep, and there was no shelter from the wind. However, the *Visitor's* survivors were out in an open boat in a winter gale, and the Whitby men, led by Gibson, showed considerable determination and resourcefulness to effect a rescue.

A group of about sixty men were sent ahead to clear the snowdrifts so the lifeboat could pass. *Robert Whitworth* was brought out of her boathouse, manhandled along Haggersgate, over the bridge and into Church Street where horses were harnessed to her carriage. As the lifeboat came through the town, many men rushed to help, taking shovels to clear the way while local farmers brought their plough. No fewer than eighteen horses hauled the boat along a road cleared by more than 200 men. Gibson and Freeman directed operations as far as Stainsacre, from where Matthew Welburn took charge. He had to order a gateway to be widened, and then the lifeboat left the road to follow a shorter and easier route over farmland.

The Whitby men eventually linked up with a party which had been working its way from Robin Hood's Bay for the difficult and dangerous descent of the long bank through the small town. With ropes attached to the carriage, volunteers controlled her as she was taken down the steep and twisting road to the sea,

The message reached Captain Gibson, the Whitby Secretary, at about 10am and he promptly called out the crew to discuss the situation. The weather was still appalling, with a tremendous sea running, the wind to the north-east, and blinding showers of snow and hail sweeping the town. To take the lifeboat by sea was impossible in these conditions, even if she could have been towed part of the way by a steam tug. The only alternative was to take her by land, a journey of six miles

Robert and Mary Ellis (ON.180) putting out on service to the steamship Isle of Iona, of Newcastle, on 7 December 1906. The ship was stranded in heavy seas on Whitby Rock and her eleven crew were saved by the lifeboat. (By courtesy of Whitby Lifeboat Museum)

Lifeboatmen on the steps of Leeds Town Hall in 1893 dressed for participation in the city's Lifeboat Saturday from both Whitby (W) and Upgang (U). Left to right, back row: William Harrison (U), Edward Gash (W), Joseph Tomlinson (W), William Afleck (Bowman, W), Pounder Robinson (Second Coxswain, W), Walter Corrie (W). Left to right, front row: Thomas McGarry Kelly (Bowman, U), Robert Richardson (U), Richard Eglon (Second Coxswain, U), Henry Freeman (Coxswain, W), Thomas Langlands (Coxswain, U) and James Elder (U).

with little more than an inch to spare as she passed the Laurel Inn. The lifeboat was launched at 1.30pm with Coxswain Henry Freeman in charge, and was rowed through the heavy seas. Although the crew were tired after their exertions, they struggled for an hour to reach the *Visitor's* boat, which was about two miles from the launch site. Several times, the lifeboat was almost swamped, and she was hit by one tremendous wave which broke six of the oars. At this point, two men were only partly conscious, several others were exhausted, and the steering oar was useless so Freeman put back to the beach. Second Coxswain John Storr obtained oars from the local lifeboat and Freeman called for volunteers to replace the exhausted men. With a crew of eighteen, *Robert Whitworth* was launched once more.

According to Captain Gibson's account, she 'was right nobly pulled through the seething mass of broken and terrific seas to the frail craft containing the crew of the ill-fated brig, all of whom had to be lifted into the lifeboat'. The rescued men were suffering badly from exposure and when the lifeboat returned to the beach, at about 4pm, the local people immediately offered hospitality to both rescued and rescuers. *Robert Whitworth* was left at Robin Hood's Bay until the storm subsided a few days later, and then her crew walked from Whitby to row her back to her station.

Following the rescue of the crew

of *Visitor*, the courage, bravery and endurance shown by the lifeboatmen were extolled in the national press, and the RNLI thanked the crew for their services, both to *Lumley* and to *Visitor*, and paid double the normal rates for both launches. Locally, the crews were entertained to dinner, a subscription was raised for their benefit, and they were invited to attend a thanksgiving at St Michael's Church.

Freeman had been coxswain for four years, and in that time had built up a tremendous reputation, both for the lifeboat service and for himself. Tall and well-built, with a commanding presence and a forceful personality, he came to be regarded as almost the ideal of a lifeboatman. The photograph of him in his cork life-jacket, taken by the famous Whitby photographer Frank Meadow Sutcliffe, has endured as an image of the typical nineteenth century rescuer.

Following the incredible efforts made by the Whitby lifeboatmen and townsfolk in going to the aid of *Visitor*, the RNLI took over the lifeboat station at Robin Hood's Bay, at the suggestion of the Rev Jermyn Cooper, who became the station's first Honorary Secretary, and completely renewed it. The old lifeboat was broken up and a new brick-built lifeboat house erected on the site of the old one. The RNLI provided a new 32ft self-righting lifeboat, named *Ephraim and Hannah Fox*, with a launching carriage and equipment.

Some of Whitby's nineteenth and early twentieth century Coxswains, from left to right: Joseph Tomlinson, David Harland, Thomas McGarry Kelly, James Murfield, Richard Eglon, Thomas Welham and Robert Harland. (By courtesy of Whitby Lifeboat Museum)

A problem with local men volunteering to crew the lifeboat was overcome when Whitby lifeboatmen agreed to form a crew, and John Storr was appointed Coxswain. On 26 September 1881 the new lifeboat arrived at her station and launched, but only one Bay man was in her crew, Second Coxswain Matthew Cooper.

Ephraim and Hannah Fox served at Robin Hood's Bay for twenty-two years, launching eleven times on service and saving twenty-four lives. She went out once with Storr at the helm, in December 1882, to a small vessel ashore near Saltwick and a boat in trouble at sea, but both were empty when the lifeboat reached them. In 1885 Matthew Cooper succeeded Storr as coxswain and Storr became second coxswain at Upgang, a post which he held until his death in 1888, at the age of thirty-eight. In 1902 *Ephraim and Hannah Fox* was replaced by a new lifeboat, *Mary Ann Lockwood*, which had been built for the station by Thames Ironworks at Blackwall. She was a standard 34ft self-righter, pulling ten oars, and served until the station closed in 1931.

Robert and Mary Ellis
1881 – 1909

The service to the brig *Visitor* proved to be the last undertaken by *Robert Whitworth* as the No.1 lifeboat and towards the end of 1881 a new lifeboat was allocated to the No.1 Station. The boat, named *Robert and Mary Ellis*, was a standard 34ft ten-oared self-righter, built by Woolfe, of Shadwell, at a cost of £363. While being taken north to her new station, she was taken to York to be displayed to the public and was formally christened there on 2 December. She had been funded from a gift of £800 from Mrs Mary Ann Ellis, of York, which had come to the Institution through the 'zealous' efforts of C. H. Dunhill, Honorary Secretary of the York Branch. The boat was named in memory of the donor and her late husband.

The ceremony in York was quite an event, with the new lifeboat at the centre of a procession which went through the streets of the city led by the band of the York Artillery Volunteers. Coxswain Henry Freeman and his crew, plus various Whitby station officials, attended the ceremony. Large crowds watched the event, and at the Blue Bridge, over the river Ouse, where the ceremony took place, several thousand people were present. The Rev F. L. Palmes formally presented the lifeboat to the Institution, and she was accepted by Cdr St Vincent Nepean, RN, District Inspector of Lifeboats, who stated that 'at no place would a Lifeboat have a better opportunity of seeing good service than at Whitby, where the men were always ready to risk their lives in order to save others, and where he was sure that its interests and efficiency would be well looked after.' Edward Chapman, Chairman of the Whitby Branch, thanked the donor, on behalf of the local committee, for her 'valuable and munificent present'.

After the formalities, Mrs Ellis broke a bottle of wine over the boat's bow to christen her *Robert and Mary Ellis*. The boat was then launched from her carriage into the river, with the Dean of York and Captain Nepean accompanying the crew afloat. She was deliberately capsized in the Foss, near Castle Mills Bridge, and righted herself immediately to demonstrate her self-righting abilities. After what was a major event for people of the city, the new lifeboat was taken by rail to Whitby. She arrived there on 5 December and *Harriott Forteath* was withdrawn from the No.2 Station and replaced by the former No.1 lifeboat, *Robert Whitworth*, which was renamed *Harriott Forteath*.

Robert and Mary Ellis recorded her first rescue on 20 September 1882 when she went to the aid of the Danish schooner *William*, which had anchored in a dangerous position off the harbour in heavy weather. The lifeboat stood by for about two hours until a steam tug was sent for. Her first life-saving service took place a few months later on 6 December 1882, when she went to the brig *Star of Hope*, of Newcastle, which stranded between Whitby and Upgang Rocks, about 250 yards north of the West Pier. The brig, bound for Dieppe in ballast, had been caught in heavy seas. The lifeboat launched amidst snow showers and

was, according to the RNLI's account, 'gallantly pulled though the heavy sea, and in about twenty minutes from the time of the vessel stranding, her crew, consisting of six men, were safely landed.'

After a routine service on 20 April 1883 to three local fishing cobles, supplying their crews with life-jackets so they could cross heavy seas on the bar in safety, *Robert and Mary Ellis* was not launched on service for almost a decade. Her next call did not come until 8 October 1892, when she went to the local coble *Palm Branch*, with a crew of three, which had been driven towards Whitby Rock in heavy weather. Heavy seas were breaking up the gangway which led down to the beach, as it was high tide, so the lifeboat was lowered into the harbour using a crane at Scotch Head. Coxswain Henry Freeman and his crew then battled their way out through heavy seas, watched by a large crowd and, after an hour, succeeded in saving the coble's crew of three.

Almost four more years passed before *Robert and Mary Ellis* was called out again. On 1 August 1896, she launched in conjunction with the No.2 lifeboat *John Fielden* to the steamship *Lady Gray*, of West Hartlepool, which had stranded on Whitby Rocks about half-a-mile from the West Pier head. The master had come ashore in the ship's boat to contact the

The crew of the second Robert and Mary Ellis (ON.588) outside the double boathouse. Pictured, back row left to right, are: John Dryden, Thomas Welham, Jim Middlemass, Edward Gash, Richard Eglon, Thomas Langlands, Robert Richardson and Frank Clarkson. Front row, left to right: John Richardson, John Robinson, Christopher Eglon, Robert Harland and Harry 'Lal' Richardson. (By courtesy of Whitby Lifeboat Museum)

owners, but he was unable to get back to his vessel due to worsening weather so the lifeboats were launched to reboard him. They also took about 150 shore men to the vessel to throw the cargo of coal overboard. After several hours of hard work, and with the aid of five powerful steam tugs, the steamer was dragged clear, and immediately headed for Hartlepool to have the damage to her hull repaired while the lifeboats returned to station.

Robert and Mary Ellis was involved in a difficult service on 21 February 1898 when she assisted several local cobles which were caught out in a north-westerly gale and rough seas. The first one succeeded in getting across the bar unaided, but the second, R. W. Jackson, was caught by a huge wave and almost lost. The lifeboat crew immediately came to her aid and brought her to safety. Although one of her crew was washed overboard during the incident, he grabbed hold of the coble and was saved by the lifeboat. With conditions on the bar worsening, the lifeboat was instructed by

the harbour master to warn the other two cobles, Tranquil and Martha Dryden, to anchor their boats and come ashore in the lifeboat. The crews were landed by the lifeboat, but the anchors holding the cobles parted in the night and the craft were wrecked on the rocks.

The majority of the services undertaken by Robert and Mary Ellis were to local fishing cobles. On 18 March 1901 she stood by in heavy seas as some local cobles returned home, and on 7 February 1902 landed the crews from the cobles Thomas and Richard and Lady Morris which were unable to cross the bar due to heavy seas. On 15 April 1904 she again launched to Lady Morris and saved her crew of three. On 24 March 1905, she stood by the coble May Blossom, which had been out tending to crab pots but had difficulty crossing the bar when returning to harbour. Just over a month later, Robert and Mary Ellis stood by six cobles as they crossed the bar through strong northerly seas.

On 20 May 1905 Robert and Mary Ellis was launched to a steamer, Cogent, of Sunderland, bound to Lisbon with coal, which was aground in thick fog halfway to the rocks off the pier. The casualty was spotted when the fog lifted at 10am, and the lifeboat immediately went to help. The coxswain boarded the steamer, and the lifeboatmen were engaged in salvaging the vessel. The No.2 lifeboat John Fielden was launched and her crew helped with the salvage. Anchors were run out from the casualty to help the distressed vessel which, when the tide flooded, managed to get clear. With the north-easterly wind

The scene on the West Beach during the unique double naming ceremony involving the new Whitby No.1 and Upgang lifeboats in August 1909. (By courtesy of Whitby Lifeboat Museum)

increasing and the seas getting rougher, the steamer had been in a very dangerous position, and had she not been refloated she would have been totally wrecked.

After this service to a steamer, the next rescue by the No.1 lifeboat was a particularly fine one. At 11.30am on 14 May 1906, six local cobles headed back towards Whitby, in rough seas and a strong north-easterly wind. Four made harbour safely, the last of which was *Thankful*, which was manned by Coxswain Thomas Langlands and two other men. However, as the fifth boat, *William and Tom*, attempted to follow them in, a huge wave crashed over her stern, nearly filling the boat. She was swept forward by the wave and then swung broadside to the next one, which broke right over her, and she sank within minutes. A buoy attached to a line was thrown from the pier to the three men in the water and two of them managed to cling to it.

Meanwhile, Coxswain Langlands had taken his coble *Thankful* back to the harbour entrance just in time to save the third man, who had been swept away from the pier. By that time, the other two men were very close to the Pier and in some difficulty. Thanks to superb seamanship by Langlands, who had to keep the coble's head to sea in a strong ebb tide, the men were hauled aboard after he had a line thrown to them. As the rescue was executed, two of the coble's oars were washed away, but she got clear of the broken water once the survivors were aboard. *Robert and Mary Ellis* had been launched by this time, and she took the three rescued men off *Thankful* and landed them. She then put out again to assist the coble *Jane and Mary*, landing that coble's three crew. For this outstanding rescue, Langlands was awarded a Silver medal by the RNLI in recognition of his 'conspicuous gallantry and skilful seamanship'.

During her last two years of service at Whitby, *Robert and Mary Ellis* completed ten effective services, all to assist local fishing cobles. On 23 March 1907, she stood by the fishing coble *Robert and Mary* as it crossed the bar. On 3 and 5 April the same year she was again employed in standing by as fishing cobles returned to their home port in difficult conditions

at the harbour bar. On 28 October, she helped three cobles return to harbour, making one trip to sea for each one.

During 1908, she performed several more services of a similar nature to local cobles. In one incident, on 15 July, one of the cobles caught in the heavy ground swell outside the harbour was swamped by a large sea, and her three crew were saved by another coble, *Blanche*, from which the lifeboat landed them. On 9 September, the lifeboat was watched by a large crowd on the pier as she helped the coble *Salmo*, saving its three occupants and then towing the empty coble near enough to the beach for her to be washed ashore safely. The final service by *Robert and Mary Ellis* took place on 27 November when she escorted nine cobles across the bar.

The second Robert and Mary Ellis 1908 – 1934

In October 1907, the Local Committee had written to the RNLI urging that a new, larger No.1 lifeboat be supplied and the following month the RNLI allocated a new lifeboat to the station. In January 1908, the coxswain and crew expressed their preference for a 35ft self-righter with a four-inch cork wale, and fitted with square-loomed oars and holes. A new carriage provided with pushing poles was also requested. The new boat was ordered from Thames Ironworks, where all RNLI's lifeboats were being built at the time, and on 28 November 1908 the new boat was reported by the builder to be ready.

The new lifeboat was forwarded to Whitby on 9 December 1908, carried

Line drawing of the first service undertaken by the second Robert and Mary Ellis (ON.588) when she went to the ketch Gem of the Ocean on 15 February 1909.

The second Robert and Mary Ellis (ON.588) lifeboat on her carriage, which is fitted with Tipping's plates, with her sail raised for what is most likely a posed publicity picture. (By courtesy of Whitby Lifeboat Museum)

north free of charge by the Great Northern and North Eastern Railway. A new carriage, fitted with modified launching poles as well as Tipping's plates to make it less likely to sink in soft sand, was also provided and sent direct from Bristol via the Midland Railway. Both the old lifeboat, which had been condemned as unfit, and the carriage were returned to London. The new boat was a 35ft self-righter pulling ten oars and fitted with eight relieving tubes and a 6ft wood and iron keel. Built at a cost of £887 0s 8d, she was funded, like her predecessor, from the legacy of the late Mrs Ellis of Harrogate and was named *Robert and Mary Ellis*.

Before her formal naming ceremony took place, the second *Robert and Mary Ellis* took part in a fine service on 15 February 1909, together with the Upgang lifeboat, to the local ketch *Gem of the Ocean* (see chapter on Upgang). Her public inauguration and naming took place several months later, on 23 August 1909, and was a unique event in that both she and the new Upgang lifeboat *William Riley of Birmingham and Leamington* were christened at the same ceremony. Large crowds had gathered on the beach and the cliffs for the event, with both boats 'decorated with flags and bunting, and presented an exceedingly pretty sight to those who were fortunate enough to get a close view of them', according to the RNLI's account of proceedings.

On behalf of the Institution, Lieut Basil Hall, District Inspector of Lifeboats, formally handed the two lifeboats over to Jefferson Suggit, Chairman of the Local Committee. After the service of dedication, with the choir of the Seamen's Institute leading the singing, the Hon Mrs Gervase-Beckett, wife of the local MP, named the two boats. A bottle of champagne, in a bouquet of sweet peas over the stem of each boat, was smashed by Mrs Beckett against the ironwork as the craft were formally christened. The lifeboats were then launched amid much cheering with Thomas Langlands in charge of the Whitby boat and Robert Eglon as Second Coxswain, and 'Pounder' Robinson in command of the Upgang boat, with T. G. Kelly as Second Coxswain. Thus, amid

Robert and Mary Ellis (ON.588) afloat for the formal opening of the new bridge across the Esk in 1911, with crowds gathered to watch the event and the temporary wooden bridge yet to be removed.

The second Robert and Mary Ellis (ON.588) lifeboat under oars in the harbour with Coxswain Thomas Langlands at the stern. This picture was taken on the day of her naming ceremony, as a very similar one of William Riley (see page 82) was taken at the same time. (By courtesy of Whitby Lifeboat Museum)

much pomp and ceremony, the two new lifeboats entered service.

Robert and Mary Ellis served at Whitby for twenty-five years and was the last pulling lifeboat to operate from the No.1 station. During her time in service, she launched twenty-five times and is credited with saving eleven lives. These figures show that demand for her was comparatively little and this is particularly so after 1919, when the station's first motor lifeboat arrived. Even during the First World War, which was a busy time for many lifeboats on England's east coast, *Robert and Mary Ellis* completed only two effective services.

The first rescue she undertook after her naming ceremony was to the fishing coble *Eliza Jane* on 9 March 1913, almost five years since the ceremony. The coble was reported to be in difficulty at 3pm, about five miles east of the harbour, and as darkness was approaching the lifeboat was launched. After an hour of rowing, the lifeboatmen found the coble, which had a broken rudder and was drifting with the strong flood tide. Her three crew were exhausted, and so the lifeboat took them in tow. She was forced to tack into the wind on the return journey, reaching port after a tow lasting more than three hours. A crowd had gathered on the piers to watch

The second Robert and Mary Ellis (ON.588) launching off the West Beach. (By courtesy of Whitby Museum)

The second Robert and Mary Ellis being launched off the West Beach. The carriage is fitted with Tipping's plates, and shore helpers are pushing the boat into the water. In severe weather, launching off an open beach was very difficult and could sometimes be impossible.

the two vessels return and the coble's three occupants were safely landed.

During the First World War, *Robert and Mary Ellis* was launched to assist only two vessels. The first was the timber-carrying steamship *Skane*, of Helsingborg, which stranded on Whitby Rock on 30 November 1915 and remained there while attempts were made to salvage her. On 23 December, the lifeboat went to help the salvers after they had been caught out in heavy weather. She landed ten of them, and then returned manned by a different Coxswain and crew and brought two ladies ashore. She was later launched a third time to the vessel and brought ashore a further eight people.

The other wartime service took place in November 1916. On 20 November the lifeboat launched to the Grimsby steam trawler *Eagle*, which had stranded whilst bound for Grimsby to unload her catch. The trawler's nine crew were landed by the lifeboat, which, the following day, assisted to refloat the vessel.

Robert and Mary Ellis performed only two effective services during her last eighteen years at Whitby, the first on 15 July 1919 when she went out to assist the schooner *Fern*, of Hull, which was bound for the Tyne from London and grounded on the bar as she was coming into harbour. Heavy seas continually filled the lifeboat as she went to the schooner's

aid, and she was damaged after being driven against the end of the pier. But the schooner's three crew were taken on board and landed in the harbour, while men on the pier extension hauled the casualty in and beached her.

After this service, *Robert and Mary Ellis* had her planking repaired at a cost of £12, and she was partially overhauled at the same time. In 1921, she had a complete overhaul, and her starboard seams and air cases were repaired. The second service, the last by *Robert and Mary Ellis*, came almost exactly three years later, on 19 July 1922. She launched at 8.15am to the fishing coble *May Blossom*, which had stranded off Whitby harbour, and escorted the vessel into port.

Robert and Mary Ellis was withdrawn from Whitby in January 1934 and, from then on, the motor lifeboat became the Whitby No.1 lifeboat. Since the service to *May Blossom* in 1922, *Robert and Mary Ellis* had not been called on, and the No.2 lifeboats were used in preference as these were kept afloat and thus easier to launch, although the motor lifeboat was of course used on the majority of services. *Robert and Mary Ellis* remained at Whitby until 1934, however, before being removed. She was then sold out of service to Captain W. Milburn for £60. He converted her into a houseboat named *Highlander* and she was kept at York for many years.

No.2 lifeboats

The RNLI became responsible for the running of the Whitby station in 1861 and the Institution continued to operate two lifeboats well into the twentieth century. This chapter describes the East Side, or No.2 lifeboats, and the major rescues which they undertook. With the 1861 takeover, the East Side lifeboat, un-named since being built in 1822, came under the Institution's auspices. Although a new lifeboat was supplied for the West Side (described in the previous chapter), the East Side boat was retained by the RNLI. She was smaller than the new RNLI lifeboat, and it is questionable whether she would have been kept had she not proved such a valuable rescue tool during the particularly notable service to the Whitby-owned barque *Royal Rose*, described in the section on *Lucy*. Following the *Royal Rose* rescue, one local newspaper argued for the retention of a second smaller boat, stating that:

> 'Had there been no other than the National boat, it is almost certain that another tragic history of twelve fellow mortals buried in the sea . . . would have had to be written. We do not say that the National boat is unsuitable, but are emphatic that there should be a second boat, lighter and easier to handle.'

The local committee requested one of the RNLI's smallest and lightest boats, well suited to being transported along the coast, and even suggested that she should be housed on the West Cliff. However, the RNLI's Inspector, Captain Ward, was against this idea and stated emphatically that a lifeboat should never be lowered down a cliff to be launched at high tide. In the end, it was agreed to have the small lifeboat repaired.

After the repairs had been completed in 1863, she was given the name *Petrel* and remained at Whitby for a further ten years,

during which time she was used only once. In 1871 she was again renamed, *Gertrude*, although details of her cost being appropriated to any donor are lacking. The decision to repair and retain this boat in 1863 was made because of her size – it was believed that two boats were needed at Whitby, even though it seems the RNLI would have preferred to have only one.

Competition from the fishermen's lifeboat was probably also a factor in the RNLI's decision. This was the Sunderland-built boat of 1822, which had been replaced on the West Side by *Lucy*. A group of fishermen had purchased the boat for £3 3s 10d despite the craft having been condemned by the RNLI in 1859. But the fishermen must have favoured this boat for they began collecting money to pay for repairs and by 1862 she was seaworthy and operating under the name *Fishermen's Friend*. Many experienced lifeboatmen from the pre-RNLI era had shares in her and were thus not available to the National Institution. The private boat showed her worth in March 1862 when she went out to the steamship *Deptford*, which had grounded on Whitby Rock in fog. The No.1 lifeboat *Lucy* also launched to the vessel, but *Fishermen's Friend* was lighter and faster so reached the casualty first and, with the steam tugs, was able to share in the salvage award.

In the mid-1860s, the boat's owners collected money to buy life-belts and a launching carriage, which was built locally. An appeal was also made to have a boathouse built, and a site was provided by the Railway Company next to the RNLI's boathouse, which adjoined the Harbour Master's house. The Treasurer of the Appeal Fund, J. J. Rigg, proved a generous man and bought out some of the original shareholders. But he was also, apparently, 'obstinate and dictatorial', and his involvement may have caused the initial enthusiasm for the private lifeboat to wane. Her efficiency was also open to question as *Fishermen's Friend* could not launch to the barque *Royal Rose*, while details of any subsequent rescues she performed are not recorded. However, she remained in use until at least the mid-1870s and was not sold until 2 September 1889, although in what condition she was by then is unknown.

Meanwhile, in 1864, a decision was made to establish a lifeboat station at Upgang, to the north of Whitby, with the lifeboat manned by a Whitby crew, described in a separate chapter. With the stationing of a lifeboat at Upgang, the Institution took the opportunity to suggest that *Petrel* should be removed. They wanted the boat taken to London and her shed disposed of, even though it was little more than a year old. The local committee met on 4 January 1865 to consider their response to this proposal,

and sent a resolution to the RNLI which stated that they were 'deeply convinced of the great importance of retaining the *Petrel* lifeboat', and 'urgently request that she may be allowed to remain in her present boathouse.' The Institution acceded to this request and the lifeboat remained at Whitby for a further six years.

However, during this time *Petrel* was involved in only one more rescue, on 6 December 1871, when several local fishing cobles got into difficulty approaching the harbour in a full north-easterly gale and heavy seas. *Petrel* was launched and saved six men from two of the boats. However, the lifeboat sprang a serious leak and could not be used, so *Robert Whitworth* was launched and saved a further twelve men from four cobles. The year after this service, *Petrel*, which had been built in 1822, was found unfit for further service and so was replaced by a new lifeboat.

The Harriott Forteath lifeboats 1872 – 1887

The new boat on the East Side was a 30ft eight-oared Peake self-righter, built in 1864 by Forrestt which, named *Dorinda and Barbara*, had been stationed at Theddlethorpe in Lincolnshire for seven years. She was sent north from the RNLI's storeyard in London on board the Whitby Steam Shipping Company's steamship *Captain Cook* and, together with a new launching carriage, arrived at Whitby on 12 March 1872. Renamed *Harriott Forteath* after being appropriated to a gift of £680 from Mrs H. Forteath of Nottingham, she was the first of three lifeboats to serve the station under this name. She was on station for eight years, during which time she is credited with saving thirty-four lives.

Her first services took place during 1874. On 14 February she launched to five fishing cobles, which were in difficulty in heavy seas off the harbour, and saved a total of fifteen people. On 9 December she put out to the schooner *Pride*, of Southampton, which had gone aground at Whitby Sands in a north-easterly gale and saved two lives. She put off to the same vessel a week later and saved a salvage party of eight men who were stranded on board the wreck in heavy seas.

A map from the 1890s showing Pier Road and the location of the two lifeboat houses. The most northerly house was for the No.2 lifeboat and the other for the No.1 boat.

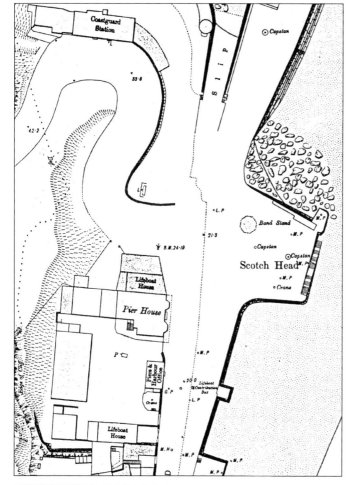

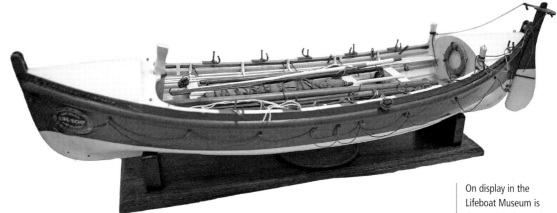

In 1877, *Harriott Forteath* was involved in a tragic incident which raised questions about the suitability of the life-belts then in use. In a prolonged period of bad weather at the start of the year, the small ketch *Agenoria*, carrying coal, arrived in Whitby Roads late in the evening of 9 January. Entering the harbour was impossible because of the heavy seas, and the harbour master, Captain Gibson, signalled to the vessel to stand off. But despite all warnings, the vessel still attempted to come in, and in the heavy seas she became unmanageable, and went ashore just north of the harbour entrance about a quarter of a mile from the West Pier.

It was impossible to launch the No.1 lifeboat as the main sewer from the cliff to the harbour had given way creating a deep trench in front of the boathouse. So, led by Coxswain Samuel Lacy, the lifeboatmen launched *Harriott Forteath* at about 1.30am across the sands in pitch darkness and into the heavy seas. Meanwhile, the Harbour Master and Coastguard took the rocket apparatus down the face of the West Cliff, having to struggle through slippery clay and deep mud to reach the beach. But they managed to set up their apparatus close enough to get a line aboard and *Agenoria's* crew of three were saved.

Although the crew had been saved, the lifeboat was still at sea and had succeeded in getting through the surf. But as she approached the stranded vessel, an enormous wave crashed over her, forcing her lee bow under the water and capsizing her. All but one of her eleven-man crew were thrown into the water. The lifeboat quickly righted herself and six of the crew were able to get back on board again,

while one man, John Storr, whose father had been drowned in the 1861 disaster, managed to struggle ashore.

He was wearing his cork jacket and reached the beach close to where the Harbour Master had set up the rocket apparatus. Unfortunately, three of the lifeboatmen were drowned: Coxswain Lacy, veteran lifeboatman Richard Gatenby, and John Thompson. A few moments later, the lifeboat, without oars or rudder, drifted close to the stranded vessel, and was washed up on the beach.

At the inquest following the capsize, the coroner concluded that the overturning of the boat was accidental, caused by the severe conditions, while the committee heard Second Coxswain Thomas Hartley's account of the events. He stated that the boat had been launched using a rope from the West Pier and then rowed north until the lifeboat crew were close to where they expected to find *Agenoria*. They put out a drogue and pulled towards the casualty.

Several big seas broke before reaching the lifeboat, but then a huge one broke over her, filling her to the gunwales and overwhelming and capsizing her. The crew were flung into the water, apart from one whose feet were tangled in some rope. The men in the water helped each other back on board, but could hear the cries of other men who were lost in the darkness. All but one of the oars were found to be broken or lost, and the boat was held by the drogue and the grapnel ropes, which had to be cut with a knife. By the time this was done, the boat and her crew were close inshore, and unable to help the drowning men.

The RNLI were satisfied with the account of events, which showed that the

The original service board for the No.2 station lifeboats Christopher and John Fielden is on display in the Lifeboat Museum. (Nicholas Leach)

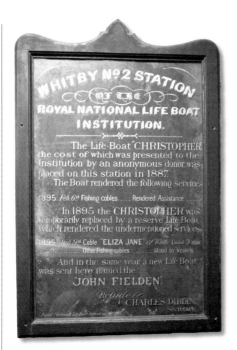

built in 1866 for the Wexford No.2 station as *Civil Service*, was a 32ft self-righter pulling ten oars. She had been unfit for further service at Wexford in 1878, so was overhauled by Woolfe, at Shadwell, and sent to Whitby the following year. However, whether she was in particularly good condition after this overhaul is questionable as she only stayed at Whitby for just over two years.

The first service she performed took place on 2 December 1879 after four fishing cobles got into difficulty while trying to enter harbour. *Harriott Forteath* was launched and supplied the crews with life-belts before escorting each boat over the bar. Her next launch was on 15 April 1880, also to fishing cobles, which got caught out in a strong easterly gale while trying to reach harbour. They were in danger of being swamped by the heavy seas, so the lifeboat went to their aid, taking out cork life-belts for the fishermen and standing by until their boats were safely beached. On 1 October 1880, *Harriott Forteath* was again launched to help some fishing boats, this time taking four crew out to the Cornish fishing boat *Matchless*, which was at anchor near Whitby Rock, and then bringing ashore a man from a coble which was unable to get into harbour or land on the beach.

The last service by the second *Harriott Forteath* took place on 28 October 1880, when she went to the schooner *Elizabeth Austin*, of Rye. Just over a year after this service, she was replaced by another lifeboat, the third to be given the name *Harriott Forteath*. This boat, formerly named *Robert Whitworth*, had been built in 1869 for the No.1 station and was transferred to the No.2 station after a new No.1 lifeboat had been completed in December 1881. The third *Harriott Forteath* was a 32ft self-righter and, as the No.2 lifeboat, she launched on service four times, saving five lives.

She undertook two life-saving services, both during 1885. The first came on 3 May when she went to the aid of the sloop *Wear*, of Sunderland, bound from Hartlepool to Walcott with coal, which got into difficulty while entering the harbour in heavy seas. The sloop missed the harbour entrance, drifted into the heavy breakers north of the West Pier, and

crew had taken all precautions with the drogue line, and had worked well together. However, the strings on many of the life-belts were found to have snapped and an explanation for this was harder to find. The belts were made of cork and fastened with strings, and they had been examined a few weeks earlier. Two of the life-belts washed up after the capsize had all their strings broken, while the stitching of several others had given way.

Hartley stated on oath that, when he and Lacy examined them some weeks earlier, the life-belts had been in good condition. It was suggested that the strings might have broken as the men struggled to climb back into the boat, or they might have deteriorated by being kept in the damp boathouse. The matter, however, was never satisfactorily explained, but attention was drawn to the weakness in the design of the belts. As a result, the RNLI sent a circular out drawing attention to the importance of renewing belt strings as soon as they showed even the slightest wear.

The last service performed by *Harriott Forteath* took place on 12 September 1878 when she launched to some fishing vessels in the Roads, boarded their crews and then stood by the vessels. In February 1879, the crew reported that they had lost confidence in the boat and so, in July, she was replaced by another lifeboat, also named *Harriott Forteath*. This lifeboat, stranded on the beach. The lifeboat was launched and, watched by thousands of spectators, saved the two men who were on board and who, with the decks awash, had been forced to take to the rigging.

The second service was on 20 August after the local fishing coble *Robert and Henry* was stranded on the beach during a northerly gale. The lifeboat launched to the coble at 6.30am and rescued the three men on board. *Harriott Forteath's* last two services were undertaken in 1886, the first on 20 January when she stood by five fishing cobles as they were crossing the bar, and the second on 5 October when she put out again to help local fishing cobles, *Lady Morris* and *Anne Elizabeth*, which were caught out by heavy seas and dense fog while trying to enter harbour.

Christopher
1887 – 1895

The third *Harriott Forteath* was withdrawn from service in August 1887 and returned to the RNLI storeyard in London. In her place, a new 34ft self-righter pulling ten oars, built by Forrestt of Limehouse, in London, at a cost of £325 7s 0d, was sent

to the station. The new lifeboat arrived on 8 August having been transported north by the Great Northern Railway. Provided out of an anonymous gift, she was named *Christopher* at the donor's request.

She served for just over eight years as the No.2 lifeboat, and was launched twice on service. Her first service launch was on 27 November 1888 when she put out to assist the Staithes lifeboat, which capsized when returning from service, but *Christopher* returned to Whitby without being able to offer any help. Her next service took place on 6 February 1895, when she stood by as the local fishing fleet returned to harbour in heavy seas.

A few weeks later, *Christopher* was withdrawn from service, having been found to be unsuitable, her keel being described as 'too deep', and she had become unfit for service. She was sent to London for repairs but, found to be in 'very defective condition', was condemned in September 1895 and broken up a few months later. Until a new lifeboat was ready, a temporary lifeboat was sent to the No.2 station but exact details of this boat are not recorded, although she did perform one rescue. She was launched

The No.2 lifeboat Christopher on her carriage on the West Side. The Tipping's plates on the carriage prevented the wheels from sinking into the soft sand on the beach. They were supplied in late 1894 together with a new carriage, which was built by Bristol Wagon Works Company.

WHITBY'S BRAVE HEARTS

The Pier Road No.1 lifeboat house can be seen centre left; it was built in 1847 and used until 1894 when the new double boathouse was built to the north on the site of the two boathouses seen behind the Scotch Head crane. Of these two houses, the one nearer to the Khyber Pass roadway housed the Fishermen's Friend lifeboat. It was built in 1864 and removed in 1889. The other was used for the No.2 lifeboat. (By courtesy of Whitby Museum)

An early view of the two lifeboats inside the double boathouse, probably taken shortly after the building was completed and showing the first Robert and Mary Ellis (ON.180) on the left and the No.2 lifeboat John Fielden (ON.379). (By courtesy of John Harrop)

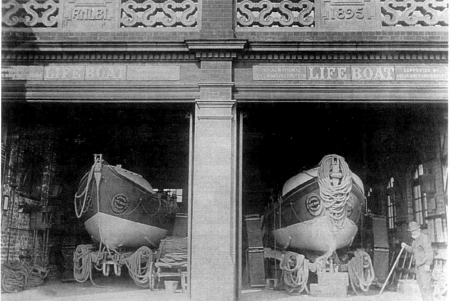

at 11am on 9 August 1895 and, in heavy seas, stood by while the town's fishing fleet returned to harbour. The lifeboat landed the crew of three from the coble *Eliza Jane*; they had been rescued by another boat after a huge wave washed them out of their own boat.

As *Christopher* was ending her career, plans were being drawn up for a new double boathouse after new launching carriages had been supplied. In December 1894 a new carriage, built by Bristol Wagon Works, arrived for the No.2 lifeboat and in February 1896 another came for the No.1 boat. Both carriages were fitted with Tipping's plates, which made crossing the soft sands much easier, and as they had proved so successful at Upgang they were supplied to the Whitby stations. However, the carriages fitted with the plates were too wide for both the existing boathouses and the slipway so the RNLI looked at ways to improve the situation. The road to the beach was repaired and widened, the retaining walls by the slipway were straightened, and a lowering bollard with deadman and chain was put in place to ease the boat down to the sand.

In September 1894 the RNLI's architect agreed a site for the new boathouse in conjunction with Sir George Elliott's Agent and Honorary Secretary Robert

Gibson, with the Corporate Seal of the Institution being affixed to the lease at the same time. In December 1894 a tender of £913 was accepted from Messrs Langdale & Sons for removing the present boathouse which occupied the site and constructing a new double boathouse. Work began in early 1895 and by May 1896 the new boathouse was ready. During the year, in December 1895 a low boundary wall with iron railings was erected on the seaward side of the lifeboat house to prevent the brick and stone wall being defaced at an additional cost of £28. With the completion of the new boathouses, the old No.2 house was handed over to the Harbour Trustees.

John Fielden
1895 – 1914

The new No.2 lifeboat was sent to Whitby on 20 November 1895, transported free of charge by the London and North Eastern Railway, and the reserve lifeboat was returned to London. The new boat was a standard 34ft self-righter, fitted with a water ballast tank, pulling ten oars and built by Waterman Bros at a cost of £305. She was provided by and named after John Fielden, of London, and served as the No.2 lifeboat for almost twenty years, in which time she saved sixty-two lives.

John Fielden was the busiest No.2 lifeboat and undertook many rescues, the majority of which were to local fishing cobles in danger while crossing the notoriously dangerous bar at the entrance to the harbour. She saved her first lives on 15 January 1896 when she rescued the crew of four from the local coble *Secret*, and put out again to local fishing cobles on 13 February and 27 July the same year. On 12 March 1897, she was again launched to assist fishing cobles, putting out at 5.15pm to the cobles *Mary Alice* and *Tranquil*. The lifeboat crew supplied the fishermen with cork life-jackets, and assisted the former vessel onto the beach. The crew of *Tranquil* decided to enter harbour, and managed to get in safely with the lifeboat in close attendance.

Following further services to local fishing cobles, *John Fielden* took part in a rather unusual service on 20 November 1901. Just before midnight on 19 November, the steamship *Cygnet*, of London, was seen approaching Whitby, with a light burning at her masthead and a north-westerly gale blowing. When the steamer dropped anchor, dangerously close to the Whitby Rocks, in rough seas she was thought to be in difficulty. *John Fielden* was launched at midnight and the lifeboatmen found that the steamer, bound for the Tyne, had almost run out of coal. Helped by one of the larger cobles, the lifeboat took some coal out to the steamer, which resumed her passage at 10am.

In the early hours of 2 June 1902, *John Fielden* was called out to assist the three-masted schooner *Frier*, of Poole, which,

The scene at Scotch Head during the naming ceremony of No.2 lifeboat John Fielden (ON.379) during the summer of 1896. She had been built by Waterman Bros at Cremyll, near Plymouth, and arrived at Whitby in November 1895.

Coxswain Thomas Langlands with John Fielden (ON.379) on her carriage in the doorway of the lifeboat house. (By courtesy of Whitby Lifeboat Museum)

Inside the boathouse on Pier Road showing William Riley of Leamington and Birmingham (ON.594), on left, and the No.1 lifeboat Robert and Mary Ellis (ON.588). The board in the centre is dated June 1910, although this image was used on an RNLI centenary postcard during 1924. (By courtesy of John Harrop)

the south. The lifeboat approached the steamer to ask for help, and the steamer agreed to tow *Frier* to safety. The lifeboat assisted in transferring a towing hawser between the two vessels, but this parted and *John Fielden* had to give further assistance in restoring contact. The second rope held, and the lifeboat, after escorting the schooner out to sea as she was towed by the steamer, returned to station.

Another service to the fishing fleet took place on 12 September 1909 after fourteen local fishing boats left port, but were caught out in bad weather which forced them to return. At midnight, when four of the boats returned, conditions were worsening and so *John Fielden* put out to help. Between then and 5am, she escorted nine craft into safety. During April 1910, the lifeboat was again busy helping fishing cobles. On 6 April she took out spare life-jackets to the crews of seven fishing cobles and escorted the vessels into harbour one at a time. At times heavy seas were breaking over the whole area between the piers and one coble narrowly escaped being totally swamped. On 22 April, the lifeboat launched to assist the cobles *Robert and Mary* and *Brotherly Love*. She stood by as it was not safe to enter harbour, but as the weather worsened it became too dangerous for their crews to remain in them, so the seven men were taken on board the lifeboat, and the cobles

carrying coal, had anchored about a quarter of a mile off Whitby Rock Buoy, close to rocks in a dangerous position. The lifeboat proceeded to the vessel, which could not get under way and to safety without assistance in the thick fog. The schooner's master asked the lifeboat to stand by until the fog lifted, when a steamer was seen approaching from

were cast adrift to wash up on the beach.

On 30 November 1911 *John Fielden* went to the aid of a steamship, *Vostizza*, of Andros, carrying coal and bound from Shields. She launched at 5.30am to the assistance of the steamship, which was stranded about four miles north of Whitby. The lifeboat reached the vessel, but her captain stated that he did not then require immediate assistance. As the vessel was in a dangerous position, the coxswain decided to stand by until the next high water as, in the event of the steamer not floating, assistance would be required. At 9am, a passing steamer came to the aid of *Vostizza*, and an hour and a half later succeeded in towing her into deep water so *John Fielden* returned to station.

During her last three years of service, *John Fielden* was further used to help local fishing cobles. On 3 December 1912, she launched at 9.45am and stood by eleven local cobles which were outside the harbour in a heavy ground sea, returning to station after almost four hours afloat. On 17 March 1913, she stood by two fishing cobles for an hour and a half in heavy seas, and on 16 March 1914 assisted five cobles which had been caught out in a strong north-easterly gale and rough sea.

This proved to be her last service as, during her next launch, to the hospital ship *Rohilla*, she was so badly damaged

that she had to be broken up. This epic service, and the part in it played by *John Fielden*, is described a later chapter.

Forester (Reserve No.4) 1914 – 1919

The damaged *John Fielden* had to be broken up on the rocks after she had performed so well during the *Rohilla* rescue leaving Whitby a lifeboat short. To remedy the situation, a temporary boat, Reserve No.4, was supplied and became the No.2 lifeboat. A 34ft self-righter, this boat had been built in 1900 as *Forester* for the Tynemouth No.2 station and arrived at Whitby on 3 November 1914. Between Tynemouth and Whitby, she also served at both Haisborough and Runswick on a temporary basis, and was one of the first lifeboats to be used as a reserve boat.

Although intended to serve only temporarily at Whitby, Reserve No.4 stayed for just under five years, and, saving ninety-eight lives during this time, was far busier than previous No.2 lifeboats, mainly because she was operating during the First World War years. Wartime operation was particularly difficult as aids to navigation were often removed so they could not help the enemy, and thus night-time rescues were much more hazardous. However, to help the lifeboats, in November 1915 the Admiralty allowed the harbour authorities

The 34ft self-righter John Fielden (ON.379) on her launching carriage. She served as the No.2 lifeboat from 1895 to 1914. (By courtesy of Whitby Lifeboat Museum)

The double boathouse completed in 1895 greatly improved accommodation for the lifeboats and is still standing, largely unaltered externally, in use as the lifeboat museum. (By courtesy of Grahame Farr)

to display lights as necessary to guide the lifeboats if they went out on service.

After arriving on station, Reserve No.4 was soon in action, saving the steamship *Ingrid II*, of Christiania and her crew of sixteen on 25 November 1914, after the vessel had gone aground on the Whitby Rocks. She was out again in December 1914, launching first on 24 December to save the steamship *Fane*, of Bergen, which stranded on the Whitby Rock while bound from South Shields to Rouen carrying coal. The crew salvaged the vessel, and succeeded in refloating her on the night of 26 December. In between, on Christmas Day, the lifeboat saved the local coble *Harvest Home* and her sole occupant, who had also been involved in the salvage.

The most notable service of 1915 involved the steamship *Skane*, of Helsingborg, which went aground on Whitby Rock on 1 December, while bound from Stockholm to Calais, and was beached almost a mile north of the West Pier. Between 2 and 20 December, Reserve No.4 was launched on numerous occasions to stand by and assist with salvage work on the vessel.

In 1917, the lifeboat undertook three services, the first on 20 February to the Sunderland steamship *Braeside*, which had stranded on Whitby Rock. The

lifeboat stood by until, eventually, local motor boats managed to refloat her. On 8 and 9 October, Reserve No.4 launched four times to the steamship *Carlotta*, of Chevant, which had stranded on Whitby Rock, and saved nineteen people. On 9 December she saved eight from the steamship *Venetia*, of Glasgow, which had been torpedoed from Middlesbrough; the other members of the steamer's crew were saved by a patrol boat.

The reserve lifeboat's last services were undertaken in 1918. On 23 January she went to the steamer *Portaferry*, of Glasgow, which had stranded on Whitby Rock in very heavy seas. The lifeboat launched at 6.45pm and spent an hour and a half at sea, saving the steamer's eight crew. On 14 February she went to the steamer *Spurt*, of Christiania, saving three from the vessel. Her last service was on 25 March when she saved twenty-three from the steamer *Nordstrand*, of London, which had gone aground on Upgang Rock in a strong northerly wind and rough seas.

In 1919, a new pulling lifeboat was sent to the station to replace the reserve lifeboat, which was sent to the RNLI's storeyard in November 1919 and sold out of service the following year. She gained a fine record of service at Whitby, and is credited with saving ninety-eight lives.

Upgang lifeboat station

In August 1864, the local committee at Whitby suggested to the RNLI that another lifeboat station should be established at Upgang, a small village about a mile north of the harbour. Launching the lifeboats at Whitby in certain conditions, particularly northerly gales, often proved very difficult and a lifeboat at Upgang, where getting afloat would be easier in such conditions, was seen as the answer. The lifeboat would be manned by a Whitby crew, and come under the Whitby committee.

The RNLI agreed to this request and, within two months, set about establishing the station. A boathouse was built at Upgang by Robinson and Smales at a cost of £220 16s 0d, and Thomas Smith Langlands was appointed Coxswain. The former Penzance lifeboat, a 30ft self-righter built in 1860 and originally named *Alexandra*, was sent, being altered from rowing six to rowing ten oars before being sent north. She was then appropriated to a gift from Dr H. W. Watson, of Derby, who had presented the RNLI with £180 for a new lifeboat. His late sister, Miss Watson, had wanted to fund a lifeboat and, as she had died intestate, Dr Watson carried out her wishes. On 4 July 1865 the boat, with a launching carriage which had been provided at a cost of £32 12s 0d, was forwarded to Whitby, where she was christened *William Watson* according to the wishes of the donor. After her christening, she was rowed round to the new lifeboat house at Upgang and recovered onto her carriage for the first time.

William Watson served for fourteen years but was never launched on service, suggesting that a lifeboat may not actually have been needed at Upgang. In 1878, she was renamed *Joseph Sykes* after being appropriated to the legacy of the late Mrs A. E. Sykes of Butharlyp Howe, Grasmere, in grateful remembrance of the rescue of Lieut J. Sykes, RN, saved from HMS *Alert* which was wrecked in 1817.

But the following year *Joseph Sykes* left the station and was replaced in July 1879 by a new 32ft self-righter. Built by Woolfe, of Shadwell, at a cost of £282, she was also named *Joseph Sykes* having been appropriated to the same legacy as her predecessor. This second lifeboat served at Upgang for just six years, and neither of her two launches resulted in effective services.

January 1881 storms

Although not used to save any lives, the second *Joseph Sykes* was involved in the most significant incident in the station's history, in January 1881, when a series of storms battered the country and the Whitby lifeboat was dragged over the moors to Robin Hood's Bay, as described in Chapter 2. During the terrible weather, shipping was forced to seek shelter. A schooner with coal from Hartlepool stranded on a sandbank inside Whitby Harbour and became a wreck, another was damaged on Tate Hill sand, while a brigantine narrowly escaped destruction on the bar. Outside the harbour, the seas got steadily worse, creating a considerable swell at the harbour entrance.

At about 9.30pm on 11 January, a Coastguard lookout saw a distress signal somewhere off Upgang, and called out the lifeboat. In the darkness, seeing the vessel was very difficult, but the Coastguard thought she might be on Upgang Rock, and guessed she was about a mile offshore. The rocket apparatus was taken along the beach, but getting the rockets to reach the wreck was a hopeless task in the strong winds and total darkness. By this time, the vessel was burning a tar barrel and, unable to help immediately, the Coastguard men separated to patrol the beach with lanterns, ready to help any of the shipwrecked crew should they be washed ashore.

Meanwhile, *Joseph Sykes* was launched, under the command of Coxswain Thomas Langlands, into heavy seas. The launching party watching from the shore soon lost sight of the lifeboat in the darkness, but knew the lifeboatmen would have a considerable struggle to reach the wreck in the difficult conditions. As she cleared the surf, however, the lifeboat was hit by a huge wave which almost overwhelmed her. She was thrown back towards the beach a dozen times, but each time the crew continued determinedly with their task of getting through the breaking surf and reaching the wreck.

Huge waves repeatedly swept over the boat, throwing some of the crew out of their seats, which left two unconscious. Despite the boat gradually becoming ice-covered, the crew continued pulling at the oars, some of which broke in the extreme conditions. Finally, after almost two hours of struggling in horrendous seas, the lifeboatmen saw the wreck, about 150 to 200 yards away, with the tar barrel still burning. They were suffering considerably in the extreme cold, as snow continued to fall. Their clothing was frozen, their hands and arms were numb and so Langlands, realising that his exhausted crew could offer no practical help, reluctantly decided to return to shore.

Captain Gibson, the Honorary Secretary, had remained at Upgang throughout and watched the lifeboat launch; he had seen the crew struggling to row through the breakers and then watched as she disappeared in the darkness and snow storms. After two hours of anxious waiting, the lifeboat was seen making for the beach. When she landed, several of the crew had to be helped out, with some unconscious, and all were taken inside to get warm. Gibson then went with one of the Coastguard men to bring the Whitby boat and crew to Upgang, but found that Coxswain Henry Freeman had already launched *Robert Whitworth*, taken the boat clear of the slipway, and commanded the crew to undertake the long pull of over two miles in heavy seas towards the wreck.

A massive effort by the lifeboatmen, which exhausted and numbed them, resulted in the lifeboat getting to within sight of the wreck. At this point, however, they saw what appeared to be a green or blue flare from the beach, the signal that the Upgang boat had completed the rescue, while the disappearance of the lights on the wreck seemed to confirm that the crew had been taken off.

Freeman showed a light indicating he intended to return, and with no signal instructing him to remain with the wreck, made for home. The return journey was as bad as the outward one for his crew and the boat, which was almost swamped several times. The lifeboatmen were wet, cold and some were frozen to their seats when the boat eventually came ashore close to the Spa Pavilion. Most of the crew went home, thinking that they would not be needed again that night, while others

A rather faded photograph showing the second Joseph Sykes lifeboat on her carriage on the beach, with her crew at the oars and the launchers on the ropes. (By courtesy of Whitby Lifeboat Museum)

went to Upgang, leaving Freeman and a group of launchers to get the boat back on to her carriage.

As the boat was being recarriaged, Gibson arrived with the news that the Upgang boat had not succeeded in rescuing the crew of the wreck. Freeman then agreed to take the boat to Upgang, but by the time a crew had been assembled the tide had risen and it was impossible to take the boat across the beach. Consequently, *Robert Whitworth* was taken up Khyber Pass, along Skinner Street and via St Hilda's Terrace to Upgang Lane. But before the boat reached Upgang, the wrecked ship started to break up. She had her sails set and, in the glare of the tar barrel, stood out against the bleakness of the night as thousands of people watched from the cliff tops. Huge waves were crashing against her sides and over her decks, where for four hours her half-frozen crew awaited salvation. But when the flames of the tar barrel died down, the spectators on the cliffs could no longer see the vessel until a brief break in the clouds, just after 2am, gave them a glimpse of the ship as she rolled onto her side and disappeared.

The next day, little was left to indicate what had happened during the night. About a hundred yards from Upgang Bank lay the overturned bottom of the brig. Half-a-mile to seaward were her spars, close to where she had gone aground. Amongst the wreckage on the beach were two bodies, and a board bearing the name *Lumley*, which was a 285-ton brigantine of South Shields commanded by John Woodhouse. The bodies of the other eight members of the crew were never recovered and the original cause of the disaster was never ascertained: the casualty may have sprung a leak or been in a collision, but in the terrible seas which eventually overwhelmed her, and prevented a rescue, none of her crew survived.

Joseph Sykes' next call, in October 1882, did not result in an effective service being completed, and less than three years later she was replaced. In August 1885, the former Bamburgh lifeboat, another 32ft self-righter, arrived at Upgang and was renamed *Joseph Sykes*, having originally been christened *John and Betty Cuttell*.

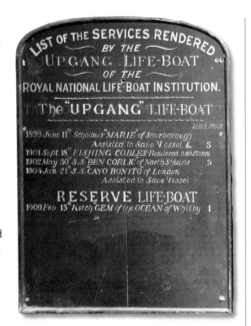

The service record board for Upgang lifeboat station is preserved and on display in Whitby Lifeboat Museum. (Nicholas Leach)

Built by Woolfe, like her predecessor, the new lifeboat had spent only two years at the Northumberland station before her move south. But at both her stations she was never launched on service, and, in November 1890, was withdrawn from Upgang.

The new lifeboat Upgang

A new 34ft ten-oared self-righter, built by Watkins & Co at a cost of £413 16s 8d, was sent to the station on 26 November. This boat had been provided by a donor who wished to remain anonymous and was named *Upgang*. She was fitted with bilge keels, two masts and sails, and two water-ballast tanks. She served the station for almost eighteen years and was the busiest of the Upgang lifeboats, launching six times on service and saving eight lives during her career.

Upgang was launched on service for the first time on 18 November 1893, when the steamer *Southwark* was driven ashore in a severe storm during which several of the neighbouring lifeboats were also called out. But as Coxswain Thomas Langlands and his crew fought their way out through the very heavy surf, the Rocket Brigade succeeded in getting a line aboard the steamer and the thirteen men on board were all saved.

Almost six years passed before the lifeboat recorded her next service, the first life-saving service by an Upgang lifeboat. On 11 June 1899, *Upgang* was launched at 1.15am, into rough seas, to go to the aid of the schooner *Marie*, of Scarborough, bound from Whitby for Blyth with a crew of three. She had dragged her anchors and was in a dangerous position amongst the breakers near Upgang rocks. With the help of the lifeboatmen, the vessel was saved and taken into Whitby harbour.

After standing by some local cobles in heavy seas on 18 September 1901, *Upgang* was next launched on service at 10.30pm on 30 May 1902, after the steamship *Ben Corlic*, of North Shields, ran aground off Upgang. The steamer, carrying coal from the Tyne to the Mediterranean, stranded in dense fog and rough seas. When the distress signals had been seen, not enough men were at Upgang to form a crew, so a message was sent to Whitby calling for more men. Once they arrived at Upgang, the lifeboat was launched and saved five of the ship's crew. Before the lifeboat had launched, however, some of the steamer's crew attempted to get ashore in a couple of their own boats. Unfortunately, these boats capsized in the heavy breakers on the beach and, while thirteen out of fifteen got ashore, two of the men were drowned. After returning ashore, the lifeboatmen patrolled the beach for two hours hoping to recover the bodies of the two men who died, but without success.

Both Upgang and Whitby No.1 lifeboat *Robert and Mary Ellis* were launched late on the evening of 21 January 1904, after the 2,000-ton steamer *Cayo Bonito*, of London, bound from the Tyne in ballast, came ashore near Upgang. The No.1 lifeboat from Whitby was launched and went to the steamer's assistance on what was a cold, frosty night. On reaching the vessel the coxswain boarded her, and at the request of the captain helped to run out a kedge anchor. Upgang lifeboat was also launched and came alongside the steamer to assist with the anchors. At about 4am the next day, the steamer got clear of the rocks and, once refloated, made for the Tyne while the lifeboats returned to their respective stations.

This was the last service performed by *Upgang*, which was withdrawn on 9 June 1908 and replaced by a reserve lifeboat, another 34ft self-righter, *James and Caroline*. Built in 1890, this lifeboat was stationed at St Agnes (Isles of Scilly) until 1904 and saved thirty-two lives during her time there. She spent just over a year at Upgang, and undertook one service, a fine rescue that earned her Coxswain formal recognition from the RNLI.

The rescue took place during the afternoon of 15 February 1909 when a small vessel, being driven southward by a fresh northerly wind, was seen to be in difficulty. At about 4.15pm, the vessel, the ketch *Gem of the Ocean*, belonging to Whitby, which had left Hartlepool earlier in the day carrying coal, was off Kettleness. The Upgang crew assembled, proceeded to the boathouse and launched the lifeboat at Lector Hole, with Coxswain 'Pounder' Robinson in command.

The vessel was driven ashore in heavy breakers south of Lector rocks, and the

Robinson Pounder Robinson was one of the best known of Upgang's Coxswains. He served in the post from 1899 until the station closed in 1919. (By courtesy of Whitby Lifeboat Museum)

lifeboat made for her. Once close enough, the lifeboat crew got a line across, but an extremely heavy sea swept the lifeboat round the stern of the ketch. As huge seas crashed over the lifeboat, one man was rescued, but an enormous wave then drove the lifeboat hard against the casualty's side, smashing the lifeboat's rudder and several oars. The rope parted and, before the boat could be got under control, she was swept ashore. The launchers waded into the pounding surf and pushed the lifeboat afloat again, some of the men going in up to their necks. The crew on the lifeboat made heroic efforts to rescue the second man on the ketch, but each time they were beaten back by the tremendous seas

Seeing that their Upgang colleagues had only managed to save one man, the crew of the new Whitby No.1 lifeboat *Robert and Mary Ellis*, under the command of Coxswain Thomas Langlands, launched their boat and, approaching the wreck from the shore side, succeeded in rescuing the remaining survivor. The vessel, not more than 400 yards from the shore,

broke into pieces a few minutes after the Whitby lifeboat got clear. Both the lifeboats then made for the beach to be hauled to safety. This fine service was described in the RNLI's official account as 'a splendid one, and the pluck displayed was much extolled in the press'. The Committee of Management accorded the Thanks of the Institution on Vellum to the two Coxswains involved, Robinson and Langlands in addition to monetary rewards. These awards were subsequently presented publicly to the two men by the Archbishop of York.

Just over five months after playing a major part in this daring rescue, the reserve lifeboat was replaced by a new lifeboat. She was a 34ft Rubie self-righter, a type of self-righter lighter than the standard version and thus more suitable for launching off flat, open beaches. Weighing just over two tons, the boat was built by Thames Ironworks at Blackwall in London at a cost of £722 9s 1d, and was provided from the legacy of William Riley of Leamington. She was fitted with

The Upgang lifeboat crew with the lifeboat Upgang outside the boathouse.

The remains of the slipway at Upgang photographed in 1963. There is no trace of the station today. (By courtesy of Grahame Farr)

six relieving tubes, a full-length keel five inches wide made of wood and iron, 16ft bilge keels, two water ballast tanks, no masts or sails, and was pulled by ten oars. The new lifeboat completed her trials out of the RNLI's storeyard on 18 June 1909 and was then sent north to her station. She arrived at Upgang on 21 July 1909 and was christened *William Riley of Birmingham and Leamington* on 23 August 1909 at a unique double naming ceremony held on the beach at Whitby, which is described in Chapter 2.

William Riley served at Upgang for a decade, and carried out two launches during that time but saved no lives. The demand on her services, like most of her predecessors at Upgang, was negligible and, by the end of the First World War, a lifeboat at Upgang was not needed. A new motor lifeboat was under construction for Whitby as the war was drawing to a close, manning had become difficult due to the demands of the conflict and in July 1919 the Chief Inspector of Lifeboats, H. F. J. Rowley, recommended that the station be closed immediately. The new Whitby motor lifeboat had undergone her final trials two months before, and the Upgang station was no longer needed.

So the dismantling of the station began and on 13 November 1919 it was officially closed after fifty-five years of service. *William Riley* was sent to Whitby as the No.2 lifeboat, while the carriage, stores and equipment were returned to the RNLI's storeyard in London. The boathouse remained standing for many years, but was gradually destroyed as the cliff behind it slowly shifted. During the latter years of the twentieth century, the house and launchway disappeared leaving no trace of the station.

The gravestone of Thomas Smith Langlands in Whitby cemetery. A pulling and sailing lifeboat in relief adorns the top. (Nicholas Leach)

The Rohilla Epic

During the years leading up to the First World War, the two Whitby lifeboats were often called out to render assistance to local fishing boats, undertaking relatively routine services. However, in 1914, they were involved in one of the finest lifeboat services in the history of the RNLI. The episode began on Thursday 29 October 1914 when the 7,409-ton hospital ship *Rohilla* sailed from Queensferry, bound for Dunkirk. Registered in Glasgow and owned by the British India Line, *Rohilla* was built in 1906 by Harland & Wolff at Belfast as a passenger and cruise liner. She was initially used on the London to India service, operating from Southampton to Karachi during the winter. In 1908 she was converted for use as a troopship and in August 1914 was requisitioned as a naval hospital ship.

In this capacity she left the Forth in late October 1914 to head south with 229 people on board, including a full medical staff and five nurses. Without any coastal aids to navigation showing because of the war, steering was calculated using 'dead reckoning', and thus prone to error. As the ship passed the Northumberland coast, in the pitch dark, she was inadvertently steered closer to the rocky coastline than her crew realised. And just after 4am on 30 October, in steadily worsening weather, she ran aground on the rocks off Saltwick Nab, about a mile south of Whitby. Stranded, the ship was pounded by mountainous seas, and soon broke in half. Many on the aft part were immediately washed away and drowned.

The dangers of this reef were, of course, well known to locals and as soon as the ship went ashore Coxswain Thomas Langlands was alerted. In the prevailing conditions, it was impossible to launch the No.1 lifeboat across the west beach and then row her round to the wreck. From 1907, the No.2 lifeboat *John Fielden* had been kept afloat at moorings in the

Rohilla wrecked at Saltwick Nab on 30 October 1914. This photo was taken early in the afternoon of the day the ship went aground.

During the early stages of the rescue attempts, the Rocket Brigade repeatedly fired rocket lines to those on board the wreck of Rohilla, but without success.

harbour during the winter months, and so Langlands decided that she should be hauled out of the water and manhandled to a suitable launch site, as rowing her out of the harbour would also be inadvisable.

But getting her into a position near Saltwick Nab was fraught with difficulties as it involved dragging the boat under the Spa ladder, a gangway from the East pier to the cliff, and then along the beach over skids. An 8ft sea-wall also had to be negotiated and the endeavour was declared impossible by many watching. However, the lifeboat was successfully brought into a position opposite *Rohilla*, although she was holed twice during the short journey. That she got there at all was due 'to the indomitable perseverance of Coxswain Langlands . . . with the help of many willing hands working under his direction', according to *The Lifeboat* Journal.

In spite of the tremendous surf that was pounding the beach, *John Fielden* was launched at 7am and, after a desperate struggle for her crew, reached the wreck, by which time the vessel had been on the Scar for just over five hours. The ship lay about 450 yards offshore surrounded by jagged rocks, but the lifeboat managed to get alongside. The five nurses and twelve of the men were rescued, having to climb precariously down a swaying rope ladder in order to get on board the lifeboat. They were landed ashore, after which the lifeboat immediately put off again.

Considerable effort was required by the lifeboat crew to get back to the wreck, but they succeeded in rescuing another eighteen men. The lifeboat sustained more damage on the rocks during her second journey and, when she was hauled ashore, it was realised that she had been too badly damaged for further use.

Captain James Milburn then sent for the Upgang lifeboat, which was brought from her boathouse, two miles west of Whitby, to the scene. This involved transporting the boat through Whitby town, with horses pulling her carriage, and over the fields to the top of the cliffs. From there she was lowered by ropes onto the beach, down the almost vertical face of the cliffs, with the assistance of not only the horses but also well over 100 willing helpers. Despite all this effort, an attempt to launch the lifeboat had to be postponed as the seas were by this time too heavy and a launch too risky in the dreadful conditions. But the Upgang Coxswain and crew remained on stand by in case they were needed.

Meanwhile, telephone calls had been made to Scarborough and Teesmouth lifeboat stations, asking for assistance. At Scarborough, preparations were made to launch the lifeboat *Queensbury*, but the crew had to wait until conditions improved before going afloat. She eventually got away at 3.30pm and, because rowing to Whitby was an almost impossible task, was taken in tow by the steam trawler *Morning*

Star. After an extremely rough passage, the trawler and lifeboat reached Saltwick Nab at about 6pm. By then, it was pitch dark and, with enormous seas breaking all around *Rohilla*, it was impossible for the lifeboat crew to get close to the wreck.

The lifeboat and trawler remained a few hundred yards offshore throughout the night, in case an opportunity came for them to get alongside the wreck. But the hopes of those on board were dashed as it became clear the boat could not get close enough. During the night, the Scarborough lifeboatmen endured the terrible conditions, as huge seas repeatedly filled their open boat. On the Saturday morning, they made a further valiant attempt to reach *Rohilla*, but were again beaten back by the huge waves. Having been at sea for almost eighteen hours, in the most appalling conditions, the Scarborough men were forced to return home. The lifeboat was towed back to station by the trawler, while the situation for those on the wreck remained perilous.

The Teesmouth lifeboat *Bradford IV* was the next to launch in the hope of reaching *Rohilla*. She was based in a boathouse on the South Gare, twenty-two miles north of Whitby, and was a 42ft self-righter built in 1893 as a pulling and sailing lifeboat for the Ramsgate station, but fitted with a 35hp Tylor petrol engine in 1906. As she crossed the bar at the entrance to the river Tees, *Bradford IV* ran into mountainous seas and heavy waves which swept over the boat. In the terrible conditions, she sprang a serious leak, placing her crew in serious danger. Fortunately, the steam tug *Sir Joseph Pease* was following the lifeboat out of the river, so took the stranded lifeboat crew aboard the tug and then towed the damaged lifeboat back to Middlesborough. So another rescue attempt ended in failure.

During the early morning on Saturday 31 October, two further attempts were made by lifeboats from Whitby. At 7am, the No.1 lifeboat *Robert and Mary Ellis* was launched into the harbour and taken to sea under the command of Coxswain Langlands. She waited for the steam trawler *Mayfly*, which had been summoned from Hartlepool by telegram, and which arrived off Whitby at 8am. The trawler took the lifeboat in tow but was unable to get the lifeboat any closer than half-a-mile from the wreck. After a discussion between Coxswain Langlands and James Hastings, Second Coxswain of the Hartlepool No.2 lifeboat who was on board *Mayfly*, it was reluctantly agreed to return to Whitby harbour.

A couple of hours later, at 9am, the Upgang lifeboat *William Riley of Leamington and Birmingham* was launched

The No.2 lifeboat John Fielden is dragged across the beach by hundreds of helpers to get into a position to launch to the stranded hospital ship.

A dramatic photo showing the lifeboat John Fielden just getting afloat ready to make one of her rescue attempts. This image shows clearly the raging seas around the wreck which made the rescue so difficult and, ultimately, proved too much for the pulling lifeboats. (By courtesy of Whitby Lifeboat Museum)

after her crew had waited throughout the night for a suitable opportunity. Once at sea, Coxswain Pounder Robinson and his crew desperately battled for over an hour to reach *Rohilla*, but eventually they became exhausted and were also forced to return ashore. The heavy seas and strong currents running between the Nab and the wreck proved too strong, although the lifeboat had at one point got to within fifty yards of the wreck.

Those on board the wreck watched as the lifeboat was swept back and, in desperation, some of them decided to jump overboard and swim ashore. As they did so, some of the onlookers, 'with heroic disregard for their own safety', rushed into the heavy surf and dragged the survivors

ashore. A number succeeded and were saved, but several others failed to reach the beach safely and died before they could be hauled ashore.

With huge seas still sweeping over *Rohilla*, it became apparent that only a motor lifeboat stood any chance of rescuing the remaining people on the wreck, which was surrounded by rocks preventing deployment of an anchor which could have been used to veer down on the ship. The Tynemouth motor lifeboat was therefore summoned by telegram.

The message reached the Tyne at 4.15pm on Saturday 31 October and within fifteen minutes the 40ft self-righter *Henry Vernon*, a 1911-built motor lifeboat powered by a 40hp Tylor petrol

The William Riley lifeboat is hauled round Saltwick Nab onto the beach after her attempts to save the survivors from the wrecked Rohilla, seen in the background. (By courtesy of Whitby Lifeboat Museum)

engine, set off on the hazardous journey south. The forty-four-mile trip was undertaken in total darkness, tremendous seas and without the aid of any of the coastal navigation lights which had been extinguished because of the war. At the helm was Coxswain Robert Smith, who was assisted throughout by the Second Coxswain, James Brownlee, and Captain Herbert E. Burton, the Honorary Superintendent of the motor lifeboat, together with eight other crew.

The motor lifeboat reached Whitby harbour at 1am on Sunday 1 November, just as arrangements were being made by Lieut Basil Hall, RN, Inspector of Lifeboats for the Southern District, to make another attempt to launch the Upgang lifeboat *William Riley* at daybreak. A supply of oil was being loaded onto the boat to be discharged into the sea to reduce the severity of the waves around the wreck. However, with the arrival of the Tynemouth lifeboat the Inspector transferred the oil onto that boat which, at 6.30am on the Sunday morning, headed out of Whitby harbour with Lieut Hall on board as well as the Whitby Second Coxswain Richard Eglon, acting as Pilot.

Henry Vernon made her way out to sea and round to the wreck, over which

heavy seas still crashed two days after *Rohilla* had run aground. When about 200 yards from the wreck, *Henry Vernon* stopped and turned seawards in a move that appeared to those onshore as though she was heading back to harbour. But in fact, her crew were ready to discharge the several gallons of oil to calm the foaming white water. Within minutes, the effect was

Thomas Smith Langlands, Coxswain at Upgang from 1877 to 1899 and Whitby from 1899 to 1920, was awarded the RNLI's Gold Medal for his part in the rescue of the Rohilla survivors. He played a key role in getting the local lifeboats to sea during the initial attempts to effect a rescue from Rohilla. One of the most famous lifeboatmen in Whitby's history, he joined the crew in 1871 and served as Second Coxswain at Upgang for two years before becoming Coxswain. In almost fifty years of service, he helped to save more than 200 lives.

The lifeboat John Fielden on the rocks where she was driven lying next to remains of the Rohilla.

close to the steamer's bridge, from where the survivors looked on in hope and amazement, and held her in position to effect the rescue. Within seconds, those on board had lowered ropes down to the rescue boat, and were sliding down them to safety. Forty men were taken aboard quite quickly, but then, according to the *Yorkshire Post's* eyewitness account,

'two enormous waves were seen rolling up from the sea at tremendous speed. One after the other they swept over the bridge and across each end of the remnants of the deck on to the Lifeboat at the other side, enveloping it fore and aft. Each time the tough little craft disappeared for a moment beneath the spray, reappeared, tottered, and righted herself gamely. Indeed, not a man was lost, not a splinter broken.'

The lifeboat, having cleared herself of the tons of water that crashed down on her, remained in position as the remaining ten men got off the wreck and were taken safely aboard. A man fell overboard at one point, but he was picked up and pulled into the lifeboat, while last to leave the wreck was the Captain, David L. Neilson,

The lifeboatmen involed in the rescue attempt included, seated, from left to right, Pounder Robinson (from Upgang), Thomas Langlands and Richard Eglon. (By courtesy of Whitby Lifeboat Museum)

quite dramatic and the huge breakers were flattened out into a heavy swell. Coxswain Smith then brought *Henry Vernon* towards the wreck at full speed, with little time to lose before the sea dissipated the oil.

With superb skill, he brought the lifeboat alongside the remains of *Rohilla*,

who brought with him the ship's cat. The whole rescue had been completed in just over fifteen minutes, and with the fifty survivors on board the lifeboat turned away from the wreck to make for harbour.

However, getting the lifeboat clear of *Rohilla* was no easy task as the effect the

The Tynemouth lifeboat crew involved in the Rohilla rescue using the 40ft motor lifeboat Henry Vernon, depicted in the inset, and led by Coxswain Robert Smith and Captain Herbert Burton.

The funeral procession crossing the bridge in memory of those who lost their lives on Rohilla.

oil had on calming the waves was starting to diminish and the heavy waves were again breaking all around. As the lifeboat was brought clear of the stern of the wreck, she was struck on her broadside by an enormous wave, which rolled her right over on her beam ends. But within seconds, she came upright and continued out to sea before Coxswain Smith turned her shoreward and brought her safely into harbour. Lifeboat, crew and survivors were met by rousing cheers from hundreds of townspeople who had rushed to the quayside on the western pier with blankets, tea and other comforts for the survivors.

The fifty survivors were helped ashore, many into waiting cars and ambulances to be taken to hospital. They had endured over two days on the wreck, without food or drink, awaiting help in perishingly cold conditions, and most wearing very few clothes. Watching the survivors come ashore was the *Yorkshire Posts's* eyewitness, who concluded his account:

'Dr Lomas, the chief of the medical staff on board, though he bore himself bravely, was evidently very greatly exhausted, but the captain seemed to be a man of iron. Unassisted, he walked firmly up the steps, wearing his great overcoat and pincenez, and looking as unperturbed as if he were returning from a pleasure trip.'

Of the 229 people on board *Rohilla* when she struck the rocks, eighty-four lost their lives. The bells of St Mary's Church, on the cliff top above the wreck, were tolled to signal the end of the tragedy and allowed all those involved to take stock of what had happened. The rescue was hailed as one of the greatest in the history of the RNLI, and numerous awards for gallantry were made by the Institution in recognition of the tremendous bravery, courage and great determination displayed by the various lifeboat crews during the prolonged efforts to save the lives of those on board the stricken hospital ship.

The monument in Whitby cemetery designed and crafted by Thomas Hill & Sons, made from West Yorkshire granite. It occupies a central position over a long trench, and pays tribute to those lost in the tragedy. The cost of £200 was met entirely by the British India Steam Navigation Co who requested that the names of those lost be engraved on the monument.

The 50th anniversary of the Rohilla rescue was commemorated in 1964 with a service near the memorial in the cemetery. Centre right, wearing the RNLI pullover, is former Coxswain Henry 'Lal' Richardson. The others pictured are survivors from the disaster. (By courtesy of Whitby Lifeboat Museum)

Gold medals were awarded to Coxswain Thomas Langlands, of Whitby and to Coxswain Robert Smith and Captain Burton, of the Tynemouth lifeboat. Silver medals were awarded to the Whitby Second Coxswain Richard Eglon and to the Tynemouth Second Coxswain James Brownlee, as well as to Lieut Basil Hall. A Silver medal was also awarded to George Peart, who had 'behaved with conspicuous bravery' in repeatedly braving the surf to help several men to safety after they had attempted to swim ashore from *Rohilla*.

The RNLI's Thanks Inscribed on Vellum were accorded to Coxswain Pounder Robinson and to Second Coxswain Thomas Kelly, both of the Upgang lifeboat, with additional monetary awards to all the lifeboatmen involved, as well as the crews of the two steam trawlers which had given their services. A special Letter of Thanks and a telescope were awarded to Captain John Milburn, who was Acting Honorary Secretary at Whitby as the permanent Secretary, John Foster, was seriously ill.

The impressive memorial pictured in 1997 standing more than nine feet in height and surrounded by various graves of local lifeboatmen. (Nicholas Leach)

The first motor lifeboat

Powered by an engine, the next lifeboat at Whitby was significantly different to her predecessors. While in some quarters scepticism about the benefits of motor power had been expressed, the *Rohilla* rescue had shown that motor lifeboats represented the future for life-saving at sea. The famous rescue from the hospital ship, a decade after the RNLI had first introduced motor power to lifeboats, showed beyond doubt that a powered lifeboat provided distinct advantages over one relying on sails and oars. Although crews in the pulling and sailing lifeboats often performed remarkable and extraordinary feats of life-saving, motor power gave a boat greater range, better manoeuvrability near a casualty and the ability to make headway against the wind.

Motor lifeboat development began in 1904 when the RNLI had an existing lifeboat, the 1893-built *J. McConnell Hussey* from Folkestone, fitted with a two-stroke Fay & Bowen petrol engine which gave her a speed of approximately six knots. This first motor lifeboat then went to the coast for evaluation at a number of stations and proved quite a success, although numerous technical problems had to be overcome in operating the engine. These included keeping it dry, even in the event of a capsize, ensuring it was totally reliable both when starting and when running, and ensuring the propellers were protected from damage. As the problems were gradually surmounted, lifeboats powered by the internal combustion engine began to be built. Some existing lifeboats were converted to motor during the 1900s and, as the RNLI's engineers gained confidence and experience with the new technology, the first purpose-built motor lifeboats were completed in 1908.

The motorisation of the fleet was delayed by the First World War, but in 1918 the RNLI made up for lost time by embarking upon an ambitious building programme, and Whitby became one of the first stations to receive a new powered lifeboat after peace had been declared. Plans for a motor lifeboat had, in fact, initially been made in late 1914 when, first, Basil Hall, RN, the RNLI's District Inspector, stated that a motor lifeboat

Whitby's first motor lifeboat, Margaret Harker-Smith, was broadly similar in outward appearance to her pulling and sailing equivalent with the box housing the motor amidships being fairly inconspicuous. The boat was built at a total cost of £5,022 15s 11d.

should be built for Whitby; and, second, the executors of the late Miss Margaret Harker-Smith agreed to defray the cost of the new boat. Hall then recommended that members of the Whitby crew and committee should visit other stations which operated motor lifeboats to select a suitable class of boat.

Meanwhile, the RNLI's Architect drew up plans for a boathouse to house the new craft. At the time, no motor lifeboat type had been designed which could be launched by carriage, and so the boat would either be kept afloat in the harbour or housed in a boathouse with a launching slipway. Although the Chief Inspector initially believed it possible to keep the boat afloat, building a new boathouse and slipway was the preferred option.

In January 1915, Mr Lewis, of the engineering firm Douglass, Lewis & Douglass, who had been commissioned to design and build the house, submitted several schemes for launching the new boat. They proposed a boathouse, 50ft by 24ft internally, built on a substructure of reinforced concrete piles and braces, and fitted with a galvanised steel movable platform on which the boat would be lowered and raised, with a short slipway from the house to the bottom of the slope, and an electric winch at the back of the house to haul the boat up the slipway on to the platform. Power would be supplied by the council at a cost of £5 per annum per kilowatt demand and per unit registered, and the house would be fitted with electric light, a luxury not afforded at the time to the existing boathouse.

A site for the proposed building was found in April 1915 on the East Side, just to the south of the Fish Pier. The Harbour Commissioners agreed to this location on condition that the toe of the slipway did not project into the navigable river, and the rear of the house was a certain distance from the adjacent buildings. The Commissioners also stipulated that the colour of paint used on the house 'must harmonise with surrounding tiles'. The cost of this scheme was estimated at £3,190, and it was considered the most suitable because of the small amount of space in the harbour it occupied.

In May 1915, the plans were finalised and a tender for the building work from T. D. Ridley & Sons of Middlesbrough of £2,880 11s 0d was accepted. However, a few days later, Whitby Urban District Council objected to the proposed site, and so an amended plan had to be drawn up. The Council wanted the house built about 17ft further back, a change that added an extra £172 to the cost. In altering the plans to meet the Council's requirements, the engineers abandoned the lifting mechanism in favour of a conventional slipway, and corrugated asbestos was substituted for galvanised corrugated steel. A new tender from Ridley of £3,061 2s 3d was accepted and work then commenced. In December 1915, Flavell & Churchill tendered £155 for an electric winch.

Construction of the new boathouse was rather slow due to wartime shortages of both labour and materials, and it did not proceed altogether smoothly. In March 1917, questions were raised over the wages paid to the Clerk of Works overseeing construction of the new house. He had received £290, whereas the amount authorised was £170. The excess was because he had spent longer than allowed in the contract due to increased difficulties in obtaining labour. At the same time, Ridley had to be paid an extra £100 after constructing the toe of the slipway proved more difficult than anticipated because of unfavourable tides during the year.

Then, in July 1917, alterations were made to the plans, including partially blocking an open well in the floor of the house, which would have been dangerous for the crew when using the building

Margaret Harker-Smith at full speed during trials shortly after she had been completed. (By courtesy of Whitby RNLI)

Inauguration of Whitby's first motor lifeboat, Margaret Harker-Smith, on 28 June 1919. Funds for the new boat came from the estate of Miss Margaret Harker-Smith, of Sheffield, whose executors, in January 1915, agreed to add £6,000 to the initial £1,000 bequest towards the cost of endowing the new lifeboat. An additional £1,668 16s 1d was raised locally by an appeal organised in the wake of the Rohilla wreck. George Shee, at the naming of Margaret Harker-Smith, said, 'She adds to the strength, beauty, and seaworthy qualities of her predecessors the powerful help of her fine engine, which is able to drive her at eight knots per hour; but there is one thing in which I am glad to say there is no change. She will not have a better crew than the John Fielden, for she will have the same crew and the same Coxswain, and a better Coxswain and crew are not to be found on the coast of the United Kingdom.' (By courtesy of Whitby Lifeboat Museum)

at night. The delays and alterations all added to the cost, and in December 1918, the RNLI allocated a further £250 to complete the building, in addition to amounts already totalling £3,391 12s 3d. An extra £45 was also found for building a reinforced concrete petrol tank.

While the new boathouse and its roller slipway were being planned and built, a decision about the type of lifeboat was taken in February 1915, with the crew choosing a 40ft motor self-righting type similar to that at Tynemouth. However, small tanks, one in the fore and one in the aft end-boxes, were requested so that oil

could be carried, 'to distribute overboard in rough weather to calm dangerous waves', according to the RNLI's minutes.

In March 1915, the new motor lifeboat was ordered from the yard of S.E. Saunders of Cowes. The following month, £402 was paid to Tylor & Sons for a 40bhp motor, and £55 to Henry & Gardner for a No.4 Gardner Reverse Gear. However, the engine was not delivered until February 1918, and considerably delayed the boat's completion. Once the engine had arrived, fitting out of the boat commenced and, by July 1918, subject to the delivery of a few

THIS·BOATHOUSE·WAS·ERECTED·IN
1918·AS·A·GIFT·TO·THE·INSTITUTION
FROM·MRS·TRUMBLE·IN·MEMORY·OF
HER·SON·LIEUT·F·H·G·TRUMBLE·RN
WHO·WAS·KILLED·IN·ACTION·ON
H·M·S·WARWICK·IN·THE·ATTACK·ON
OSTEND·10TH·MAY·1918·AGED·24

The bronze tablet in the lifeboat house in memory of the donor. The tablet was ordered in January 1919 from Osborne & Co at a cost of £22 5s 0d and fixed to the boathouse in memory of Lieut Trumble, a soldier killed in action off Ostend on 10 May 1918 while serving on HMS Warwick, in whose name the new boathouse was dedicated. (Nicholas Leach)

Richard Eglon, who took over as Coxswain of the motor lifeboat in 1920 having served on the pulling lifeboats for many years. He spent three years on the motor lifeboat before retiring. (By courtesy of Whitby Lifeboat Museum)

fittings, the new craft was ready for trials.

At the same time, the Honorary Secretary was endeavouring, through the Labour Priority Department, to find a suitable motor mechanic for the boat. He had no need to rush, however, as not until March 1919 was the new lifeboat actually completed while almost another three more months passed before she reached her station. Final trials took place during April and May 1919, with the District Inspector reporting that 'the machinery ran well and gave every satisfaction'. The new boat eventually sailed for her station on 31 May 1919. She was taken by sea to Portsmouth, then on board the Admiralty steamship *Buccaneer* to Grimsby, and onwards by sea to Whitby, with Coxswain Thomas Langlands at the wheel for

the last leg of the journey. The cost of conveying the new boat was £57 11s 10d, including £33 8s 2d for insurance.

Whitby's first motor lifeboat arrived in early July 1919. She was 40ft in length, 10ft 6in in beam, and was fitted with a single 40hp Tylor C.2 four-cylinder, six-and-a-half-stroke petrol engine. She was a self-righting type, built along basically the same lines as a pulling and sailing lifeboat but fitted with an engine. A number of 40ft self-righters were built during the 1920s and all provided good service at the stations they served. On trials, the Whitby boat reached a maximum speed of seven and a half knots, with the engine developing 825rpm. She had a radius of action of fifty-two nautical miles at full speed, carried a total of sixty gallons of fuel and consumed thirty-four pints per hour. Her propeller was twenty-two inches in diameter and she was fitted with a Gardner No.4 Reverse gear. She could carry more than sixty survivors in addition to the nine crew and gear.

The new lifeboat was dedicated, christened and formally launched on the afternoon of 28 June 1919, with a large crowd made up of residents and visitors in attendance. A flag day was combined with the ceremony, and throughout the town collectors appealed for contributions. An exhibition of artefacts from the *Rohilla* incident and other maritime and wartime relics was held in the West Pier boathouse. The displays were formally opened by Miss Marion Beckett, eldest daughter of the Hon Gervase Beckett, the local MP, during the morning and among the many exhibits were some remains of the *John Fielden* lifeboat, damaged beyond repair while returning after her second voyage to *Rohilla*, as well as the bell salvaged from the hospital ship.

The opening ceremony for the new boathouse, and the naming of the new motor lifeboat itself, took place in the afternoon, with George Shee, Secretary of the RNLI, starting proceedings at 3pm, describing the new boat as 'in a word, the last expression of human ingenuity in Life-boat construction'. The new boathouse was dedicated to the memory of the late Lieut F. H. G. Trumble, RN, who had been killed in action off Ostend, in May 1918. Trumble had been a regular visitor to Whitby, along with his mother, whose gift had funded the construction of the boathouse and slipway. Mr Suggit, Mr Shee, the Rev Chancellor Austen and about sixty others then went into the lifeboat house for the formal dedication and christening of the boat.

The dedication was performed by the Rev Chancellor Austen, and the lifeboat was christened *Margaret Harker-Smith* by Miss Jenkyn-Brown, a close relative of the late Miss Harker-Smith, who broke a bottle of wine against the bow. As soon as she did this, the boat was launched into the harbour accompanied by cheers from spectators and sirens from several naval motor launches. The boat, with several passengers, was taken on a short trip down the harbour before being rehoused.

With the arrival of the new motor lifeboat, and her entry into service, the Whitby and Upgang station were reorganised. The No.2 lifeboat *Forester* (Reserve No.4), which had been on station since 1914, was withdrawn on 13 November 1919, and *William Riley of Birmingham and Leamington*, the lifeboat built in 1909 for Upgang, was transferred to the No.2 station. Upon her departure, the Upgang station was permanently closed. However, somewhat unusually, this was the only lifeboat to be removed immediately as a result of the arrival of the

motor lifeboat, and two pulling boats were retained at Whitby until the mid-1930s. They were left on station because of problems with the harbour silting up.

During the war, and in the years immediately afterwards, little dredging was undertaken and in July 1919 the RNLI's Chief Inspector, Captain H. F. J. Rowley RN, stated that only when the harbour had been dredged could removing one of the pulling boats be considered. By November 1919, the situation had become serious – no dredging had been carried out for six months and the District Inspector explained that, as a result, the motor lifeboat was 'put out of action for practically six hours each tide'. The silting of the harbour got so bad that, while being launched for a deputation from Tenby lifeboat station in March 1920, the lifeboat struck a mud bank and her rudder was damaged beyond repair. A new one was immediately ordered from Saunders, but the situation was clearly unsatisfactory.

Despite the difficulties in launching, *Margaret Harker-Smith* was in action soon after her arrival and, before the end of 1919, had completed four services. Her first service, on 24 October 1919, was to HM Motor Launch No.292, which she guided into harbour after the vessel and its crew of eleven got into difficulties off Sandsend in a strong north-easterly gale.

Margaret Harker-Smith launching on exercise. Coxswain Tom 'Garry' Kelly is at the wheel while the Second Coxswain is ready to drop the rudder. The District Inspector is wearing his bowler hat and holding onto the port rail while Captain Mothersdale, the Honorary Secretary, is wearing a trilby hat. She was originally launched stern first down the slipway from the new boathouse, but this was later changed to a more usual bow-first launch. (By courtesy of Whitby Lifeboat Museum)

On 5 November the lifeboat assisted to save the steamship *Bratto*, of Newcastle, which was leaking, whilst bound from Hull to the Tyne. On 19 December, the steamship *Mojave*, of Tacoma, got caught broadside to the harbour entrance in a heavy gale. Both the motor lifeboat and No.2 lifeboat were launched, standing by while motor fishing vessels got ropes from the boat to the pier, which were used to haul the vessel to safety. The final service of the year took place on 31 December when the lifeboat escorted four motor fishing boats to safety through heavy seas.

Richard Eglon took over as Coxswain of the motor lifeboat from Thomas Langlands and, in 1920, on one of his first services in the post, he and his crew completed a very fine service. *Margaret Harker-Smith* was launched at 3.30am on 15 November 1920, to the aid of the five-masted schooner *Cap Palos*, of Vancouver. More than a year before, on 24 October 1919, *Cap Palos* had been driven onto the rocks in Robin Hood's Bay in rough weather and the Robin Hood's Bay lifeboat went to assist. The vessel was abandoned, and lay ashore for nearly twelve months until attempts were made to salvage her. At the beginning of October 1920 she was brought to Whitby Harbour, and, in the early morning of 14 November 1920, two tugs towed her out to sea, intending to take her to Blyth. However, she had no rudder, was only being kept afloat by pumps and, once outside the harbour, the wind proved so strong that the tugs could not make headway, so they anchored.

During the night, as the wind increased to gale force, *Cap Palos* broke away from the tugs and was blown out into the North Sea. At 3am the tugs signalled for help, and *Margaret Harker-Smith* put out. Unfortunately, her engine broke down, and she had to be anchored while repairs were effected. By this time, *Cap Palos* was out of sight and so at 5am the lifeboat returned to station to complete the repairs. Half-an-hour later, one of the tugs entered harbour and reported that all efforts to take off the crew of *Cap Palos* had failed and the lifeboat was needed. Within ten minutes, she was on her way, battling through very heavy waves to reach the casualty. The lifeboat was continually buried by the seas, but after an eighteen-mile passage she reached *Cap Palos*, where she found the other tug was standing by. The lifeboat crew found the schooner waterlogged and drifting at about four knots, with two anchors down. She had a heavy list to starboard, and her rails were repeatedly disappearing under water as she rolled violently.

With great skill, Coxswain Eglon took the lifeboat alongside the schooner, a dangerous manoeuvre in which she could have been crushed under the vessel. She was damaged by one of the schooner's heavy chain plates, which had been torn away and, as the casualty rolled, caught the after-end box of the lifeboat and stove in one of the air cases. In spite of this, however, the lifeboat was taken alongside long enough for the sixteen exhausted crew to be rescued from their ordeal.

The twenty-one-mile passage home was very rough, and the lifeboat eventually entered Whitby Harbour at 2.30pm, nine hours after setting out. Both the rescued men and the lifeboat crew had suffered from exposure. For this excellent service, Coxswain Eglon was accorded the Thanks of the Institution inscribed on Vellum, and additional monetary rewards were made to the crew. As for *Cap Palos*, after drifting in the North Sea, derelict, for nearly a month, she was found floating keel up and

eventually broke in two and sank.

No effective services were performed during 1921, and in 1922 and 1923 the majority of services were to fishing cobles. The lifeboat either stood by or escorted them into harbour after they had been caught out in bad weather. On 13 January 1923, she was launched to the steamship *Spero*, of Newcastle, of 3,000 tons, which stranded at Kettleness Point while bound for Brussels from the Tyne carrying coal. The Runswick lifeboat *Hesther Rothschild* put out at 4am, and *Margaret Harker-Smith* reached the scene soon afterwards. An unsuccessful attempt was made to refloat the steamer using a tug, after which the crew abandoned their vessel and were taken on board the Runswick lifeboat, which the Whitby lifeboat towed back to Runswick Bay to land the survivors.

Following this service, the other rescues performed by *Margaret Harker-Smith* during 1923 were to fishing cobles. On 26 February, she went to Staithes to escort some local cobles to safety, and found the Runswick lifeboat had already helped most of them back to harbour. On her way back

Margaret Harker-Smith launching from the lifeboat house. (From an old postcard in the author's collection)

Margaret Harker-Smith under way off the harbour. She was powered by a single engine and was typical of the RNLI's early motor lifeboats.

Margaret Harker-Smith leaving harbour, passing the East Pier extension.

to station, *Margaret Harker-Smith* stood by the motor fishing boat *Remembrance*, as a south-easterly gale had created very rough seas on the bar, until the boat was safely in port. On 24 August, she saved two crew from the fishing coble *Pansy* and stood by two other cobles, *Providence* and *Maria*, which had been overtaken by a northerly gale. The lifeboat escorted the latter two vessels into harbour, watched from the pier by thousands of people.

The most notable rescue of 1924 took place on 30 May, but did not involve the lifeboat. Just before 7pm, a small pleasure boat, with five boys aged eight to seventeen on board, was approaching the harbour. Although the weather was fine and the sea smooth, a heavy swell on the bar capsized the boat as it entered. The boys were thrown into the water about

fifteen yards from the end of the Old West Pier End. A local fisherman, John William Storry, and three other men were on the pier at the time and, on seeing what had happened, Storry immediately climbed down the pier side and jumped, fully dressed, into the water. Two of the boys were able to swim to the pier unaided, where they clung to lifebuoys fastened to ropes thrown by the three men. Storry meanwhile struck out for the other three, who were struggling in the water, unable to hold on to the upturned boat.

One by one, he swam with each boy back to the pier. The last boy, also the youngest, had almost drowned by the time Storry rescued him. A line was lowered and Storry helped the three boys out of the water. But for Storry's help, they would have been swept away. Meanwhile, the men on the pier had signalled a fishing coble which was working off the West Beach, and a quarter of an hour later it crossed the bar and reached the pier so that Storry and the boys could get on board. On landing, not only was Storry exhausted but he had sprained the muscles of the arm which had held on to the rope. His rescue efforts were undertaken at great personal risk, and but for his prompt actions the three boys would undoubtedly have drowned. In recognition of this, and his considerable courage, Storry was awarded the Silver Medal by the RNLI.

On 12 June 1924, *Margaret Harker-Smith* was launched to the steamship *Redhall*, of Aberdeen, which stranded about 5.30pm on Whitby Rock during

Margaret Harker-Smith on the slipway outside the lifeboat house with her crew in their life-jackets. This posed photograph was used for contemporary RNLI publicity material and was also issued as a postcard. (From an old postcard in the author's collection)

thick fog while bound to Havre carrying coal. Several fishing vessels put off to help, but when the fog cleared and the wind strengthened causing the sea to worsen, the lifeboat went to stand by in case any assistance was needed. At 9.30pm the steamer refloated and was able to recommence her voyage. The lifeboat returned to station bringing ashore the Lloyd's Surveyor and his Assistant who had gone out to the grounded vessel.

The service to the steamer *Redhall* was one of very few performed by *Margaret Harker-Smith* which did not involve helping local fishing vessels. During her nineteen years on station at Whitby, the motor lifeboat launched 117 times and is credited with saving eighty-six lives, but more than ninety per cent of the services in which she was involved were to fishing boats. More or less all of these incidents were routine in nature, and involved the lifeboat escorting in cobles and motor fishing vessels caught out in bad weather. The large fishing fleet at Whitby would

spend much of the time at sea, and the boats would often have difficulty crossing the dangerous harbour bar, resulting in the lifeboat's help being needed. A full list of rescues can be found in the Appendix, and only a few of these are recounted below.

On 17 January 1928, *Margaret Harker-Smith* was launched to escort a number of motor fishing boats that had put off when the weather was fine early in the morning. By midday, however, rough seas were breaking over the bar, and *Irene*, *Faith*, *Diligence*, *Remembrance* and *Lady Kitchener* all needed to be escorted back into port during the afternoon. Another of the fishing boats, *Fortuna*, shipped a heavy sea as she crossed the bar and collided with the end of the pier in the rough seas, while another boat, *Guide Me*, had similar difficulties. The lifeboat was able to save both cobles and bring their crews, totalling nine men to safety.

In 1929 Whitby became one of the first lifeboat stations to receive a centenary vellum, then recently introduced. The

Margaret Harker-Smith with her sails raised. She was fitted with a No.1 rig and carried ten coble oars, as well as having a 4ft 6in steel drop keel. As she only had a single engine, sails and oars were needed in case the motor failed.

Fisherman John William Storry who received the RNLI's Silver medal for his actions in saving three boys from drowning in the harbour, May 1924. (By courtesy of Whitby RNLI)

presentation was made on 17 August 1929, also lifeboat day, although the year was not a particular anniversary in the station's history. A ceremony took place on one of the pulling lifeboats, while *Margaret Harker-Smith* and the other pulling lifeboat were launched for the occasion. The lifeboats were dressed overall, as was shipping in the harbour, and the event was attended by many notable people including the Earl of Mulgrave, Rev the Marquess of Normanby and Viscount Cranborne, MP, with the Chairman of the Urban District Council, M. Wilson, presiding. The vellum itself was presented by Sir William Milligan, MD, JP, a Vice-President of the Manchester, Salford & District Branch, to Captain Milburn, who handed it to Councillor Wilson. Wilson said it would be hung in the Council Chamber and be 'treasured with

the same pride which Whitby felt for the lifeboatmen themselves'.

On 3 February 1930, *Margaret Harker-Smith* undertook a routine service to the motor fishing boats *Pilot Me* and *Fortunas*, which were escorted back through very rough seas after the boats had not returned when expected. Three days later, she was involved in a more unusual service when she launched at 11.40am, initially to escort the fishing coble *Topsy* into harbour. While the lifeboat was helping the coble, a message was received that the steamship *Brandon*, of London, was making for the port as the Chief Engineer was suffering from appendicitis and in need of medical help. A doctor and three ambulancemen were notified, and were taken aboard the lifeboat to go out to *Brandon*.

The lifeboat soon reached the steamer, but transferring the ill man across was both difficult and dangerous. However, once this was accomplished, he was brought ashore and taken to hospital. Shortly after landing the crewman, *Margaret Harker-Smith* was called out again, this time escorting another small fishing coble, and went out for a fourth time later in the evening to stand by several motor fishing vessels. The owner of the steamer, C. Salvesen & Co, sent a donation to the RNLI.

Whitby was one of two lifeboat stations called into action on Christmas Day 1930. *Margaret Harker-Smith* was launched to the steamship *Lucy*, of Helsingborg, which had run aground on the rocks at Calder

Margaret Harker-Smith during a memorial service marking an anniversary of the Rohilla tragedy, probably during the 1920s. She was accompanied by various local fishing vessels, with wreaths cast into the sea and flags at half mast. (By courtesy of Whitby Lifeboat Museum)

Steel about four miles north of Whitby while bound from Grangemouth to Bordeaux. The lifeboat put out at 6.15pm into a strong south-westerly breeze, which was getting stronger. The steamer was in a very dangerous position and so the lifeboat saved the crew of eighteen. The rescued men were landed safely, and taken to the Seamen's Institute.

On 27 February 1931, *Margaret Harker-Smith* was launched to stand by the fishing fleet in heavy seas with a moderate westerly breeze. She put off at 8.30am and spent all day going in and out of harbour assisting a number of vessels which had gone out early in the morning and been caught in worsening conditions. The first boat escorted in was *Brethren*, and the lifeboat put off again at 11am to stand by *Guiding Star* and *Ned*. On her third trip, she escorted *Lady Kitchener*, *Guide Me* and *Radiance*. She went out for a fourth time at 2.30pm to escort *Pilot Me* and *Irene*, and her fifth and final service was to *Faith* and *Fortune*. She eventually returned at 4.45pm after a very busy day for her crew, whose efforts were recognised by the granting of additional monetary awards.

On 5 December 1932, *Margaret Harker-Smith* was again involved in standing by the fishing fleet for a few hours. During the morning, the motor fishing coble *Primrose*, of Whitby, got into difficulties about a mile from Whitby Rock buoy, and the lifeboat put out at 11.25am to go to her aid. A strong north-westerly breeze was blowing and the sea was getting rougher as a result. The lifeboat found *Primrose* at anchor with her engine flooded, and so towed the vessel and her three crew to harbour. Another ten fishing vessels were still at sea, so the lifeboat remained afloat and later escorted them to safety. She returned to her station at 2.45pm after more than three hours afloat.

Towards the end of 1935, *Margaret Harker-Smith* was needed on a couple of occasions to escort fishing boats to safety. On 4 November, she launched at 10.30am after conditions worsened and some local boats and cobles were at sea. A moderate easterly breeze was blowing, a rough sea was rolling into the harbour while, as a result of recent heavy rain, a lot of fresh water was running down the harbour. The lifeboat made several trips and escorted in

Margaret Harker-Smith returning to harbour.

Margaret Harker-Smith returning to harbour from service in 1934 with her drogue streamed. (By courtesy of Whitby Museum)

Margaret Harker-Smith, with her drogue streamed, is watched by hundreds of people on the West Pier extension as she returns to harbour from service. (By courtesy of Whitby Lifeboat Museum)

a total of eleven motor fishing boats and three fishing cobles.

On 2 December, she went out to eleven fishing boats which had put out early in moderate weather but got caught as the wind and seas worsened. Because entering harbour was a risky undertaking for them, the lifeboat was launched at 11.10am into rough seas to assist the vessels. The lifeboat crossed the harbour bar and returned eleven times, escorting the boats in one by one. Each time she crossed the entrance, she sprayed the sea with oil.

Throughout her time at Whitby, *Margaret Harker-Smith* was launched to help the same cobles many times, and her last full year on station, 1937, was no exception. On 19 January, she launched at noon, and escorted in *Pilot Me* and then *Provider*, which hit the East Pier on the way in. She then put off again to warn two other boats not to attempt to cross the bar until the tide flowed, and went out again later to escort in *Venus, Galilee* and *Progress*, and later two other boats. Eight days later she again went out to help *Pilot Me*, escorting her in from about three-quarters of a mile out. On 2 March, the

lifeboat escorted in *Provider*, which had risked going to sea despite the bad weather and heavy sea breaking a long way outside the harbour entrance.

On 11 March the fishing fleet put to sea early in the morning, but the weather got bad, and by 11am three boats had not returned so, in heavy seas and snow showers, *Margaret Harker-Smith* launched and escorted *Galilee* in through the dangerous entrance. On 20 August she went to assist *Galilee* again, as well as *Venus*, escorting both into harbour through heavy seas, returning to station at 1pm and being watched by many visitors from the piers. On 15 November the motor fishing boats *Noel II, Venus, Galilee, Pilot Me* and *Success* were caught at sea by bad weather and so the lifeboat went out when they were seen approaching harbour. She escorted them through rough seas which were breaking at the harbour entrance.

The last two services performed by *Margaret Harker-Smith* were both to local fishing boats. On 12 February 1938, she launched to the motor fishing boats *Endeavour, Pilot Me* and *Success*, which had left harbour for the fishing grounds at about 4am, and six hours later been caught in a gale with high seas and sleet showers. The lifeboat launched at 11am and stood by as they crossed the bar in very heavy seas. *Margaret Harker-Smith's* final service, on 8 April 1938, involved her escorting the fishing boats *Pilot Me* and *Provider* across the bar. As the tide ebbed, a rough sea began to break heavily outside the pier ends, making the entrance dangerous. The boats came in at 4.30pm, and the lifeboat returned to her station an hour and a half later.

The last pulling lifeboats

Whitby has the distinction of being the last lifeboat station in the United Kingdom to operate a pulling lifeboat in service. During the nineteenth century, at many lifeboat stations, two or sometimes more lifeboats were operated, but gradually this practice ceased as motor lifeboats were introduced. At Whitby, however, while the stationing of a motor lifeboat saw the closure of the Upgang station, unusually two pulling boats were retained even though the motor lifeboat was on station. But the situation did not last long. The No.1 lifeboat performed her last rescue in 1922 and, after that, was not used again, although she remained in Whitby.

The No.2 lifeboats were much busier, and complemented the larger motor lifeboat as they were smaller, lighter craft, designed for easy handling on a beach. Built to the design of Felix Rubie and known as the Rubie self-righter, no fewer than four such lifeboats served at Whitby between 1919 and 1957. All were second-hand, but all performed a good number of rescues. Rubie's design was developed in 1894 when a self-righting lifeboat, lighter than the standard design, was required for service at Dungeness. The design had a double-bottom of rot-proof canvas, divided into compartments, rather than having the space under the deck filled with air cases, and this helped reduce the weight. The boats were 34ft in length, 8ft in beam and weighed under two tons.

The first of the Rubie self-righters at Whitby was the *Forester* (Reserve No.4) lifeboat which had arrived in 1914 but, in November 1919, was condemned and returned to London. Even though by then the motor lifeboat *Margaret Harker-Smith* was on station, two pulling lifeboats were still needed because, as the Chief Inspector explained in July 1919, the

harbour needed dredging before the motor lifeboat could operate at all states of the tide. The pulling lifeboats were launched across the beach, to the west of the West Pier, and thus were not affected by the problems in the harbour.

When Upgang was closed, transferring the lifeboat from there was a logical step. It had always been difficult maintaining the Upgang station, and in September 1918 the Council's slipway, which the lifeboat used for launching, was disintegrating. It did not impede launching, but abandoning the station a year later was an easy decision given the cost of upkeep needed to maintain the slipway.

William Riley of Leamington and Birmingham 1919 – 1931

From 13 November 1919, *William Riley of Leamington and Birmingham* became the No.2 lifeboat at Whitby and was kept on her carriage in the boathouse on the West Side. Her first service was on 19 December 1919 when she launched during a north-westerly gale to go to the aid of the steamship *Mojave*, of Tacoma, which had stranded broadside across the entrance to the harbour. Motor fishing boats were also on hand, and helped to get ropes from the vessel to the pier. The vessel's steam winches were then used to haul the steamer round and she eventually got into harbour safely. The No.2 lifeboat stood by together with the motor lifeboat.

William Riley's first full year at Whitby, 1920, was also one of her busiest. On 21 January she launched at 12 noon to the steamship *Dorothy Talbot*, of London, which was caught in a north-westerly gale and got into difficulty near the harbour entrance. The lifeboat spent three hours at sea and landed eleven from the steamer.

On 3 March, *William Riley* assisted the steam tug *St Keyne*, of London, which was four miles north of Whitby. On 21 April, she went to the Danish schooner *Mathilda*, which was caught in heavy seas behind the East Pier extension. Nine days later, the lifeboat spent two hours at sea escorting six fishing cobles through the harbour entrance. Her last service of the year took place on 26 December, when she launched to an unknown vessel and once again her services were not required.

During the next three years, *William Riley's* only services were to local fishing cobles, but during 1924 the boat was involved in a rather tragic incident. As she was being taken down to the beach on her carriage for a demonstration launch on 16 August, as part of flag day, the lifeboat's shore signalman, James Harland, slipped and fell beneath the carriage. Before the carriage could be stopped, one of its wheels had run over him. Unfortunately, he died shortly afterwards.

Further routine services followed in 1925 and 1926. *William Riley's* longest service of 1925 took place on 19 April when she stood by the sailing vessel *Mimi Selmer*, of Hamburg, which was in difficulty off the harbour. The lifeboat launched at 9pm and spent more than five hours standing by in a north-easterly breeze and strong swell. On 22 December, she launched at 12.45pm to the barge *Mary Bridge*, of Hull, which had been caught in an easterly gale and heavy swell off the bar. After two hours at sea, the lifeboat saved the barge's four crew.

William Riley's most testing service of 1926 took place on 27 July. She launched at midday to help the coble *Elsie*, which had capsized at the harbour entrance. It was low water spring tide and impossible to get the motor lifeboat out of the harbour, so the pulling lifeboat was launched across the beach. Two of the coble's crew had hung on to their boat after it had capsized, and were saved when it was washed ashore. The third man had swum to a ledge of the pier, but there had become unconscious. A doctor and others climbed down to help, and later all were

brought ashore in the lifeboat. As six other cobles were out, the lifeboat was again launched and warned them not to come in until the tide flowed. She stood by and escorted each coble into harbour, watched by a large number of visitors.

During a service on 7 December 1927, *William Riley* was seriously damaged while standing by the fishing fleet, which was heading home through rough seas. Having escorted the majority of the fleet into harbour, the lifeboat went to the aid of two cobles which were disabled, one by a fouled propeller and the other by engine trouble. As the lifeboat was about to take one of the disabled cobles in tow, another motor coble came alongside to take over the tow, but rammed the lifeboat during the process. A large hole was ripped in the fore end-box, both the outer and inner skins were pierced, and the gunwale inside the end-box was fractured. Despite being damaged, the lifeboat towed in another disabled coble before being recovered. After inspecting the damage, the surveyor reported: 'The lifeboat received a severe blow . . . The iron knee inside the end-box appears to have saved the boat'.

The damage to *William Riley* was repaired and she remained in service until February 1931, having a complete overhaul in 1929 and damaged deck planking replaced in June 1930. The services she undertook during her last three years at Whitby were all to fishing vessels of one kind or another, escorting them into harbour or standing by off the bar in rough seas. Her penultimate year on station, 1929, proved to be a particularly busy one, with her first service of the year coming on 1 January when she escorted six motor fishing boats through heavy seas and into harbour.

On 27 June she launched at 1.28pm, within eight minutes of the call, to assist the coble *Silvester* which had been capsized by heavy breaking seas outside the pier extensions. Although the men thrown from this coble were picked up by other cobles, the lifeboat was able to escort the vessels to safety and then went out again to salve *Silvester*. Her final service in 1929, and indeed her last effective service, took place on 27 October when she took a doctor out to the Hull steam trawler *Earl Haig*. She stood by while the doctor

ministered to the vessel's captain, and then brought the doctor back to port while the trawler continued to Hull.

Jacob and Rachel Vallentine lifeboats 1931 – 1947

The last launch by *William Riley* took place on 15 February 1930, when she went to the local motor fishing vessel *Irene*. Almost exactly a year later, she was replaced by another 34ft Rubie self-righter, the former Palling No.1 lifeboat *Jacob and Rachel Vallentine*, which took over as the No.2 lifeboat on 14 February 1931. Although older than *William Riley*, this lifeboat was seen to be in better condition. Having served in Norfolk, originally at Happisburgh and then at Palling, she only spent seven years at Whitby. Her first service took place within a couple of weeks of her arrival, on

The first Jacob and Rachel Vallentine (ON.580) is lifted onto a railway wagon in London on 14 February 1931, prior to being sent to Whitby for the first time. Her hull has been painted in anti-fouling paint ready for service at Whitby, where she was sometimes kept afloat. (By courtesy of the RNLI)

Jacob and Rachel Vallentine (ON.580) being taken along the road to Ruswarp to help victims of flooding in September 1931. This unusual service resulted in Letters of Appreciation being sent by the RNLI to those involved. (By courtesy of Whitby Museum)

Edward Verrill, Coxswain of the pulling lifeboats from 1946 to 1952. (By courtesy of Whitby RNLI)

Jacob and Rachel Vallentine (ON.580) puts out to the assistance of the fishing coble Enterprise on 25 April 1937. (E. Coling, by courtesy of Jeff Morris)

1 March 1931, when she escorted the local motor coble *Topsy* into harbour.

Jacob and Rachel Vallentine's second service was an unusual one and was undertaken a mile and a half inland. On 2 and 3 September 1931 torrential rain caused flood water to pour down Eskdale from the hills. By the afternoon of 4 September, the river Esk was gushing through Whitby in torrents, uprooting trees and pulling boats off their moorings. As the water continued to rise, the river burst its banks and water blocked many of the roads in the area with nearby Ruswarp facing the worst of the conditions.

By 5pm on 4 September, the road to Sleights was 8ft under water and the inhabitants of two cottages at Ruswarp were in considerable danger. The Coastguard contacted the lifeboat station and, at 5.40pm, the No.2 lifeboat was taken out of her boathouse and made ready. In floods the previous year, the lifeboat crew had used a fishing boat to reach the same village, but this time the lifeboat was regarded as a better option.

The boat was hauled along the road to Ruswarp by about seventy people, and an hour after leaving Whitby, was launched into the flood water. The current was so strong that it was impossible to row against it, but with helpers hauling on ropes the lifeboat was taken upstream,

Three photos showing the first Jacob and Rachel Vallentine (ON.580), which was on station as the No.2 boat from 1931 to 1938, being launched for a demonstration and watched by a large crowd. It is likely that this was the first launch of the lifeboat after her arrival at Whitby. (By courtesy of Whitby Lifeboat Museum)

Lifeboat Day on 31 August 1938 with Richard (ON.522) being prepared for a demonstration launch. This lifeboat was subsequently renamed Jacob and Rachel Vallentine. (E. Colling, by courtesy of Jeff Morris)

through the raging torrent, for over half a mile. She was then rowed into the middle of the stream, anchored, and dropped down to the cottages to rescue two people, including a ninety-year-old bedridden lady. A small boat manned by three fishermen was used as a bridge between the cottage and the lifeboat. After picking up the two women, the lifeboat dropped down the river to Mill House where two more women and a man were rescued from a bedroom window. A ladder was used to bridge the gap between lifeboat and house. The five rescued persons were landed in the front garden of a house.

Following the rescue, the lifeboat was secured at the roadside by which time it was dark. The lifeboatmen had been at work for more than two hours in very difficult conditions, and had faced strong currents, floating trees, and obstacles such

as submerged walls and fences, with one of them injured by the hauling ropes. In appreciation of their efforts, those involved were sent Letters of Appreciation from the RNLI, addressed to Captain Milburn, Chairman of the Branch Committee, Captain Mothersdale, a committee member, and John Foster, honorary secretary, all of whom had taken an active part in the service.

Following her work inland, *Jacob and Rachel Vallentine's* subsequent services were more routine and consisted largely of escorting local fishing vessels. She did occasionally launch to other vessels, and on 25 January 1936 went to the steam trawler *Andri*, of Eskifjarder, which ran ashore at Kettleness, carrying a crew of twenty-five. The sea was smooth, but fog and heavy rain had caused the vessel to lose her way. Runswick's motor lifeboat *Robert Patton – The Always Ready* launched at 8.10pm, followed fifty minutes later by *Jacob and Rachel Vallentine*. The pulling lifeboat was taken to the trawler, which was in broken water, surrounded by rocks, and the lifeboatmen found three men in a small boat in the vessel's lee. They were taken on board the lifeboat, eight more men were rescued, and the coxswain told the master he would return for the others when the tide flowed. The lifeboat was towed to Whitby by a motor fishing boat, leaving the Runswick lifeboat at anchor off the trawler. After putting the rescued men ashore, *Jacob and Rachel Vallentine* returned to the trawler to find that the

Robert and Ellen Robson (ON.669) launching off the West Beach at high water, with the ten oarsmen ready to pull the boat through the surf. (By courtesy of Whitby Lifeboat Museum)

Robert and Ellen Robson (ON.669) being hauled out of the double boathouse on Pier Road on exercise in about 1953. The building subsequently became the boat's permanent home and is now the Lifeboat Museum. (By courtesy of Whitby Lifeboat Museum)

remainder of the crew had been rescued by the Kettleness coastguard life-saving apparatus, so she returned to station.

The last two services by *Jacob and Rachel Vallentine* were both in 1937. The first was on 25 April to the motor fishing boat *Enterprize*, which was escorted across the bar in heavy seas. When rowing out of the harbour to take life-jackets to the boat, the lifeboat shipped some big seas and one of her oars was broken. The second service, and the last by *Jacob and Rachel Vallentine*, took place on 6 December, when she stood by the motor fishing boats *Pilot Me*, *Provider* and *Success* at the harbour entrance while the boats came in. Just over a month later, on 19 January 1938, *Jacob and Rachel Vallentine* was replaced by another 34ft Rubie self-righter, the former Donna Nook lifeboat *Richard*, which had been built in 1904 and stationed at Donna Nook until 1931. Part of the Reserve Fleet when allocated to the No.2 station, she was more than thirty years old when she took up her duties at Whitby, and was renamed *Jacob and Rachel Vallentine* in 1940 or 1941.

The second *Jacob and Rachel Vallentine* served the No.2 station for just over nine years, during which she completed just five effective services, all of which were to assist local fishing boats into harbour. During the Second World War she was only called out a couple of times, and

between June 1941 and May 1946 was not called upon at all. Her last two services were performed during 1947. The first of these was on 8 April, when she launched at 10.45am to stand by several local fishing vessels as the tide was too low for the motor lifeboat to get out. Her last service was on 2 May when she launched at 9am to the coble *Floral Queen*, which was escorted in; she then stood by at the harbour bar until 11.30am to ensure seven keel boats got in safely. At the end of May 1947, *Jacob and Rachel Vallentine* was replaced as the No.2 lifeboat and two months later sold out of service to the Whitby Boatbuilding Company.

Robert and Ellen Robson
1947 – 1957

The last pulling lifeboat to serve at Whitby, and indeed the last pulling lifeboat to see service with the RNLI, *Robert and Ellen Robson*, was placed on station on 30 May 1947. Built in 1918, this lifeboat had a varied career, serving at Tramore, Aberdeen and in the Reserve Fleet before coming to Whitby. She was often kept at moorings in the harbour, although could be launched by carriage across the beach if necessary. Like her predecessor, her work involved helping the local fishing fleet, and during just over ten years on station she performed fifteen effective services. The

Robert and Ellen Robson (ON.669) being lowered down the slipway onto the West Beach to be launched on exercise, circa 1953. The Tipping's plates on the carriage's main wheels prevented them sinking into the sand. Coxswain Edward Verrill is standing to the left of the lifeboat with 'Cox' written on his life-jacket. (By courtesy of Whitby Museum)

first of these took place on 4 December 1947, when she escorted the fishing cobles *Silver Line, Good Faith, Floral Queen* and *Effort* into harbour after they had been caught in a heavy swell, which made the harbour bar dangerous.

Robert and Ellen Robson was involved in a more unusual service on 5 October 1949 after seventeen geology students from Aberdeen University were cut off by the tide off Black Nab. Three of them scrambled through deep water and breakers, and reached the shore to raise the alarm. The lifeboat was towed out of the harbour fifteen minutes later by a local fishing boat, and was then rowed close inshore. The fourteen remaining students were found clinging to the cliffs, along with two coastguards who had been lowered down to them. The lifeboat took all on board, landed them safely and arrived back at her station at 3pm.

Robert and Ellen Robson (ON.669) under oars at the mouth of the harbour. (By courtesy of Whitby Lifeboat Museum)

Robert and Ellen Robson's busiest year was 1952, when she performed three services, all routine in nature. The first was on 2 April, when she escorted the fishing cobles *Floral Queen*, *Silver Line*, *Little Lady* and *Margaret* across the bar in a strong north-easterly wind. The second was on 4 September when she again escorted two motor fishing boats, *Gem* and *Whitby Lass*, across the bar in a dangerous ground swell, launching at 8.30am as the motor lifeboat could not get across the bar due to an exceptionally low tide. The last service of the year, on 21 September, was to the motor launches *Lady Margaret*, *Georgina II* and *Pandora B*, and *Robert and Ellen Robson* was again in action because the tide was too low for the motor lifeboat to be launched. It proved to be quite a long drawn-out service, with *Lady Margaret* grounding on the bar and then, just after she had been freed, *Georgina II* also grounding, damaging her steering gear. Men on the pier helped to refloat both vessels using ropes passed to them by the lifeboat crew, after which the local motor launch *Pandora B*, which had been lying off the harbour, was escorted safely in when the tide had risen.

The last services by *Robert and Ellen Robson* took place in November 1955. On 23 November she escorted in four local fishing boats in bad weather, assisting the motor lifeboat. The following day, she

launched at noon to assist some other fishing vessels, escorted one, *Pilot Me*, into port, and stood by at the bar awaiting the return of other vessels. The weather had worsened during the day, and the pulling lifeboat was called into action as the motor lifeboat was at Scarborough following her service to another fishing boat the previous day. This proved to be a historic event as it was the last time that an RNLI rowing lifeboat was launched on service.

By the time of this rescue, the RNLI had decided to close the No.2 station and withdraw what was by then the last pulling lifeboat in the fleet. At a meeting of the Institution's Committee of Management on 14 November 1957, the decision had been taken to remove the boat from the operational fleet, but it was also decided

Robert and Ellen Robson (ON.669) is hauled into the lifeboat house on Pier Road. (By courtesy of Whitby Museum)

Robert and Ellen Robson (ON.669) under oars in the harbour. Standing at the stern are, on the left, Coxswain Edward Verrill and, on the right, Cdr Leslie Hill, District Inspector. The pulling lifeboats were retained for work either in the harbour or close inshore. (By courtesy of Whitby Lifeboat Museum)

Robert and Ellen Robson escorts the motor launch Pandora B into harbour in heavy seas on 21 September 1952.

The Lifeboat Museum was opened in July 1958 with Robert and Ellen Robson as the main exhibit. The first attendant was Harry 'Lal' Richardson, a former coxswain with a distinguished record both as a member of the lifeboat crew and as a voluntary worker. Pictured here is Captain Willison, who took over as attendant in the late 1960s. (By courtesy of Whitby Museum)

to keep the lifeboat in the old double boathouse and, in due course, adapt the building into a museum.

The driving force behind the new museum was honorary secretary Eric Thomson, who assembled a collection of models, photographs and paintings telling the history of the station from its foundation in the 1800s. The new Lifeboat Museum was formally opened on 26 July 1958, with *Robert and Ellen Robson* as the main exhibit. The opening ceremony was performed by Lady Georgina Starkey, the daughter of Earl Howe, Chairman of the RNLI's Committee of Management.

Robert and Ellen Robson, the last pulling lifeboat in RNLI service, was displayed at the London Boat Show at Earl's Court in January 1975. During her visit to the Thames, she was taken afloat on the river with a volunteer crew commanded by Sheerness Coxswain Charles Bowry. (By courtesy of Whitby Lifeboat Museum)

Mary Ann Hepworth

By the mid-1930s, *Margaret Harker-Smith* was in need of replacement after almost twenty years on station. Motor lifeboat technology had advanced considerably during the preceding two decades, and sturdier and more powerful lifeboat types had been developed. So in 1937 a new 41ft Watson class boat was ordered for the station from the Cowes yard of Groves & Guttridge. The 41ft Watson, a non-self-righting type, was designed primarily for slipway launching, weighing just over fifteen tons with crew and gear. The hull was divided into eight watertight compartments and fitted with 145 air cases.

Powered by twin 35hp Weyburn AE6 petrol engines, the new lifeboat had a top speed of just over eight knots and a cruising speed of seven knots. At full speed, she had a radius of action of sixty nautical miles, which increased to eighty-six nautical miles at cruising speed. Amongst the notable features were two cockpits, a line-throwing gun and an electric searchlight. Funded from the legacy of Mr W. W. Hepworth, of Hessle, near Hull, the new boat was named *Mary Ann Hepworth* and cost £6575 10s 3d to build. She sailed for her new station in early April 1938, and arrived on 12 April to replace *Margaret Harker-Smith*, which was sold to the Chelsea Yacht & Boat Co.

The naming ceremony of the new boat took place on 27 June 1938 with Kenneth McNeil, chairman of Whitby District Council presiding. The lifeboat was presented to the station by Sir Godfrey Baring on behalf of the donor, who could not attend the ceremony. After a service

The 41ft Watson motor lifeboat Mary Ann Hepworth, which arrived at Whitby in April 1938, on exercise in 1972.

of dedication led by the Rev Canon Sykes, assisted by the Rev Ivor J. Robertson, the boat was christened by the Marchioness of Normanby. A vote of thanks was proposed by Captain W. W. Milburn, and seconded by Captain A. D. Milner.

Mary Ann Hepworth served at Whitby for thirty-six years, making her the station's longest-serving lifeboat, and one of the longest-serving motor lifeboats in the history of the RNLI. During her unusually long career, she launched 372 times on service, and is credited with saving 201 lives. The majority of her services were routine ones to local fishing cobles and vessels, escorting them into harbour and standing by them in heavy weather. However, she was also on station throughout the Second World War, and was involved in many outstanding rescues.

Mary Ann Hepworth's first service launch was on 18 April 1938, when she escorted the cobles *Success* and *Pilot Me* through heavy seas into harbour. Her first life-saving service took place a few days later, on 29 April, when she went out to the fishing coble *Noel II* and her crew of five, who had fired a distress signal after being caught in rough seas. The coble had lost her rudder and another, *Easter Morn*, was towing her in. The lifeboat escorted the vessels towards the harbour, but as they approached the entrance the tow rope broke. The lifeboat crew immediately passed another line to *Noel II*, and safely brought the vessel into harbour.

Less than three weeks after this service, an unfortunate accident happened. On 16 May 1938, the lifeboat was called out to a speedboat which had broken down. As the lifeboat was being launched down the slipway, Coxswain David Harland received a severe blow in the face. Another boat was able to save the speedboat, but, as a result of the injuries he received, Harland had to retire from the lifeboat service.

During the Second World War, the two Whitby lifeboats were launched forty-four times on service and saved 103 lives. One of the first wartime services took place on 18 October 1939 after distress signals had been seen six miles north of Whitby. At 7.45pm *Mary Ann Hepworth* launched in a north-easterly wind to investigate and her crew searched without success, facing the danger of floating mines, before returning to station at 9.30pm. Runswick motor lifeboat *Robert Patton – The Always Ready* launched at 8.10pm to the same signals, but also failed to find anything.

It was subsequently learned that the signals had been made by the crew of a

Mary Ann Hepworth dressed overall in the harbour for her naming ceremony, 27 June 1938.

German bomber which had been shot down two days before, with two of its four crew killed. The other two, one of whom was severely injured, saved themselves in a rubber collapsible boat which came ashore at Whitby on 19 October. The two had been afloat for thirty-six hours, believing they were in the Firth of Forth rather than off the Yorkshire coast.

Less than a month after this fruitless search, *Mary Ann Hepworth* was involved in a difficult service. At about 3.30am on 12 November 1939, the Coastguard reported that a vessel was ashore under the cliffs, 200 yards south of the East Pier. Within twenty minutes, Coxswain James Murfield was taking *Mary Ann Hepworth* out of the harbour. It was pitch-black and quite foggy, and a heavy swell was breaking against the cliffs. The lifeboatmen reached the casualty fifteen minutes after launching and found the minesweeper *Cape Comorin*, with a crew of eighteen. Less than 100 yards from the cliffs and bow-on to them, she was caught in the backwash against the cliffs with the confused seas breaking right over her causing her to roll heavily.

The minesweeper was under the Coastguard station and the district officer kept his searchlight trained on her, without which the lifeboat could not have completed the rescue. With large rocks either side of the casualty, Coxswain Murfield could not drop anchor, so he had to rely solely on the boat's engines. First, he tried taking the lifeboat in stern first, but the fierce tide carried the lifeboat too far and he was forced to take her back out to sea. He then took the lifeboat in bow first, amongst the rocks and, with exceptional skill and outstanding seamanship, brought her alongside the minesweeper. She could not get to the vessel's stern, and had to go abreast the wheelhouse, but as soon as she was in position, ropes were lowered and eleven men dropped down into the lifeboat.

At this point, an enormous wave suddenly crashed over the stern of the lifeboat, carrying away the ropes, the windscreen and bending the guard rails and stanchions on the port side. The force of the wave bent the Coxswain's backrest forward by four inches and knocked Coxswain Murfield over the wheel, which was spun round so violently that it was wrenched from his hands. Water also filled the shelter where the mechanics were standing at the controls and swept the lifeboat towards the cliffs. But Murfield picked himself up and quickly brought the lifeboat under control, going astern on both engines to bring her alongside the minesweeper for a second time.

Four more men jumped aboard before the lifeboat was again swept away towards the cliffs. The Coxswain went astern again, and came alongside for the third time, enabling the last three men to be rescued. All eighteen had been saved. Very cautiously, Coxswain Murfield brought the lifeboat out stern first, away from the wreck and clearing the rocks without touching any. He headed back to harbour after a rescue that had taken just forty minutes of intense work.

The district officer of the Coastguard, who had been holding the searchlight on the wreck throughout, saw the whole rescue, and later admitted that he had thought it impossible for the lifeboat to go alongside the wreck in the foaming seas.

The youngest ever crew of a Whitby lifeboat stand in front of Mary Ann Hepworth. They are, left to right, Bob Russell, Philip Storr, Tom Welham, Tommy Lewis, Eric Russell, Robert Murfield, James Philpott and unknown. (By courtesy of Whitby Lifeboat Museum)

James Murfield took over as Coxswain in 1939, having previously been Coxswain of the pulling lifeboats and coming from one of the town's well-known fishing family. (By courtesy of Whitby RNLI)

Mary Ann Hepworth launching down the slipway into the harbour on exercise.

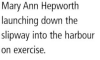

The minesweeper's chief engineer had stood at her stern holding a light to guide the lifeboat and wondered 'what it was like in the little boat below'. He could see the two mechanics at the engines under the canopy, up to their necks in water, and 'watched in admiration the way in which the lifeboat was handled, and noticed that not a voice was heard except the Coxswain's, giving his orders'.

For his tremendous courage and superb seamanship during this well-executed rescue, Coxswain Murfield was awarded the Silver medal; Acting Second Coxswain John Dryden and Motor Mechanic James Philpot were each awarded the Bronze Medal; and the other five members of the crew were accorded the Thanks of the Institution on Vellum; they were Christopher Wale, W. Dryden, R. Walker, J. Richardson and J. Hebden.

Less than three months later, on 3 February 1940, *Mary Ann Hepworth* was involved in another outstanding rescue. At 9pm the coastguard reported a vessel ashore near Saltwick in a south-easterly gale which was whipping up rough seas. Twenty minutes later the lifeboat was at sea, with Coxswain Murfield in command. The lifeboat's searchlight hardly pierced the intense darkness, which was so black that the Coxswain did not realise he was a crew member short.

Under the 200ft cliffs, nothing could be seen until the lights of the Coastguard life-saving apparatus appeared and gave the lifeboat crew the approximate position of the wreck on Saltwick Nab. They were then able to locate the casualty, the Belgian steamer *Charles*, of Bruges, which had a crew of ten and had gone aground at the same spot as *Rohilla* in 1914. Acting Second Coxswain was John Dryden, an experienced fisherman and former

A fine photograph of
Mary Ann Hepworth
at full speed off
Whitby in 1972.
(By courtesy of Whitby
Lifeboat Museum)

lifeboatman, who had returned to the crew when the regular Second Coxswain had been called up for war service.

Working together, Coxswain and Second Coxswain took the lifeboat towards Saltwick Nab, uncertain as to whether there was enough water for the lifeboat to get close to the wreck. They approached the stern of the wreck, which was projecting beyond the cliffs, feeling their way through the darkness, beam on to the heavy seas. Suddenly, an exceptionally heavy wave 'rose at her out of nowhere' and smashed into the port side of the lifeboat, knocking her right over onto her beam-ends and throwing Coxswain Murfield overboard.

In the water, he could see the lifeboat's port handrail above him and expected the boat to capsize. But she righted herself and Murfield, who had clung to the wheel with one hand, dragged himself back on board. As the lifeboat was striking the bottom, he immediately took her astern and out into deeper water and realised that the boat had been in an extremely dangerous position. She was amongst rocks which, at low water, stand ten feet high but at high water are covered.

Not until the lifeboat had reached deeper water did Murfield look round and check on the crew, realising John Dryden was not in the cockpit. The Coxswain did a quick check and discovered that not only was Dryden missing, but so too was Acting Bowman Christopher Wale, another former lifeboat man who had returned to the crew. Both had gone overboard in the darkness, unseen and unheard. Wale had been standing on the port side of the after shelter getting a rope ready. It was also thought at the time that a third man was missing and it was not until they returned to the harbour that the Coxswain learned that he had gone to sea with one man short. Another member of the crew had very nearly been lost overboard, but he had been saved by holding onto the searchlight and was then helped back on board by his colleagues.

The assistant motor mechanic was John Dryden's son who, as soon as he heard that his father had gone overboard, wanted to go after him. The others knew that nothing could be done and that if the son went overboard it would be to his

The grave of Christopher
Wale, who lost his life in
February 1940, can be
seen in Whitby Cemetery.
(Nicholas Leach)

death, but they could not convince him. The mechanic, while still looking after his engines, had to hold him in the boat by force to prevent him from attempting to follow his father.

Coxswain Murfield, meanwhile, had wrenched his arm severely when he was washed overboard and had also gashed his head so badly, with a deep cut at the top of his nose, that blood was running down into his eyes. He decided that little more could be done there and then, so brought the lifeboat back to harbour at 10.30pm and 'out of a place where it was little less than a miracle that she had not been lost with all her crew', according to the RNLI's

account. After receiving treatment for his injuries, he was sent to bed by the doctor.

Meanwhile, the Life-Saving Apparatus Team had scrambled down to the foot of the cliffs of Saltwick Nab, got a line aboard the steamer and hauled four of the crew to safety, before the rising tide forced them to abandon their efforts. One of the crew of the life-saving apparatus was John Robert Storr, a fisherman, who, when he returned to Whitby went to the coxswain's house to ask if he might get together a fresh crew and make another attempt with the lifeboat. Coxswain Murfield advised him to wait until daylight, but John Storr desperately wanted to try before then and so assembled a fresh crew, together with motor mechanic James Philpot, who agreed to go out with them despite being badly shaken by the first attempt.

Mary Ann Hepworth put to sea again at 2.30am with her scratch crew. As she was turning in the river, however, she hit the fishing boat *Easter Morn*, causing damage to both craft, but the lifeboat went on. In the intense dark, none of the crew could see anything of the wreck and John Storr realised that Coxswain Murfield had been right, as not even the lights of the rocket apparatus were available this time to act as a guide. So he took the lifeboat back into the harbour at 4.30am to await daylight. At 7.30am, with the same crew, he set out for the third attempt, and, although some of the steamer's crew had been reported to

Mary Ann Hepworth returning to harbour through breaking seas creating conditions often seen at the entrance to the harbour. Many photos exist showing the boat both leaving and entering the harbour in rough weather.

be in a life-raft, the lifeboat made for the wreck. However, no sign of life could be seen on board the steamer, so the lifeboat searched the coast for the life-raft.

She was joined in the search by the Scarborough motor lifeboat *Herbert Joy II*, which had been launched at 12.45am when it was learned that the Whitby lifeboat had had to return to station. When she reached Saltwick Nab, her crew realised it was so dark that they decided to wait until daybreak. Despite a thorough search of the coast, no sign of the life-raft could be found and, with huge seas still breaking around the wreck, it was impossible for either lifeboat to get near her so they made for Whitby Harbour, arriving there at 9.15am.

The Scarborough lifeboat returned to her own station, having been at sea for twelve hours. It seems probable that the reports of the life-raft had been misunderstood, and that what had been said was not that men were 'on a raft' but that they were 'aft'. The aft end of the steamer had been pounded by the seas, and when, later, several bodies were found they were close to this part of the wreck.

After the lifeboat had returned for the first time, two men, John Robert Dryden, home on leave from the Navy (no relation to Acting Second Coxswain John Dryden), and Norman Russell, got a rope ladder from the life-saving apparatus and, shortly before midnight, went down the 200ft cliff at Saltwick Nab in search of the two men who had been washed out of the lifeboat. The cliff face was covered with ice and snow and the descent extremely hazardous. However, they found the body of Christopher Wale on the shore and brought it up the cliff. Then they kept watch until 5am when they saw another body on the rocks, so went down again and brought up John Dryden.

So ended the gallant attempt to rescue the crew of *Charles*. Two lives had been lost, no lives had been saved by the lifeboat, but the attempt had shown 'the splendid spirit of the men of Whitby'. It was reported afterwards that John Storr had said to the District Inspector of lifeboats, 'while there are men in Whitby able to stand up, the lifeboat will never be short of a crew'. John Dryden and Christopher Wale were the first

lifeboatmen to lose their lives during the war. The Institution paid for the funerals and pensioned their widows, who were their only dependent relatives, as if the men had been sailors killed in action.

For their efforts during this difficult service, the Silver medal was awarded to mechanic James Philpot, who took part in all three launches; the late John Dryden, acting second coxswain, was awarded a clasp to his bronze medal; the bronze medal was awarded to each of the other five men who took part in the first launch, who were: Coxswain James Murfield, the late Christopher Wale, acting bowman, W. Dryden, assistant mechanic, Matthew Winspear and John Walker. The Thanks of the Institution on Vellum was accorded to John Storr, Acting Coxswain, who took part in the second and third launches. In addition the Institution paid for the repairs to *Easter Morn*, which cost £15. The Carnegie Hero Fund Trustees awarded

John (Will) Dryden, who was awarded the Bronze medal in 1940, and Mechanic James Philpot, who received the Bronze medal in 1939 and the Silver medal in 1940. (By courtesy of Whitby RNLI)

Mary Ann Hepworth returning to harbour through heavy following seas on 23 January 1939 after escorting the local motor fishing boat Pilot Me to safety.

certificates and £15 each to John Robert Dryden and Norman Russell.

Mary Ann Hepworth launched at 4.20pm on 29 April 1940 after the 400-ton steamship *White Toft*, of Middlesbrough, carrying steel and with a crew of fifteen, had been reported ashore near Robin Hood's Bay. She was aground on the rocks and heavy seas were washing over her. With great skill, Coxswain Murfield took the lifeboat to the casualty stern-first, in amongst the rocks, and the whole crew were rescued. She returned to her station at 7pm. A Letter of Appreciation was later sent by the RNLI to Coxswain Murfield for this fine service.

The services undertaken during the remaining years of the war were less dramatic than those performed in the early years of the conflict. During February 1941, *Mary Ann Hepworth* was launched twice in three days to two different vessels, one of which was a casualty as a result of the war. This was the Canadian steamship *Westcliffe Hall*, of Montreal, which had been bombed by German planes on 13 February. The steamer's steering gear was broken, she had a large hole in her side, and an unexploded bomb on board. She required a tow, so the lifeboat, which had launched to her aid, contacted a patrol ship and the lifeboat crew assisted getting a hawser from the casualty to the ship.

Two days later, *Mary Ann Hepworth* and her crew were in action again, launching this time to the steamship *Paris*, of London, which was aground off Stourpe Beck carrying a cargo of coal with a crew of twenty-two. The lifeboat landed seventeen of the crew at Whitby in the morning, then put out again at 10.20am. The captain eventually decided to abandon the vessel, and so, with the remaining five members of the crew, he was brought ashore by the lifeboat.

Launches to fishing cobles followed during the rest of 1941 and throughout 1942, although the lifeboat also launched to war casualties. On 25 March 1942, an aeroplane came down a mile off Sandsend and her crew took to their rubber dinghy. As fishing boats were at sea manned by lifeboat crew, seventy-one-year-old former coxswain Thomas Welham, who had been retired from the lifeboat for more than six years, took command, with sixty-year-old T. Peart Acting Second Coxswain and five boys aged sixteen among the crew. *Mary Ann Hepworth* was launched at 11.05am and soon found the rubber dinghy, with four airmen on board. One had hurt his leg, and all had minor injuries. The lifeboat immediately brought them in, reaching Whitby within an hour of launching.

During the last three years of the war, *Mary Ann Hepworth* completed relatively

Whitby lifeboatmen in front of Mary Ann Hepworth. They are, left to right, Dr Edward Barnes (Honorary Medical Adviser), Robert Allen, Richard Frampton, Bill Kaiser, Bill Harland, James Philpot, Bob Pennock, Eric Breckon and Eric Thomson (Honorary Secretary). (By courtesy of Whitby Lifeboat Museum)

few rescues. She performed only one in 1943, launching at 3.35pm to the motor fishing coble *Hilda*, of Scarborough, which was in difficulties in a strong southerly wind and rough seas. The coble was found five miles off Whitby with its engine broken down and so, together with her crew of three, was towed into Whitby.

During 1944 only three effective services were undertaken, the last of which was to the Harbour Defence Motor Launch D.421049. The lifeboat was asked to escort the launch, and set off at 5.20pm to find the vessel two miles off the harbour entrance. The skipper was anxious to get back to harbour as his boat was small and the weather was worsening, so the lifeboat escorted him in. The final service of the war took place on 27 January 1945 to the motor fishing boat *North Star* which was caught out in a north-easterly gale, rough seas and snow showers. All the other boats had come into harbour when the missing boat was seen four miles to the north. *Mary Ann Hepworth* launched at 3.05pm, and escorted *North Star* into harbour.

Soon after the War had ended, a service which started out as being routine in nature soon became anything but, as a fishing boat's crew got into difficulty. On 23 February 1946, with the fishing fleet out at sea, a north-westerly gale suddenly sprang up, with heavy seas building at the entrance to the harbour, and waves breaking right over the two piers. *Mary Ann Hepworth* was launched at 10.45am to stand by as the fishing boats returned and she escorted five into harbour. The lifeboat then put to sea again to escort another boat, *Easter Morn*, which was just coming in. Just as the fishing boat was trying to cross the bar, exceptionally heavy sea broke right over her and, for a few moments, Coxswain Harry Murfield lost sight of her. When the boat reappeared, the Coxswain could see men on the piers,

Mary Ann Hepworth leaves harbour, breaking through a heavy sea as she heads out, and with her crew sheltering in the aft cockpit.

Mary Ann Hepworth in Scarborough on service. When the weather was too bad to enter Whitby, she would often come south to Scarborough, usually with the casualty. (By courtesy of Whitby Lifeboat Museum)

On the afternoon of 27 July 1954 Mary Ann Hepworth was finishing a rescue demonstration by breeches buoy during an exercise in the harbour when a small boat was reported in difficulties three-quarters of a mile north-east of the station. The lifeboat towed to safety the 14ft rowing dinghy, with a young boy and girl aboard, who were being carried out to sea. (By courtesy of Whitby Lifeboat Museum)

as well as some of the crew of the fishing boat, frantically waving and pointing, with crowds on the pier also shouting. He realised that someone from the fishing boat had been washed overboard.

As the lifeboat was lifted high on the crest of the following wave, he saw a man in the water and took the lifeboat in at full speed. A lifebuoy was thrown to the man, but he made no attempt to grasp it and Coxswain Murfield shouted that he must be unconscious. As the man drifted astern of the lifeboat, lifeboatman John Robert Harland, without hesitation and in his oilskins and life-belt, jumped overboard.

He seized the unconscious man and supported him while the other lifeboatmen hauled both aboard the lifeboat, which returned ashore as quickly as possible. The lifeboat crew worked on the unconscious fisherman until the lifeboat had reached harbour, where a doctor was waiting to help bring the man round.

For this most courageous rescue, Robert Harland was awarded the Silver medal by the RNLI, with Coxswain Murfield receiving the Bronze medal for his courage and excellent seamanship. King George VI later awarded Harland the Silver medal for Saving Life at Sea, and Harland also

Whitby lifeboatmen in front of Mary Ann Hepworth in the lifeboat house, left to right: Elliott Duke (Second Coxswain), W. Harland (Bowman), Robert Pennock, William Kaiser, and William Dryden (Mechanic). (By courtesy of Whitby Lifeboat Museum)

received an Honorary Certificate from the Carnegie Hero Fund. He was later presented with the Maud Smith Award, in memory of John, Seventh Earl of Hardwicke, for the bravest act of life-saving by any lifeboatman during 1946.

During the immediate post-war years, the motor lifeboat was called out almost exclusively to local fishing boats. In November 1947 she was out on four different days to help fishing boats, helping *Pilot Me* on 14 and 15 November, after most of the fleet had got safely into harbour, and escorting *Gem* on 28 November after the vessel's rudder had broken. On 29 November *Mary Ann Hepworth* launched to the fishing vessel *Venus*, which had broken down off Staithes, and was being towed in by another fishing boat, *Galilee*.

On 17 December the lifeboat went to help the Runswick lifeboat *Robert Patton – The Always Ready* with a Whitby fishing boat, *Gem*. The Whitby lifeboat met the vessels ten miles off the port and took over escort duties so the Runswick boat could return to station. As the boats approached Kettleness, they saw distress signals from another boat, and the lifeboat went to help, finding the Danish motor fishing boat *Tut* at anchor and short of fuel. As the weather was worsening, the coxswain advised the vessel to make for Whitby under sail and use what little fuel he had left.

During May 1949 *Mary Ann Hepworth* performed services that did not involve local fishing boats. On 7 May, she launched at 6.45am after reports that the motor yacht *Red Rover*, of Southwold, had been taken in tow by the motor fishing boat *Prosperity*, of Whitby, in a strong northerly gale and rough seas. The yacht's engine had broken down and so the lifeboat escorted both vessels into harbour. She reached harbour at 8.15am with the two vessels, but went out again to escort three other fishing boats.

On 12 May *Mary Ann Hepworth* launched at 4.15pm to the motor vessel *Arbroath*, of Dundee, which had been in collision with another steamer, *Anna Maria Nurminen*, of Finland, in dense fog. The lifeboat found the ships five miles north-east of the harbour. *Arbroath* had been badly holed and her crew of eleven had been taken off by the Finnish vessel.

A tow was rigged to *Arbroath*, firstly by the Finnish steamer and then by three local fishing boats, with the lifeboat in attendance. The steamer was beached near the piers, and, when the tide rose, towed into harbour by five fishing vessels. The lifeboat stood by throughout, and returned to her station at 4.45am on 13 May after more than twelve hours on service.

During 1951, *Mary Ann Hepworth* was very busy, completing fifteen service launches, mainly to local motor fishing boats. During November, she was particularly busy, and assisted vessels from as far afield as Rotterdam and Fraserburgh. The first services of the month took place on 4 November when the lifeboat took a pilot out to the motor vessel *Gezina*, of Rotterdam, as the weather was too bad for other boats. As she was launching, at 1.15pm, a message was received that a fishing boat was in

Lifeboatman John Robert Harland receiving his Silver medal for the service on 23 February 1946, for which Coxswain Harry Murfield was awarded the Bronze medal. Accompanying the medal was a Vellum service certificate (being held by the man on the right), with the formal presentation taking place on board No.2 lifeboat Jacob and Rachel Vallentine (ON.522) some time in 1946.

Eric Taylor served as Coxswain from 1953 to 1962 and received the Bronze medal for the service to the fishing boat Foxglove. (By courtesy of Whitby Lifeboat Museum)

Mary Ann Hepworth battles her way across the bar at the entrance to the harbour.

Map that appeared in the Lifeboat Journal for September 1954 showing the service by Mary Ann Hepworth to the fishing boat Foxglove which got into difficulty off Whitby on 15 April 1954.

trouble near Robin Hood's Bay and so, after putting the pilot aboard *Gezina*, the lifeboat proceeded to the fishing boat. She found the Scarborough boat *Courage*, with five crew, making very heavy weather. The lifeboat's crew administered first aid to one of the men, who had been injured, handed out biscuits and rum to them all, and escorted the vessel to Whitby. The following day, the lifeboat was again called out to *Gezina*, which had parted her moorings and was in danger of being swept seawards by an easterly gale. The lifeboat crew passed several hawsers ashore and helped the vessel get moored again before returning to station.

The last services of the month, on 26 November, involved standing by the local fishing boats *Galilee*, *Success*, *Provider A*, *Progress*, *Venus* and *Pilot Me* as they came into harbour. On her way out to sea, the lifeboat escorted the Fraserburgh fishing vessel *Girl Ann*, which was herself leaving for her home port.

At a ceremony held at the Pannett Art Gallery on 30 October 1952, a 150th Anniversary Vellum was presented to the Whitby station. The Vellum was presented by Miss C. Yeoman, the honorary secretary of the ladies' lifeboat guild, to Councillor J. C. Stoney, Chairman of Whitby Urban District Council, and received on behalf of the Literary and Philosophical Society for safe-keeping in the Museum by Miss D. M. Walker, president of the ladies' lifeboat guild and one of the Museum's honorary curators. RNLI records up to this date showed that the station's lifeboats had rescued 813 lives, and six gold, thirteen silver and nine bronze medals had been awarded to Whitby men. During the year 1952, the lifeboat continued its fine tradition of service by carrying out more launches than any other RNLI lifeboat.

During spring 1954 *Mary Ann Hepworth* was involved in a number of fine rescues, culminating in one for which her Coxswain and crew gained formal recognition. The first service of the period, a routine affair, came on 4 March, when the local fishing fleet was caught in bad weather. The lifeboat launched at 1.46pm and, in rough seas, escorted *Lead Us* and *Faith Star* across the harbour bar. On 10 March, *Mary Ann Hepworth* launched to the 1,871-ton steamer *Guildford*, of London, which had been involved in a collision three miles north of Whitby. The vessel, manned by a crew of eighteen, had radioed for a tug and her engine-room was leaking. The lifeboat stood by for more than twelve hours, until the crew were ready to abandon ship after realising that the damage was too severe. The lifeboat crew attempted to beach the steamer, without success, which sank a mile off the South Gare light. The lifeboat then took the crew to Middlesbrough.

Although this was a long service, the next rescue was even more testing. At 9.30am on 15 April 1954 *Mary Ann Hepworth* was launched as most of the fishing fleet was at sea and the weather was rapidly deteriorating, with seas getting rougher, and a north-easterly gale blowing. As Coxswain Eric Taylor was at sea at the time, former Coxswain Harry Murfield took the wheel of the lifeboat. The lifeboat escorted several fishing boats into harbour and Eric Taylor, after returning in his own boat, assumed command of the lifeboat.

Crossing the harbour entrance was becoming increasingly hazardous and the lifeboat went out to warn the crews

The wreck of the fishing boat Foxglove on the rocks outside the East Pier, April 1954.

of two cobles, *Easter Morn* and *Foxglove*, of the danger. Closely escorted by the lifeboat, *Easter Morn* safely entered the harbour. However, just as *Foxglove* was approaching, she was hit by a particularly heavy sea which carried away her drogue and partially flooded the wheelhouse and engine-room, stopping the engine, and one of her crew was washed overboard. Coxswain Taylor immediately took the lifeboat in at full speed through a mass of white, churning water and the crew saw the man in the water. He weighed seventeen stone and only with considerable difficulty was he pulled aboard the lifeboat.

Meanwhile, the crippled *Foxglove* had drifted onto rocks east of the East Breakwater, with three men still on board her. With superb seamanship, Coxswain Taylor took the lifeboat through a gap in the rocks, the lifeboat striking the bottom several times, and then, skilfully using the

At 11.41am on 5 October 1956, the fishing vessel Galilee with five crew on board went aground near the East Pier and was in danger of being carried on to the Scaur Rocks. Mary Ann Hepworth launched at 12.15pm in a moderate sea, with a north-westerly breeze blowing and took over the tow ropes to bring Galilee to safety. (By courtesy of Whitby Lifeboat Museum)

Archer was sent to the station and, for the first time since she arrived in 1938, *Mary Ann Hepworth* went for overhaul. The reserve lifeboat, a 45ft Watson motor built in 1924 and stationed at Teesmouth for most of her career, stayed at Whitby from 18 May to 1 June 1955, launching on service twice to escort local fishing vessels.

Upon her return to station, *Mary Ann Hepworth* was called out to escort local fishing boats as usual, and on 23 November 1955 had to help the fishing fleet in difficult conditions. She launched at 11.25am after the weather worsened, and stood by as the boats entered harbour. About 1pm she had to help the fishing boat *Progress*, which had broken down three miles north-east of the harbour. The lifeboat took her in tow and, as conditions as Whitby were too dangerous to attempt to enter harbour with the vessel, headed for Scarborough. They were escorted in by the Scarborough lifeboat *Annie Ronald and Isabella Forrest*, on temporary duty at that station. *Mary Ann Hepworth* remained at Scarborough until 25 November, and so between the afternoon of 23 November and the return of the motor lifeboat two days later, the pulling lifeboat *Robert and Ellen Robson* was used to stand by the fishing fleet and escort in the boats in the rough seas prevailing at the time.

During 1956 and 1957 *Mary Ann Hepworth* undertook the usual services to fishing boats, escorting the fleet into harbour in bad weather on a number of occasions. Other services included one to the motor vessel *Spontaneity*, of London, which was on passage to Yarmouth on 16 July 1957 when help was requested for a sick crewman. The lifeboat picked up the crewman and, in the early hours of 17 July, landed him at Whitby so that an ambulance could take him to hospital.

The most notable rescue of 1958 came on 17 July after an eleven-year-old boy fell into the harbour. A woman told mechanic William Dryden what had happened and Dryden, despite being a non-swimmer, immediately jumped into the water and seized the boy. He then grabbed a mooring line from one of the fishing boats and slowly worked his way along the line to the boat, where he and the boy were helped aboard by the woman who had first raised the alarm. For this courageous rescue,

At 1.30pm on 27 June 1958 the motor fishing vessel Our Confidence, of Bridlington, broke down in dense fog. Mary Ann Hepworth was launched at 1.45pm and found the vessel three to four miles east-south-east of Whitby Rock. The vessel, with her crew of five, was towed to harbour, which was reached at 4pm.

engines, he laid the bow of the lifeboat at right angles against the fore part of the stranded fishing boat. But despite the pleas of the lifeboatmen, none of the three on board *Foxglove* would leave, and so Coxswain Taylor was forced to take the lifeboat out stern first and into position a second time. This time, the three men were taken on board after which the lifeboat was brought out into deeper water. A few minutes later, *Foxglove* broke up.

The lifeboat landed the three men and then resumed escorting the fishing boats, the last of which entered harbour at about 3pm. What had begun as a routine service ended with an outstanding rescue and, for determination, initiative, sound judgement and good seamanship, Coxswain Taylor was awarded the Bronze medal. The Thanks of the Institution on Vellum was accorded to Mechanic William Dryden, and additional monetary rewards were made to the nine members of the crew.

During 1955, the reserve lifeboat *J.W.*

On board Mary Ann Hepworth during lifeboat day 1964 are, left to right, Robert Noble, Bill Kaiser, Eric Thomson (behind), William Harland, Will Dryden, Robert Pennock, Jim Hansell, Bob Allen and Eric Breckon. (By courtesy of Whitby Lifeboat Museum)

Dryden was awarded the Royal Humane Society's Testimonial on Parchment.

Almost all of the effective services carried out in the five years after this incident involved escorting in fishing boats. On 1 July 1963 the reserve lifeboat *Rosa Woodd and Phyllis Lunn* was sent to Whitby so *Mary Ann Hepworth* could go for overhaul, and she remained on station until 30 November, during which time she launched four times on service and saved one life. The life-saving service came on 26 November 1963 when she launched in the afternoon to the motor vessel *Eminence*, of Rochester, bound from Sunderland to Goole. One of the crewmen on board was sick, and needed to be landed. The lifeboat took out the honorary medical adviser, met the vessel just over three miles north-east of Whitby

Mary Ann Hepworth at the head of the slipway, with the pulling lifeboat Robert and Ellen Robson at temporary moorings, in about 1957. The pulling lifeboats were not usually kept at moorings in the harbour during the summer months.

Mary Ann Hepworth leaving harbour, pushing her way through the swell across the bar. (By courtesy of Whitby Lifeboat Museum)

Lifeboatmen on Mary Ann Hepworth, from left to right, Mechanic Peter Thomson, Robert Second Coxswain Pennock, Robert Allen, Coxswain William Harland, John Hall and Eric Brecken. (By courtesy of Whitby Lifeboat Museum)

and transferred the doctor despite the near gale force winds and rough seas. The man was suffering from a thrombosis, and so was strapped to a stretcher for transfer to the lifeboat. Once patient and doctor were aboard, the lifeboat made for Whitby from where the sick man was taken to hospital.

Mary Ann Hepworth was back on station in November 1963 and performed a number of useful services during 1964. On 2 October she went to the coaster *Queensgate*, of Goole, which was ashore in moderate seas. The lifeboat launched at 4.30pm and found the coaster almost high and dry. The captain said he did not need assistance so the lifeboat returned to harbour, putting out again at 11am the

next day to stand by while local boats tried to refloat her and she was eventually freed during the late afternoon. On 23 October, *Mary Ann Hepworth* was launched to escort the local fishing boats *Ocean Venture* and *Lead Us* across the bar in heavy seas.

As well as undertaking some routine launches to escort local fishing vessels, during 1965 *Mary Ann Hepworth* also launched to merchant and pleasure craft. On 7 June she went to the motor yacht *Selina*, of Sandsend, which had gone onto a sandbank north of Sandsend, with four crew on board. Her engine had broken down, and so the lifeboat pulled her clear of the sandbank and into Whitby.

On 13 August the lifeboat went to the steamship *Cardiganbrook*, of London, after the vessel had radioed for a doctor as one of her crew was injured. The lifeboat launched at 6pm with the honorary medical adviser on board, and met the steamer off the harbour. The doctor went aboard to examine the boatswain, who had fallen from a hatch, and diagnosed a suspected broken arm and dislocated shoulder. The injured man was strapped to a stretcher, and taken aboard the lifeboat which was met by an ambulance at the harbour at 6.35pm.

The most notable rescue of 1965 took place in the early hours of 27 November when *Mary Ann Hepworth* went to the motor vessel *Fred Everard*, which was in difficulty with a serious list nine miles south of Whitby. *Mary Ann Hepworth* was launched at 2.30am, into a fresh south-easterly wind and heavy swell. As the lifeboat headed south, visibility was reduced by heavy snow squalls and it was bitterly cold. Under the command of Coxswain William Harland, the lifeboat crew found *Fred Everard* at 3.46am aground near Blea Wyke Point, with a heavy list to starboard. In very confined space and shallow water, it took great skill to manoeuvre the lifeboat alongside.

The lifeboat's first approach was to the starboard side, but as twelve of the crew were in a rubber life-raft on the port side, the lifeboat backed away and was taken round into shallow water to reach the raft. The twelve men were taken off the raft, and the lifeboat then returned to the coaster's other side to take off the master and mate. Shortly after 4am, the rescue was completed and the lifeboat returned to station. She put out again two hours later with the master and three crew, but when the master went aboard his vessel and found there had been an explosion in the engine room, he decided to abandon her. The lifeboat finally returned to station at 11.30am after a long drawn-out service for which Coxswain Harland was accorded the Thanks of the Institution on Vellum.

In October 1966 the lifeboat was involved in a somewhat unusual service. On 6 October, the police informed the Honorary Secretary that a motor cruiser had been reported missing from Whitby. The following morning, HMS *Wasperton* and a Shackleton aircraft began searching for the missing craft, and at 7pm the motor cruiser was spotted forty miles east of Whitby. HMS *Wasperton* proceeded to the position of the casualty, took it in tow and brought it towards the coast. *Mary Ann Hepworth* was launched at 3.30am on 8 October to assist, and found the warship and casualty two miles off. The Second Coxswain was put aboard the cruiser, *Marigella*, which was towed to harbour.

During 1967 and 1968 the usual services to escort local fishing vessels and cobles were undertaken. On 9 September 1969 *Mary Ann Hepworth* took out a doctor to the motor vessel *Sustina*, of San Francisco, and saved an injured man on board. Almost two weeks after this service, *Mary Ann Hepworth* went away

Mary Ann Hepworth launching on exercise in 1964 from the boathouse which was her home for more than thirty-five years. She had just returned from a full refit at Groves & Guttridge during which she was fitted with new diesel engines. (Arnold Taylor)

Mary Ann Hepworth on exercise with an RAF Whirlwind rescue helicopter in the early days of helicopter air-sea rescue operations. (By courtesy of Whitby Lifeboat Museum)

for overhaul and refit, and was replaced by the reserve lifeboat *Rosa Woodd and Phyllis Lunn*, which stayed from 27 September until 1 November 1969. She performed one service, saving the local fishing boat *Fairmorn* and her crew of one, while the station lifeboat was away.

During 1970, the Whitby lifeboat was involved in two outstanding services, with the first taking place in July. In the early hours of 15 July 1970, after the Coastguard had reported a small vessel making heavy weather two miles north-east of Whitby, *Mary Ann Hepworth* was launched at 5.10am to investigate. Getting out of harbour in the force nine north-westerly gale force conditions involved crossing confused seas between the piers,

which filled the lifeboat as she made her way to sea. She reached the casualty half-an-hour later and found the fishing vessel *Gannet*, with a crew of two, in difficulty. The boat's engine had been swamped and her rudder was jammed, but the two fishermen refused to leave their boat.

As it was impossible to tow the boat into Whitby harbour, Coxswain William Harland decided to head for Scarborough. But conditions for towing were very bad and the vessel's towing bollard was torn out, followed by a deck ring to which the tow line had been attached. The tow rope was then tied to the anchor cable, but when the fishing boat began to fill with water, Harland realised that the two men had to be taken off their boat as the situation had become so dangerous. The lifeboat had to go alongside three times before the men could be safely transferred across from their craft, which was sheering about wildly in the heavy seas.

Mary Ann Hepworth then headed south and, at 7.30am, the Scarborough lifeboat *J. G. Graves of Sheffield* was launched to help. She met the Whitby lifeboat at 8.30am, taking up station astern of the fishing boat. Shortly afterwards, the tow line from the Whitby lifeboat to the fishing boat parted and the Scarborough Coxswain, William Sheader, advised that it would be extremely dangerous to attempt to tow the crippled fishing boat into Scarborough Harbour. Reluctantly, her crew agreed to

Mary Ann Hepworth is recovered after escorting in the 44ft Waveney The White Rose of Yorkshire which replaced her.

The last launch of Mary Ann Hepworth, 6 December 1974. Her replacement, The White Rose of Yorkshire, is at moorings in the pen which was specially constructed alongside the Fish Pier. The lifeboat house was subsequently converted to house the inshore lifeboats. (By courtesy of Whitby Museum)

leave *Gannet* adrift and the two lifeboats entered Scarborough harbour safely at 9.30am. Later that day, when conditions had improved, the Scarborough lifeboat went out again and managed to tow *Gannet* into the harbour. For this difficult service, the Bronze Medal was awarded to Coxswain Harland, and Medal Service Certificates went to the rest of the crew, made up of Second Coxswain Robert Pennock, Mechanic Peter Thomson, Assistant Mechanic Ronald Frampton and crew Eric Breckon and Robert Allen.

Just over a month after the *Gannet* rescue, another noteworthy service was undertaken. At 6pm on 17 August 1970, the Coastguard reported that a locally-hired rowing boat, with a youth on board, was drifting towards the Scar Rocks outside Whitby harbour in rough seas and north-westerly force seven winds. *Mary Ann Hepworth* was launched under the command of Coxswain Harland, who took the boat alongside the small boat, which was on the point of sinking. The youth had collapsed and was lying in the bottom of the boat.

Two of the lifeboat crew, David Frampton and Robert Allen, immediately jumped into the rowing boat and managed to grab the youth, just as the boat sank beneath them. Although the two

lifeboatmen were non-swimmers, they held the casualty until he could be pulled aboard the lifeboat and then they too were pulled aboard. The lifeboat headed back to harbour where an ambulance was waiting to take the casualty to hospital, where he made a full recovery. For their prompt and courageous actions, which had saved the youth, lifeboatmen Frampton and Allen were each accorded the Thanks of the Institution on Vellum and Vellum service certificates were presented to the remainder of the lifeboat crew.

Following these two dramatic services of 1970, *Mary Ann Hepworth* remained on station for another four years but performed relatively routine rescue work. By the 1970s, she had been on station for more than thirty years and was in need of replacing. The RNLI was looking to introduce faster, more advanced self-righting lifeboats and had a number of new designs being developed and built and in 1973 one was allocated to Whitby.

Mary Ann Hepworth performed her final services of a long and impressive career at Whitby in September 1974. She launched on 24 September to the trimaran *Kalu Kun*, saving the boat and its crew of four, and then helping the motor fishing vessel *Sea Fisher* six days later. By the time she left, *Mary Ann Hepworth* had become the

The first inshore lifeboat, No.84, inside the lifeboat museum where she was kept when she was first on station in spring 1966. Honorary Secretary Eric Thomson is standing on the far left. The crew are, left to right, Bill Kaiser, William Harland, Ben Dean and Alan Marshall. (By courtesy of Whitby Lifeboat Museum)

station's longest-serving lifeboat and had saved more then 200 lives during her time. She was sold out of service in July 1974.

Inshore lifeboats

During the 1960s, less than a decade after the pulling lifeboat had been withdrawn, Whitby had two lifeboats again. The new boat was designed for inshore work and had been developed as a result of the growth of the leisure industry with increasing numbers of people using the sea for recreational purposes. Consequently more people were getting

into difficulty, often within sight of land and in moderate weather.

In response to this increasing number of inshore incidents, the RNLI introduced a new rescue tool in 1963, the inshore rescue boat (IRB), later designated inshore lifeboat (ILB). Conventional lifeboats were not well suited for inshore incidents, where speed was often crucial, so the small, fast inflatable rescue craft was developed. The RNLI bought its first inflatable boat in 1962 for extensive trials, and a delegation from the Institution visited France, where similar boats were in operation, to see the boats in action first hand.

The first IRBs were introduced during summer 1963 at ten stations and such was their success that more and more places began to operate the boats in subsequent years. The 16ft inflatable lifeboats, made from tough nylon with neoprene, could be launched quickly and easily, and were manned by only two or three crew. Their speed of twenty knots was considerably faster than any lifeboat in service during the 1960s, and they could go alongside other craft or persons in the water without causing or suffering damage.

In May 1966, an inshore lifeboat, No.84, was supplied to Whitby for service during the summer months. This boat was 15ft 6in in length with a beam of 6ft 3in, and was manufactured by RFD, a company well known for supplying life-rafts on

The inshore lifeboat when it first arrived in spring 1966, with crew members looking over the new and somewhat novel craft. Crouching down is the RNLI's Inspector Cdr Leslie Hill. (By courtesy of Whitby Lifeboat Museum)

Launching the station's first ILB from the old rocket house on the West Beach which served as a boathouse from 1968 until the mid-1970s. (By courtesy of Whitby Lifeboat Museum)

The first inshore lifeboat at Whitby, No.84, being launched across the West Beach from her trolley. (By courtesy of Whitby Lifeboat Museum)

The first inshore lifeboat, No.84, being recovered after exercise. (By courtesy of Whitby Lifeboat Museum)

The old rocket house on the West Beach, situated just beneath the Spa Pavilion, which served as an ILB house from 1968 to the mid-1970s. It has since been demolished. (By courtesy of Whitby Lifeboat Museum)

board ships. She was powered by a single 40hp outboard engine and was at first kept in the double boathouse which had been converted into the lifeboat museum. It was then moved to the old rocket house on the beach towards Upgang and a hand winch was installed to help with recovery.

The new ILB was launched on service for the first time on 31 May 1966, but no effective service was performed on that occasion. Her first service came a couple of months later, on 30 July 1966, when her crew gave help to the motor boat *Jackie*. During the following year, the IRB performed a number of useful services, showing her worth when assisting a boy who had fallen from a cliff and helping two men stranded on Black Rock.

On 18 August 1968, the IRB was used to undertake an outstanding rescue after a 20ft speedboat capsized in heavy surf about 150 yards from the IRB house. The IRB was launched, manned by Mechanic Peter Thomson and lifeboatman John

Anderson, and sped to the scene through north-westerly winds and breaking surf. The casualty was 120 yards offshore, head to sea, with three men clinging to it. As the lifeboat approached, the lifeboatmen were informed that some people were trapped beneath the boat. As the casualty was thrown up in the surf, two people could be seen clinging to part of the hull.

To reach them, the IRB was driven under the bows of the upturned boat as it lifted on a wave and, with great difficulty, two men and a girl were pulled out. All three were in a very poor state and so were immediately rushed ashore by the IRB, whose crew intended to return to pick the other three up. But as the IRB was about to put to sea again, the speedboat grounded in the surf and the three men clinging to the hull scrambled ashore. For this excellent service, Peter Thomson and John Anderson were accorded the Thanks of the Institution on Vellum.

The first IRB, No.84, served the station until October 1970 and was replaced the following season by a new inshore lifeboat, D-193, which was placed on service on 7 May 1971. This boat was provided by the South Kirkby (Emsall) Round Table and was, like the boat she replaced, a 15ft 6in RFD PB16 type inflatable. The first effective service by D-193 was undertaken on the afternoon of 27 June 1971 when she assisted the motor yacht *Philander*, of Hull, which was on fire six miles offshore. Apart from part of the 1973 season from May to September, when relief ILB D-87 was on station, D-193 served at Whitby until June 1977.

Man overboard exercise undertaken by the crew of D-193 in the early 1970s. (By courtesy of Whitby Lifeboat Museum)

The White Rose of Yorkshire

On 24 November 1974, *Mary Ann Hepworth* was withdrawn from service to be replaced by a new 44ft Waveney class, steel-hulled, self-righting lifeboat, built by Groves & Guttridge, of Cowes, at a cost of £79,018. The Waveney was based on a United States Coast Guard (USCG) design for a steel-hulled all-weather lifeboat, self-righting by virtue of its inherent buoyancy. The RNLI purchased one of these boats from the USCG in 1963 and took it on a tour of lifeboat stations in Britain and Ireland to assess its suitability and ascertain crew opinions. With a speed of around fifteen knots, it was the first design of 'fast' lifeboat and, as such, represented a radical departure from the traditional designs used hitherto.

After the design proved its capabilities during the trials, an initial construction programme of six boats was embarked upon. Further Waveneys were built once the first craft of the class to enter service had proved to be excellent lifeboats. The boat allocated to Whitby was the twelfth of the class and one of eight Waveneys built in the mid-1970s by Groves & Guttridge. She was powered by twin 260hp General Motors 8V-53 diesel engines. The hull design, necessary to achieve the higher speed, meant the new lifeboat had to be kept afloat at moorings and a berth was found adjacent to the boathouse.

On 21 May 1975, HRH The Duchess of Kent, wife of the President of the RNLI,

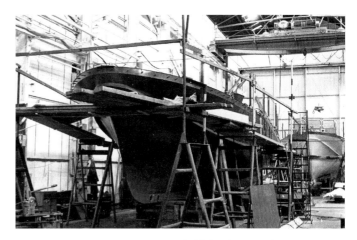

Two photographs showing The White Rose of Yorkshire in build at Groves & Guttridge yard, Cowes, at different stages of the build. The photo on the left was taken as she was nearing completion on 8 July 1974. (Jeff Morris)

The Waveney lifeboat The White Rose of Yorkshire arrives on station for the first time. (By courtesy of Whitby Museum)

The Waveney lifeboat The White Rose of Yorkshire arrives on station with Mary Ann Hepworth on hand to greet her replacement.

Crew of The White Rose of Yorkshire who brought her to Whitby were, left to right, Tom Howard, Alf Hedlam, Coxswain Robert Allen, Mechanic Peter Thomson and Dennis Carrick.

THE CREW OF WHITBY LIFEBOAT "THE WHITE ROSE OF YORKSHIRE"

visited Whitby to formally name the new lifeboat. The Marquis of Normanby, president of the station branch, opened proceedings by inviting the Duchess to present a framed photograph of the new boat to the donor, Miss Gwynaeth M. G. Milburn, of Harrogate, who up to then had remained anonymous. Miss Milburn had been honorary secretary of the Harrogate ladies' guild from 1952 to 1961. She was a life governor of the Institution and became an honorary crew member of the station in recognition of her support.

During the ceremony, the new lifeboat was formally delivered to the station by

Commander F. R. H. Swann, chairman of the RNLI, and accepted by Honorary Secretary David Stevenson. After a service of dedication, the Duchess christened the lifeboat *The White Rose of Yorkshire* and then boarded the boat and met the crew, before going for a short trip out to sea.

The White Rose of Yorkshire served at Whitby for fourteen years, during which time she launched 239 times on service and saved more than fifty lives. Indeed, by the time of her naming ceremony, she had undertaken a number of services, all routine in nature. During December 1974 she had been out on service a couple of times to local fishing vessels, and on 23 December went to the Dutch motor vessel *Mercurius*, from which she landed an injured crewman. She was also launched on service on Christmas Day 1974, putting out at 10am to go to the cabin cruiser *Care Free* which had broken down a mile from the station in a force six wind and moderate seas.

During 1975, the inshore lifeboat was involved in a number of excellent rescues. On 25 July D-193, which had been on station since 1971, was launched at 6.20pm to go to the aid of a man cut off by the tide at Saltwick Nab. Manned by Helmsman Michael Coates and lifeboatman David Wharton, the ILB

Lifeboat crew on board The White Rose of Yorkshire for her naming ceremony on 21 May 1975, with the Scarborough lifeboat J. G. Graves of Sheffield behind. The crew on board are, from left to right, Coxswain Robert Allen, Mechanic Peter Thomson, Dennis Carrick, Alf Hedlam and Howard Bedford. (Jeff Morris)

At the naming ceremony of The White Rose of Yorkshire were the Scarborough lifeboat J. G. Graves of Sheffield and the Runswick lifeboat Amelia, a relief boat on temporary duty and which later went on to serve as station boat at Scarborough. (Jeff Morris)

was taken towards the reported position. Arriving on scene, the two crewmen saw the casualty clinging to the cliff face 12ft above the water but slowly slipping down as his hand holds gave way. The lifeboatmen dropped anchor and, with its head to sea, veered the ILB towards the cliffs. Helmsman Coates then attached a line to his life-jacket, jumped overboard and swam to the foot of the cliffs.

With the heavy surf pounding the foot of the cliffs, Coates persuaded the man to slide down and drop into the sea. As soon as the casualty entered the water, he was grabbed by the lifeboatman and both were then hauled aboard the ILB. The man was landed at Whitby at 6.55pm, just over half an hour after the ILB had launched. For his actions during this fine rescue, Helmsman Coates was awarded a Bronze Medal and David Wharton was accorded the Thanks of the Institution on Vellum.

Just over three weeks later, on 18 August 1975, the ILB took part in another very fine service. D-193 was launched at 6.25pm, five minutes after

Inshore lifeboat D-193 served at Whitby from 1971 to 1977. (Jeff Morris)

the Coastguard reported that a speedboat had been swamped in rough seas 400 yards offshore and that its two crew were in the water. Manned by Brian Hodgson, David Wharton and Barry Mason, the ILB headed out of the harbour at full speed and the crew then began searching for the casualty. Eventually, one man was sighted just outside the line of the breakers on the beach, and the ILB headed for him.

A second man was then spotted, fifty yards away, almost caught in the heavy surf. Lifeboatman Hodgson jumped into the water to support the first man while the ILB made for the second man, who was rescued just as he was about to be engulfed in the surf. The ILB then returned to Hodgson and the first casualty and both men were pulled aboard. The ILB returned to harbour at 6.50pm and landed the two survivors. For his courageous actions, Hodgson was awarded the Bronze medal, and Medal Service Certificates were presented to David Wharton and Barry Mason.

During 1976 *The White Rose of Yorkshire* went away for a routine overhaul in April and May, with the prototype Waveney 44-001 standing in. She returned and resumed service, but on 21 September 1976, while on service to the fishing boat *Anmara*, one of her engines broke down. When she returned to station after the service, it was decided to undertake repairs in Whitby and, as an emergency relief, *William and Mary Durham*, a 42ft Watson built in 1957 for Berwick-on-Tweed, was used. This lifeboat was on passage south from Berwick, having left there for the last time, and was on duty at

Whitby for less than two weeks while the Waveney's engine was replaced. Just over a week after she had arrived, however, she was involved in an outstanding rescue which tested the Whitby crew to the limit. On 30 September she was called to the fishing vessel *Admiral Van Tromp*, which had radioed for assistance after going aground under cliffs near the High Light.

The lifeboat slipped her moorings at 3.26am and headed out to the last reported position of the casualty. With visibility reduced to about forty yards by thick fog, Coxswain Robert Allen radioed to the casualty to fire flares to indicate their position, which enabled the lifeboat crew to see where the vessel was ashore. The nearer the lifeboat got to the casualty, and the closer inshore she went, the heavier the seas became. Suddenly, an enormous wave, estimated at about 20ft in height, crashed right over the

The stranded fishing vessel Admiral Van Tromp to which the Whitby lifeboats went on 30 September 1976.

Two dramatic photos showing The White Rose of Yorkshire on service in heavy surf off the West Beach to the cabin cruiser Wyndways, which was wrecked on 19 October 1980. Conditions were so bad that the casualty was unable to enter harbour and broke up, with her two crew being washed overboard. One of them was washed up on the beach and survived, but the other was never found despite a long and difficult search in heavy seas and gale force winds. The lifeboat was operating inside the harbour wall, but failed to find anything and so, despite the conditions, this was classed a 'no service'. On the bow in the lower photo is Keith Stuart, keeping a lookout for the body. (By courtesy of Whitby Lifeboat Museum)

lifeboat, forcing Coxswain Allen to back the lifeboat out. He decided that reaching the fishing vessel would be easier when the tide had risen. Desperate efforts were made by Coastguards to get a line aboard the casualty, but with tremendous seas constantly sweeping over her, the fishing boat's crew could not venture out on deck to secure them.

At 4.15am, the crew of *Admiral Van Tromp* radioed that their situation was becoming critical and that they would soon be forced to abandon ship. Coxswain Allen decided to make another attempt to reach the wreck and took the lifeboat stern first towards her, dropping anchor and then veering down to within 60ft of the stranded vessel. The lifeboatmen

fired three lines over the wreck, but the fishermen were unable to secure any of them. The lifeboat then began to drag her anchor and she was swept broadside towards the rocks. Coxswain Allen put the engines full ahead and, with the wheel hard to port, succeeded in bringing the lifeboat round, head to sea, just as she was about to strike the rocks. The anchor was recovered and the lifeboat taken out to sea, where the crew realised that the fluke had broken off the anchor.

Coxswain Allen went to two fishing boats and borrowed two anchors from them, as well as two more line-throwing guns. The larger of the two anchors was attached to the lifeboat's anchor-cable and the lifeboat taken in again. This anchor was dropped so that the lifeboat could veer down, getting within 28ft of the wreck. At this point, two enormous waves crashed right over the lifeboat, knocking three crew off their feet and sweeping them aft. One, Raymond Dent, dislocated his shoulder and another, Howard Bedford, was knocked unconscious.

Coxswain Allen slammed both engines full ahead and the anchor cable was immediately cut. The lifeboat was driven back out to sea through enormous breaking seas. Lifeboatman Dent was transferred to the fishing boat *Jann Denise* and brought ashore for treatment, while Bedford recovered consciousness and remained on board the lifeboat. Coxswain Allen then made another attempt to reach the wrecked fishing vessel, but once again, the lifeboat was hit by several tremendous waves, damaging some of her stanchions and breaking the VHF radio handset. No sign of life could be seen on the wreck and so Coxswain Allen took the lifeboat into deeper water to await daylight before another rescue attempt would be made.

Lifeboatmen Michael Coates and Brian Hodgson were taken out to the lifeboat by *Jann Denise* to make up a full crew. At 8am, in better visibility, Coxswain Allen made another attempt to reach *Admiral Van Tromp*. The lifeboatmen had been informed by radio that two men from the fishing vessel had got ashore, but three remained unaccounted for. One of those men was then spotted on a rock known as the Black Nab, but the lifeboat could get no closer than fifty yards and so, while the Coastguard tried to get a line to this man, the inshore lifeboat was called out.

Helmsman Richard Robinson took the ILB well out to sea to clear the heavy breakers and went alongside *William and Mary Durham* at 8.45am, narrowly avoiding a capsize as the ILB headed back towards the shore. Helmsman Robinson then took the ILB through broken water and into Saltwick Bay, going inshore of the Black Nab. On seeing this, the man on the rock began to clamber across the rock, while heavy seas swept over it. Realising that the man could be washed off the rock, Robinson drove the ILB at full speed onto a small ledge and the other two lifeboatmen, David Wharton and Anthony Easton, grabbed the man just as a huge

wave crashed over the rock, filling the ILB and sweeping the boat off the ledge.

The ILB's propeller was fouled by one of the gun-lines in the water and so the crew got out the oars as huge waves continually swept them. One of the lifeboatmen grabbed a gun-line and used it to hold the ILB head to sea while the anchor was dropped and the propeller cleared. The engine was restarted, the anchor recovered and Robinson took the ILB out through broken water and back to the lifeboat to transfer the rescued man across. As the other two men from the fishing vessel were dead, the lifeboats returned to the harbour at 9.30am.

For this outstanding and most courageous service, Coxswain Allen was awarded the Silver medal by the RNLI, and Helmsman Richard Robinson the Bronze medal. The Thanks of the Institution on Vellum was accorded to the other two ILB crew and to each of the crew on the offshore lifeboat who had taken part in the first four rescue attempts.

Robert Allen was the first Coxswain of the Waveney lifeboat The White Rose of Yorkshire and served in the post until March 1977. (By courtesy of Whitby RNLI)

With the departure of Mary Ann Hepworth from the boathouse, the inshore lifeboat was transferred there in 1974 and the slipway was altered so that it could be used for the ILB's launching trolley.

The White Rose of Yorkshire returned to station in late November 1976 and completed a number of routine rescues during the first half of 1977, helping a number of fishing vessels. The most outstanding service of the year came on 5 June 1977 and involved the inshore lifeboat. At 4.30pm that day, reports were received that a man was cut off by the tide below the cliffs a mile from the station in force six winds and heavy seas.

Within ten minutes of the alarm being raise, D-193 was at sea manned by Helmsman Michael Coates and crew Brian Hodgson and Tony Easton. They spotted the man on the beach and dropped anchor to bring the ILB head to sea. She was then veered down towards the beach and Tony Easton entered the water to help the stranded man out to the ILB. But, in the pounding surf, he experienced considerable difficulty and so Helmsman Coates fastened a line to his own life-jacket and waded ashore to help. But, in the heavy seas, both lifeboatmen were swept off their feet and, together with the casualty, were carried onto the rocks.

At the same time, Brian Hodgson, in the ILB, shouted that the anchor-line had parted and the inflatable lifeboat was being swept towards the beach. Several times, the ILB was dashed against the rocks, but the other two lifeboatmen and the casualty somehow managed to get on board and, after several attempts, the outboard engine was restarted and they headed out through the heavy surf. But just as they were clearing the breakers, the engine suddenly stalled and the boat was rapidly swept back onto the beach.

To assist in what had become a difficult situation, The White Rose of Yorkshire was called out, slipping her moorings at 5pm. However, in the very shallow water at the scene of the accident, she could not get close enough to help and so a helicopter was tasked from RAF Leconfield. At 5.40pm, the crew of the ILB reported that they were abandoning the ILB because of the state of the tide and sea. Coastguard Officer Alan Martin was lowered down the cliffs and tried to get a line across to the stranded men, but his efforts were foiled by the heavy surf which smashed the whip box against the cliff.

The helicopter arrived at 6.11pm and winched up the casualty and the three lifeboatmen, as well as the Coastguard, and landed them on top of the cliffs. The casualty was taken to hospital as he was suffering from exposure, The White Rose of Yorkshire returned to station but the inshore lifeboat D-193 was a total loss. For their courage and determination during this very demanding service, the RNLI awarded its Thanks of the Institution on Vellum to Helmsman Michael Coates and lifeboatmen Brian Hodgson and Anthony Easton. A framed letter of thanks signed by Major-General Ralph Farrant, RNLI Chairman, was presented to Coastguard Officer Alan Martin.

In place of D-193, which had been damaged beyond repair, came a relief ILB, D-114. Built in 1966 for Mablethorpe, the relief boat served at Whitby until the end of the season, undertaking a number of rescues including being involved in a long search for a missing diver on 4 September in winds gusting to force seven. The following year, a new boat was allocated to the station, D-260, and entered service in March 1978. She was funded by Miss Gwynaeth Milburn, the donor of The White Rose of Yorkshire and, to meet the wishes of the crew, she was named Gwynaeth after the donor. The ILB was formally christened on 3 May 1978 with branch chairman Alan Marshall naming the boat by pouring champagne over her bows, as the donor looked on.

Before the new ILB had been placed on station, The White Rose of Yorkshire had undertaken a long service to four

Naming ceremony of the inshore lifeboat D-260 Gwynaeth in the boathouse, 3 May 1978. The donor (back to camera) looks on as the boat is formally christened.

Lifeboat crew on board The White Rose of Yorkshire in her pen. Standing at the back are, left to right, Dave Smith, Keith Stuart, Peter Thomson, Nick Botham and Peter Sellers. At the front is Barry Sneddon and behind him is Glenn Goodberry. (By courtesy of Whitby Lifeboat Museum)

fishing vessels which got into difficulty fifteen miles off Whitby on 11 January 1978. In force eight northerly winds, the vessels *Michaela Christopher*, *Rachel Claire*, *C. K. S.* and *Wakeful* got into difficulty, and the lifeboat put out at 10.42am to escort them through the difficult conditions and into harbour. From October 1977 until 21 April 1978, the relief lifeboat *Edian Courtauld*, a 46ft 9in Watson built in 1953 for Walton & Frinton, was at Whitby as an emergency relief boat. She stood in for *The White Rose* on two occasions, from October to December 1977 and again from January to March 1978, performing two routine services during this time. The Waveney was taken to Amble Boat Company in Northumberland for maintenance.

The next significant rescue at Whitby saw lives saved through the quick thinking of a young man at Robin Hood's Bay. On the afternoon of Sunday 10 June 1979, two youths launched a home-made raft from the Bay, but the heavy seas quickly swept the raft towards Gunney Hole, where it began to break up. One of the boys tried to swim to safety, but got into difficulties. On seeing this, sixteen-year-old Simon Hall launched an 8ft dinghy and rowed eighty yards out through the breaking seas to rescue the youth.

Hall then rowed across to a moored fishing boat aboard which both boys climbed. The inshore lifeboat D-260

Gwynaeth was called out and landed both boys from the fishing boat. The second youth who had been on board the raft managed to swim ashore safely. For showing considerable courage and initiative, Simon Hall was awarded a Bronze Medal by the RNLI.

During 1980 and 1981, the relief 47ft Watson *T. G. B.* stood in twice for *The White Rose of Yorkshire*, although she did not perform any services. The Waveney was taken to Robson's boatyard at South Shields for an inspection in 1980 and maintenance work in 1981. Before going

The White Rose of Yorkshire heads out of harbour. (By courtesy of Whitby Lifeboat Museum)

The crew on board The White Rose of Yorkshire in Scarborough harbour after the service in April 1982 to the fishing boat Rayella. (By courtesy of Whitby RNLI)

aft cabin. Another of the lifeboatmen, Keith Stuart, was knocked overboard, but his colleagues pulled him back aboard within minutes. The Scarborough lifeboat *Amelia* was called out to escort *The White Rose of Yorkshire* and *Rachel Clare* into Scarborough Harbour, and just after 10am the boats were safely secured.

The other long service took place on 26 May 1981 after a sick man needed evacuating from the fishing vessel *Carlo*, which was about forty miles off Whitby. The lifeboat put out at 11.25am with a doctor on board, and reached the fishing vessel three hours later. The injured man was subsequently taken off, and the lifeboat returned to station after almost seven hours at sea.

At 8.15am on 8 April 1982, *The White Rose of Yorkshire* slipped her moorings to go to the 60ft fishing vessel *Rayella*, which had broken down three miles off Whitby in a north-westerly gale. As the lifeboat left harbour, Coxswain Peter Thomson had to reduce speed as the lifeboat encountered rough seas and heavy swell. The casualty was reached at 9.15am and the lifeboat then stood by while arrangements were made for a sister ship to come down from the Tyne to take her in tow. The crew of *Rayella* had dropped anchor, but when this began to drag the lifeboat had to take her in tow. Coxswain Peter Thomson manoeuvred the lifeboat close to the port bow of the casualty and a tow-line was secured. The casualty's anchor was then

away to South Shields, *The White Rose* was involved in a couple of long services, the first on 22 March 1981 when she was called out at 4.30am after the fishing vessel *Rachel Clare*, with six crew on board, broke down off Robin Hood's Bay. The lifeboat, with Second Coxswain Michael Coates in command, took the fishing boat in tow and, in steadily worsening conditions, headed for Whitby.

On arrival off the harbour there, however, it was found that conditions were too bad to tow the vessel in and so the lifeboatmen began the long haul south to Scarborough. During the difficult tow in heavy seas, a huge wave struck the lifeboat and knocked lifeboatman Brian Hodgson off his feet, causing his head to strike the

The White Rose of Yorkshire at speed off the harbour with Brian Hodgson and Tony Easton standing by the aft cabin, Keith Stuart amidships wearing cap, and Alf Hedlam on right.

Relief Waveney lifeboat Wavy Line on duty at Whitby in August 1983. She served from June to September 1983, and came for relief duty at the station again in 1985, 1986 and 1987. (Nicholas Leach)

Relief lifeboat Wavy Line returns to harbour in foggy conditions.

slipped and, with the full length of the tow-line paid out, the tow got under way.

In the prevailing conditions, it was impossible to turn and run downwind to Scarborough or enter Whitby Harbour, so Coxswain Thomson headed slowly away from the coast, into the wind and seas, knowing that *Nimrod*, another fishing vessel, was on her way from the Tyne to take over the tow. *Nimrod* arrived at 3pm, about five miles north of Whitby, and by 3.30pm had connected her own tow-line to the casualty and began heading slowly north towards the Tyne, thirty-four miles away. The two fishing vessels reached port safely after more than twelve hours.

Meanwhile, the lifeboat headed back to station in the extremely heavy seas, accompanied by snow showers, with the gale by now force nine. At 3.45pm, a report was received by the lifeboat that conditions at the harbour entrance were bad, but it might be possible to enter if the lifeboat waited for a 'smooth'. Coxswain Thomson cautiously approached the entrance to assess the situation, but after ten minutes decided conditions were too bad and so he swung the lifeboat round and headed out towards the Bar Buoy, intending to head south to Scarborough.

However, at 4.15pm an exceptionally large wave, estimated at 25ft high, suddenly rose up on the lifeboat's port bow. Coxswain Thomson opened the engines to full power to climb it, but as the lifeboat did so, the wave began to break and the lifeboat, on clearing the top,

corkscrewed off the top of the wave and fell heavily down to starboard into the following trough, hitting the bottom of it at an angle of forty-five degrees.

The impact was extremely severe, throwing the crew across the wheelhouse. Alf Headlam hit the Coxswain's seat with such force that the seat was bent and buckled, and three of his ribs fractured. Brian Hodgson broke his arm when he was thrown against the inside of the wheelhouse, and Keith Stuart suffered cuts to his face. Coxswain Thomson received a severe blow on the head, but he quickly brought the lifeboat under control.

Alf Headlam was in such severe pain that his colleagues could not move him and so he had to remain where he fell, secured by a safety-line and packed round with spare life-jackets and blankets. Coxswain Thomson headed south at reduced speed, so as to lessen the motion

A fine photograph showing The White Rose of Yorkshire at speed off the harbour. She served Whitby for fourteen years and saved fifty-one lives.

The White Rose of Yorkshire punching her way through heavy seas at the harbour entrance.

of the lifeboat. In the heavy seas, it was not until 5.20pm that they approached the harbour at Scarborough, which was entered safely despite conditions. The lifeboat was moored and the injured men were taken to hospital by ambulance. Alf Headlam and Brian Hodgson were detained, and the others returned by road.

The lifeboatmen went back to Scarborough the following day when *The White Rose* was examined by RNLI officials. She was then sailed back to Whitby where the Coxswain's seat

was replaced and arrangements made to examine her hull. For his courage, determination and fine seamanship during this extremely demanding service, which lasted more than nine hours, Coxswain Thomson was accorded the Thanks of the Institution on Vellum, with Vellum Service Certificates being presented to the other lifeboatmen involved, Second Coxswain/ Assistant Mechanic Michael Coates, Keith Stuart, Alf Headlam and Brian Hodgson.

The White Rose of Yorkshire continued on station for the rest of the year, undertaking several routine services to fishing cobles and pleasure craft. Between June and September 1983, the relief Waveney lifeboat *Wavy Line* was on duty, while the station boat went to Robson's yard, and completed six effective services. During lifeboat day that year, 6 August 1983, she was on hand as a number of events were organised. Shortly before 3pm, the crew prepared to escort the station's former lifeboat *Mary Ann Hepworth*, under private ownership, into harbour. As they were about to cast off, a swimmer, wearing sub-aqua gear, got into difficulties a few feet from the stern of the moored lifeboat, so Coxswain Peter Thomson and lifeboatman Brian Hodgson immediately jumped in to help. The water was about 25ft deep

The White Rose of Yorkshire acting as a brake to the fishing vessel New Success, which is towed into harbour by another vessel. (Nicholas Leach)

but visibility was almost nil because of silt so, after two unsuccessful dives, Peter Thomson put on a pair of goggles.

The inshore lifeboat and the Atlantic 21 from Staithes & Runswick, both of which were afloat in the harbour, immediately rushed to the scene and Second Coxswain Michael Coates was taken by the Staithes ILB to get help from some sub-aqua divers who were just outside the harbour while David Smith, who was crewing the ILB, dived into the water. With the aid of the goggles, Peter Thomson saw something on the bottom, but was unable to reach it before having to come up for air.

Again he dived and this time saw what looked like a diver's air bottle. Forced to come to the surface for air, he indicated the spot to David Smith, who took a deep breath and dived to the bottom. Smith found the man and, with great difficulty, managed to get him to the surface. The weight of the man with all his diving gear was pulling Smith down again, but helped by Peter Thomson, Brian Hodgson and Michael Coates, who had returned with two more divers, the man was pulled across to *Wavy Line*. A heavy line was thrown from the lifeboat, but, just as it was being made fast to the diver's harness, the man slipped from the harness and sank.

Repeated attempts were made by the lifeboatmen and the divers to find the body, but without success. The body was eventually recovered at 6.45pm by a team of police frogmen. For their tremendous, selfless efforts during this incident, framed letters of thanks, signed by the RNLI Chairman, His Grace The Duke of Atholl, were later presented to Coxswain/

Mechanic Peter Thomson, Second Coxswain/Assistant Mechanic Michael Coates and lifeboatmen Brian Hodgson and David Smith.

Having returned from refit in September 1983, *The White Rose of Yorkshire* performed a number of long services during 1984. On 9 March she launched at 5.15am to the Grimsby fishing vessel *Navell*, which was on fire sixteen miles off Whitby, and stood by for two hours while the fire was got under control. On 22 June she went to the yacht *Highfly*, which was unsure of its position twenty miles from the station. The lifeboat found the yacht struggling in force eight winds so brought it back to harbour. On 24 August the fishing vessel *Trudella* was in difficulty thirteen miles off Whitby and the lifeboat put off at 4pm, spending more than four hours towing her safely to harbour.

On board The White Rose are, left to right, Keith Stuart, Mike Coates (Second Coxswain), Peter Thomson (Coxswain), Alan Fairclough and Robert Brookes. (By courtesy of Whitby Lifeboat Museum)

The White Rose of Yorkshire with lifeboats on passage north, destined for Longhope and Thurso. The Tyne lifeboat Lord Saltoun (47-025 on bow) was heading for Longhope while City of Bradford IV, the former Humber lifeboat, was on her way to Thurso to become the first Arun to serve there. (By courtesy of Whitby Lifeboat Museum)

During 1985 *Wavy Line* and the inshore lifeboat D-260 *Gwynaeth* worked together to execute an unusual rescue on 19 March 1985 after a party of twenty-seven schoolchildren and three teachers were cut off by the incoming tide 250 yards to the east of Whitby harbour. The lifeboat and inshore lifeboat put to sea at 12.40pm and, with *Wavy Line* standing by 400 yards offshore, the ILB was taken to the beach and the stranded group. In seven trips, the inflatable ferried them out to the

waiting lifeboat, which landed them at the harbour. The children were cold and wet, several were seasick as the sea was very choppy, with a 5ft swell and strong south-westerly wind blowing, but most were none the worse for their experience.

A long service was undertaken on 25 August 1985 when the lifeboat was called out to the yacht *Floozie* after a female member of the yacht's crew had been washed overboard fifty miles east of Whitby. The lifeboat launched at 12.15pm,

heading into very rough seas and a force eight south-westerly gale. At 4pm, the crew of a helicopter reported that they had located the yacht and radioed her position to the lifeboat crew, who reached the casualty two hours later. The yacht's skipper was in a state of shock after losing his companion and so he was taken aboard the lifeboat, while two lifeboatmen were transferred to the yacht. A tow-line was secured and the yacht was brought to harbour, where an ambulance was waiting to take the skipper to hospital. The woman who washed overboard was never found.

The next notable rescue also involved both lifeboats and took place on 9 April 1988 after the 24ft yacht *Cymba* headed out of Whitby harbour, with two men on board, and ran into heavy breaking seas, with waves up to 15ft high. The yacht was swamped and swept back towards rocks west of the harbour. The Coastguard were alerted but, as the situation had rapidly deteriorated and the need for help was extremely urgent, they immediately alerted the ILB crew. Within minutes D-260 *Gwynaeth* was on her way, manned by Helmsman Nicholas Botham and lifeboatmen Robert Brooks and Andrew Jordan. As the ILB set off at 8.44am, Coxswain/Mechanic Peter Thomson rushed to the lifeboat station and the Coastguard agreed that the Waveney should launch as well so *The White Rose of Yorkshire* slipped her moorings a minute later and headed out of harbour.

The crew of the ILB safely negotiated heavy seas over the bar and then turned west, towards the casualty, which was being driven rapidly towards the shore. As Helmsman Botham took the ILB into the very rough, broken seas, the crew spotted something in the water. Course was altered and they made for the spot, speed having to be adjusted frequently, as the ILB headed directly into the head seas. Although the crew had seen a pot

Peter Thomson took over as Coxswain of The White Rose of Yorkshire in March 1977. He joined the crew in 1966, was appointed full-time mechanic in 1967, and become Second Coxswain/Mechanic in 1974. From 1977 to 1993 he served as full-time Coxswain/Mechanic. He has been heavily involved in the running of the Museum from the mid-1980s, and since retiring in 1993 took much more time and interest in the Museum as its official curator. In September 1993 he was awarded the MBE for services to the RNLI. (By courtesy of Whitby Lifeboat Museum)

The White Rose of Yorkshire breaking through swell as she heads out of the harbour. (By courtesy of Whitby Lifeboat Museum)

marker, as they approached it a man was spotted nearby in the water. Waiting for a chance to come about, Botham turned and headed down past the man, then swung the ILB round to reach the man in the water. He was pulled aboard the ILB at 8.49am, but sadly was found to be dead.

Helmsman Botham saw that the offshore lifeboat was approaching the yacht and, as the seas closer to the shore were beyond the ILB's capabilities, decided to return to harbour. The extra weight of the body caused the ILB to frequently take heavy seas, so the boat was taken further out to sea before entering harbour where the body was landed.

Meanwhile, Coxswain Thomson, seeing that *Cymba* was in imminent danger of being driven onto the rocks, realised that he had to act very quickly. The yacht was beam on to the seas with one man

in the water astern of her, apparently still attached by a lifeline. The lifeboat approached the yacht but, when about thirty yards off, two very heavy seas struck the lifeboat from astern. The Coxswain realised that he would not be able to keep the lifeboat under control unless he went in stern first, and kept the lifeboat head to sea. Skilfully, he worked the lifeboat towards the yacht, having to go ahead on both engines each time a large wave came crashing over the lifeboat.

On the first attempt, the lifeboat was too near to the bow of the yacht and so the lifeboat was taken out again, with a danger that the lifeboat could get swept onto the rocks in the shallow water. The second attempt had to be abandoned when a massive wave lifted the lifeboat into the air and threatened to smash her down onto the yacht. The third attempt, however, was successful and a line was thrown to the man in the water. He unzipped his safety line and was hauled alongside and onto the lifeboat amidships, where he was held until Coxswain Thomson had taken the lifeboat back out through the heavy, breaking seas. He was then put into the aft cabin and wrapped in blankets as the lifeboat entered harbour at 9.04am.

At 9.30am, while the crew was still at the lifeboat house, Les Heath, the Honorary Secretary, was informed that two cobles were approaching the harbour and facing conditions at the entrance which were still very bad. So *The White Rose of Yorkshire* put to sea again

Relief lifeboat Khami approaching the harbour. She was on station from June to September 1988. (By courtesy of Whitby Lifeboat Museum)

immediately and escorted the cobles *Alliance* and *Progress* into harbour and returned to moorings at 10.30am.

For their courage, determination and excellent seamanship during the service to *Cymba*, Coxswain/Mechanic Thomson and Helmsman Botham were each awarded a Bronze medal by the RNLI, and Medal Service Certificates were presented to the lifeboatmen involved in these services. The eight lifeboatmen from the two lifeboats were later awarded the Silk Cut Seamanship Award for 1988. At

a ceremony at the Dorchester Hotel in London on 24 November 1988, Coxswain Thomson, on behalf of the lifeboat crew, received the Gold and Glass Plaque.

On 10 August 1988, a new D class inshore lifeboat, D-369, arrived at Whitby. The new boat was an Avon EA16 type inflatable, 16ft 3in in length, slightly larger and better equipped than her predecessor. Costing approximately £9,000, the new boat was provided from the bequest of the late Jack Wilson in memory of his wife Hilda Mary and, at a ceremony at

The White Rose of Yorkshire on exercise. (By courtesy of Whitby Lifeboat Museum)

The scene on Fish Quay during the naming ceremony of inshore lifeboat D-369 on 23 October 1988. (By courtesy of Whitby Lifeboat Museum)

Inshore lifeboat D-369 on exercise outside Whitby harbour. (By courtesy of Whitby Lifeboat Museum)

Whitby on Sunday 23 October 1988, she was formally handed to the station. John Wilson, son of the donor, handed the boat over and she was accepted by Gilbert Gray QC on behalf of the RNLI who, in turn, handed her to Les Heath, Honorary Secretary. A service of dedication was conducted by the Rector of Whitby, the Rev Ben Hopkinson, after which the ILB was launched for a short demonstration.

By the time this ceremony took place, the new ILB had already been involved in thirteen services, including one on 9 October, which nearly ended in a tragedy. The ILB was called out after three people had been trapped by the tide at cliffs near Saltwick Nab. By the time the ILB reached the spot, one of the trapped men had managed to scramble up to a relatively safe ledge, some way up the cliff face, but the other two men were still trapped at the foot of the cliffs. The ILB was taken in and the three lifeboatmen, Barry Snedden, Brian Hodgson and Howard Fields got out to turn the boat round and hold her steady while the two men were helped aboard.

With conditions worsening all the time, by the time the trapped men had been reached, the waves were up to 8ft high and, as the men were being helped into the ILB, a very large wave lifted the boat up, throwing it and all five men against the face of the cliffs and swamping the boat. *The White Rose of Yorkshire* was called out and she towed the ILB back to the

harbour after the three stranded men and the three lifeboatmen had been winched to safety by an RAF helicopter.

The final services performed by *The White Rose of Yorkshire* took place during the last two months of 1988. On 2 November 1988 she went to the 40ft fishing vessel *Nova Venture* on board which one of the crew had received a head injury and needed to be taken ashore. In force five winds, the lifeboat put out just after midday and reached the vessel half an hour later. It was decided not to transfer the patient because of the sea conditions, so the lifeboat escorted the vessel to Whitby where a Coastguard Land Rover was waiting to take the patient to hospital.

On 27 November 1988 the lifeboat went to the fishing vessel *O. B. J.* which was ten miles from the station and had lost steering and power, so the lifeboat towed her back. On 1 December 1988 she went to the fishing vessel *Eventide* which was escorted through a heavy swell at the harbour entrance.

The White Rose of Yorkshire left Whitby in December 1988 having proved her worth during many difficult and dangerous rescues off the Yorkshire coast. In April 1989 she went to Invergordon and served there for just over seven years. After three years in the Relief Fleet, she was sold out of service in March 1999 to the Canadian Lifeboat Institution for service as a lifeboat at Roberts Bank, near Vancouver.

City of Sheffield

In May 1987, the RNLI had announced that a new and more capable offshore lifeboat had been allocated to Whitby to replace *The White Rose of Yorkshire*. She was a 47ft Tyne class steel-hulled self-righter, a type developed principally as a slipway-launched lifeboat, although at Whitby she lay afloat in the pen at Fish Quay. The basic lines plan for the hull of the 'fast slipway boat' (FSB), as the Tyne was known during development, was provided by the National Maritime Institute and featured a semi-planing hull with a shallow draught, long straight keel and flared bow above the waterline.

Protection for the propellers was given by partial tunnels, substantial bilge keels, and a straight wide keel. The wheelhouse had a low profile to fit into existing lifeboat houses, with a flying bridge amidships and a separate cabin aft of the upper steering position. Twin propellers were driven by twin 425hp General Motors 6V-92-TI diesel engines. The design had a top speed of approximately eighteen knots. The two main tanks carried 510 gallons of diesel between them, with a reserve tank of 102 gallons, giving a range at full speed of 238 nautical miles.

To fund the new boat for Whitby, which was the twenty-first of the class to be built, an appeal was made to the people of Sheffield with the intention of raising £300,000. The appeal was formally launched on 16 May 1987 in Sheffield Town Hall by Andrew Thompson, chairman of the Appeal Committee, supported by the Lord Mayor of Sheffield,

47ft Tyne City of Sheffield emerges from the building yard of Wrights at Derby, on 5 November 1987, ready to be transported to Souters Shipyard for fitting out. (Tony Denton)

City of Sheffield at full speed during trials shortly after being completed. (By courtesy of Jeff Morris)

The hull was built by R. Wright & Son, Derby, and then taken to the Isle of Wight to be fitted out by Souter Shipyard, Cowes, between November 1987 and July 1988. A series of initial tests followed, and in early November 1988 the boat underwent her forty-hour trials from the boatyard prior to being handed over to the RNLI. Crew training took place during late November when Coxswain Peter Thomson, Second Coxswain Keith Stuart, and crew members Barry Sneddon, Alan Fairclough and Nick Botham went to the RNLI's Depot at Poole to be familiarised with the new boat. At the end of the training, the boat set off for her new station on 26 November. During the passage north, she called at Ramsgate and then Grimsby, reaching Scarborough on 28 November, with the Whitby crew accompanied by Divisional Inspector Tom Nutman and Divisional Engineer Eddie Irwin. The following day she arrived at Whitby and was welcomed home by *The White Rose of Yorkshire*.

Further crew training followed once the new boat had arrived, and *City of Sheffield* was placed on service on 12 December 1988. She carried out her first service on 22 January 1989, when she launched at 9.09am to three people on board the 18ft pleasure boat *Billy B II*, which had engine failure. In light seas, the vessel was towed into harbour and moored at the marina. This was the first of many services for the Tyne lifeboat, which served at Whitby for just over seven years, during which time she launched 239 times on service and saved eighty-eight lives.

The naming ceremony of the new boat took place on 28 July 1989, when HRH The Duchess of Kent visited the town to formally christen the boat. Over £435,000 towards the cost of the lifeboat had been raised by the Sheffield Appeal and many supporters from the city were present at the ceremony. The ceremony was opened by James Hall, Chairman of the station, who introduced Arthur Thompson, Chairman of the Sheffield Appeal Committee, for the formal handing over of the boat to the RNLI. She was accepted by Michael Vernon, Chairman of the Institution who, in turn, passed the boat into the care of the station and Honorary Secretary Les Heath. After a service

47ft Tyne City of Sheffield undergoing her self-righting trials at Cowes, Isle of Wight, attended by Coxswain Peter Thomson. She was hauled upside down and righted herself in about six seconds. (By courtesy of Jeff Morris)

Councillor Frank Price, the Lord Mayor elect Councillor Peter Horton, Gilbert Grey of the RNLI's Committee of Management, Captain Nick Barker RN of HMS *Sheffield*, and Coxswain Peter Thomson. The boat, to be named *City of Sheffield*, cost £566,000 to build and the appeal, with the bequest of Mrs Mary Mabel Walker and other gifts and legacies, provided the funds for its construction.

of dedication led by the Rev Benjamin Hopkinson, Rector of Whitby and lifeboat chaplain, the Marquis of Normanby, president of the station, invited the Duchess of Kent to christen the lifeboat *City of Sheffield* and, after the formalities, the Duchess went for a short trip to sea.

City of Sheffield's first full year on station, 1989, proved to be a busy one. Before her naming, she was involved in a number of services, one on 26 February 1989 when she helped the motor fishing boat *Sophie Louise* after the fishing boat had inadvertently caught a 1,000lb mine in her nets. The fishing boat headed towards Whitby and, while a Royal Navy Bomb Disposal Team from Rosyth was tasked, the fishermen lowered the mine onto the seabed about a mile north-west of Whitby. The following afternoon, the lifeboat took Navy divers and their equipment to the scene. The lifeboat moved away while the divers, working from their own inflatable boat, attached a detonating explosive to the mine and lit a three-minute fuse.

With the fuse set, however, the helmsman of the Navy inflatable was unable to start the boat's outboard engine. Seeing the problem, Coxswain/Mechanic Peter Thomson immediately took the lifeboat in at full speed and a tow line was thrown to the men in the inflatable which was towed clear. After about fifty yards, the inflatable's engine was restarted and both boats got clear, getting away just before the mine exploded and sent a

Whitby lifeboat crew on board 47ft Tyne City of Sheffield during crew training at the RNLI Depot, Poole. Left to right: Nick Botham, Peter Thomson, Barry Sneddon, Alan Fairclough and Keith Stuart. (By courtesy of Jeff Morris)

column of water 200ft into the air, shaking the Coastguard lookout over a mile away. For the quick thinking, courage and excellent teamwork shown by Coxswain Thomson and his crew, a Letter of Thanks signed by the RNLI's Chief of Operations, Captain George Cooper, was later sent to the lifeboat station.

On 30 May 1989 *City of Sheffield* launched at 7.40am to escort the small fishing vessel *Dominator A* into harbour in rough seas and a northerly gale. The boat was escorted safely in, after which the lifeboat put to sea again to escort another fishing vessel, *Blenheim*. As the lifeboat approached the harbour while on escort duty, she was overtaken by a very large breaking sea, about 15ft high. The lifeboat ran down the face of the wave, rapidly

City of Sheffield arrives on station for the first time, November 1988, after her passage north from Poole. (By courtesy of Whitby Lifeboat Museum)

Lifeboat crew on board 47ft Tyne City of Sheffield shortly after she arrived at Whitby, left to right, Nick Botham, Peter Sellers, Keith Stuart, Peter Thomson, Mike Coates, Alan Fairclough and Barry Sneddon.
(By courtesy of Whitby Lifeboat Museum)

gathering speed and, in order not to catch the fishing vessel ahead of her, Coxswain Peter Thomson put both engines full astern. Immediately, the lifeboat's starboard engine stopped and all attempts to restart it failed, while the engine room was found to be full of smoke.

With the lifeboat by that time only about fifty yards from the harbour entrance and being carried rapidly towards the West Pier, Coxswain Thomson drove the boat hard to starboard and just cleared the

end of the Pier. Two more attempts were then made to enter harbour, but each time without success. A third attempt failed when the lifeboat was forced rapidly to port by the heavy seas and, being very close to the East Pier, she had to be turned hard to port, heading straight for the Whitby Rocks and very heavy, breaking seas. But, with outstanding seamanship, Coxswain Thomson brought the lifeboat round and clear of the rocks. On the fourth attempt, the lifeboat was safely brought into the harbour. A Letter of Thanks, signed by the Director of the RNLI, Lieut Cdr Brian Miles, was later sent to Coxswain Peter Thomson, for his perseverance and skilful boat handling which had prevented damage to the lifeboat and possible injury to the crew.

Early on the morning of 1 June 1989, after the Coastguard had reported that the 31ft fishing vessel Karoline, of Kirkwall, with a crew of six, had broken down forty miles south-east of Whitby, City of Sheffield put to sea at 5.15am and headed out into choppy seas and force six northerly winds. Three of the men on the fishing

47ft Tyne City of Sheffield moored at Scotch Head for her formal naming and dedication ceremony on 28 July 1989, with former lifeboat Mary Ann Hepworth moored in the background.
The three on the bow are, left to right, Keith Stuart, Peter Thomson and Mike Coates.
(By courtesy of Whitby Lifeboat Museum)

HRH The Duchess of Kent goes aboard City of Sheffield after the naming ceremony on 28 July 1989, and is introduced to some of the crew on board. (By courtesy of Whitby Lifeboat Museum)

With HRH The Duchess of Kent on the flying bridge, City of Sheffield puts to sea at the end of her naming ceremony on 28 July 1989, escorted by Staithes & Runswick's Atlantic 21 lifeboat. (Tony Denton)

vessel had acute food poisoning. An RAF helicopter flew to the vessel and winched off one of the men who was flown straight to Scarborough Hospital. Once on scene, the lifeboat took the disabled vessel in tow and Coxswain Thomson headed for Scarborough, arriving there at 1pm. Permission to enter harbour was refused, however, until the hospital had carried out tests on the man brought in earlier. The lifeboat eventually brought the fishing vessel into the harbour at 1.45pm. After having something to eat and drink, the lifeboatmen returned to Whitby, arriving back at station at 3.56pm.

In October 1989, the relief lifeboat *Owen and Anne Aisher*, a 47ft Tyne built in 1988, came to the station and stayed for nine months, undertaking a number of services during her stay, mainly to broken-down fishing vessels and pleasure craft. *City of Sheffield* returned to station on 20 July 1990 and three days later she was called out on a routine service to the yacht *Karen Kelly* which had broken down twelve miles off Whitby in moderate seas.

In August 1991, *City of Sheffield* was twice involved in services to injured

people. Late on the morning of 3 August 1991, she was called out after one of a party of anglers on board the fishing boat *Sea Roma* had been taken ill. *City of Sheffield* slipped her moorings at 11.39am and, after picking up a doctor at Scotch Head, headed out to the fishing boat, which was twelve miles north-east of Whitby. The doctor was put aboard and the unwell man, who had become seriously ill, was transferred to the lifeboat, with a

City of Sheffield leaving harbour with the historic church and ruined abbey providing the backdrop during a photoshoot in January 1989.
(By courtesy of Whitby Lifeboat Museum)

colleague. They were landed at Whitby where an ambulance took them to hospital.

The other medical evacuation took place the following morning. She was called out at 6.57am after a crew member on board the fishing vessel *Nova Venture* was injured. The man had been hit on the head by a piece of metal which had been hauled up in the nets. He was taken aboard the lifeboat and landed at Whitby, and an ambulance took him to hospital.

In very rough seas, late on the morning of 18 January 1992, the cabin cruiser *Coronet*, with two people on board, broke

down half-a-mile south-east of Whitby harbour. *City of Sheffield* put to sea at 11.25am and reached the casualty five minutes later. Attempting to get the lifeboat alongside the smaller vessel could have resulted in a severe collision, so the lifeboat was swung to starboard to bring her stern close to the casualty and, after two attempts, a line was passed across and secured. The two people were then taken off the disabled boat, which was towed out to sea to clear the rocks in the area, and then brought safely into harbour where the survivors were landed just before noon.

City of Sheffield standing by the fishing boat Blenheim as the vessel returns to harbour and crosses the bar in heavy seas, 30 May 1989.
(By courtesy of Whitby Lifeboat Museum)

Relief lifeboat Owen and Anne Aisher heading out through the harbour entrance on 3 April 1990 for the third service of the day, this time going to the fishing vessel Sophie Louise. The casualty was towed to Scarborough as entering Whitby harbour was too dangerous after the vessel damaged her rudder when she touched the bottom in a trough. (By courtesy of Whitby Lifeboat Museum)

Owen and Anne Aisher came to the station again at the end of September 1992 for relief duty. She stayed until 7 December and, just before she left, was involved in a very fine service. Late on the afternoon of 2 December 1992, the fishing vessel *Darren S*, with a crew of three, became disabled after the rudder was damaged while the vessel was two-and-a-half miles south-east of Whitby. *Owen and Ann Aisher* put to sea at 4.48pm in very rough seas and near gale force north-westerly winds. She arrived on scene ten minutes later and took the disabled boat in tow. However, in the prevailing conditions and with the casualty's rudder jammed, the tow proved extremely difficult.

Conditions at the harbour entrance were made worse by an unusually heavy outflow of fresh water, the result of several days of torrential rain in the hills. As the lifeboat tried to tow the casualty into harbour, both boats nearly collided with the piers several times. But with great skill, Coxswain Peter Thomson brought the lifeboat and casualty safely in, and *Darren S* was berthed at 6.50pm. For his fine boat handling, Coxswain Thomson was sent a Letter of Appreciation, signed by the RNLI's Chief of Operations, Commodore George Cooper.

In heavy seas, late on the morning of 20 February 1993, a 21ft rigid-inflatable boat capsized to the east of the harbour entrance as it was returning to Whitby. The crew of two were thrown into the water. One man was picked up by another rigid-inflatable, which itself was nearly overturned by a very heavy wave. In the prevailing conditions, the helmsman of the other boat realised he could not operate safely and so made for harbour as quickly as possible to raise the alarm. With only two hours of flood tide to go, the depth of water was not enough for the Tyne lifeboat to get close inshore, so Coxswain Thomson asked for volunteers to man the ILB, D-369, even though she was off service for the winter months and did not have a radio fitted.

With volunteers ready, the ILB was launched and at 11.35am *City of Sheffield* put to sea followed by D-369. As the lifeboats approached the Whitby Rocks, nothing could be seen of the missing man but he was then spotted in the turbulent, breaking seas. Slowly, Coxswain Thomson took *City of Sheffield* towards him but, with just 3ft of water showing on the lifeboat's echo-sounder and with heavy seas breaking over her stern, could get no closer and so he waved the ILB in.

Relief lifeboat Owen and Anne Aisher at moorings in the pen. (By courtesy of Whitby Lifeboat Museum)

Helmsman John Pearson skilfully took the ILB at full speed to the man in the water, 100 yards away. In the heavy, breaking seas, it was impossible to turn the ILB and so she was taken past the man before being brought round.

While making a first attempt to reach the survivor, the ILB was forced away by a large, breaking wave and another attempt had to be made. This second attempt was successful and the man was hauled aboard even though the ILB could not be stopped in the conditions. With heavy swell driving onto the rocks, the breaking seas were estimated at 12ft high and, with the other two lifeboatmen in the bows to prevent the ILB from capsizing, Helmsman Pearson kept the boat head to sea as he brought her clear. On several occasions the ILB left the water as she battled the waves.

Aware that conditions had been worsening, Coxswain Thomson had carefully edged City of Sheffield closer to the shore and the crew prepared heaving lines in case the ILB should capsize. But eventually the ILB reached the Tyne safely and both lifeboats headed into deeper water. The rescued man, who was suffering from shock and cold, was transferred to the all-weather lifeboat which landed him at 12.11pm, with an ambulance taking him to hospital.

For his superb seamanship and tremendous courage, Helmsman John Pearson was awarded a Bronze medal by the RNLI. The other two crew of the ILB, Nick Bentley and Glenn Goodberry, were each awarded the Thanks of the Institution on Vellum. A collective Framed Letter of Appreciation signed by the

City of Sheffield escorting a small fishing vessel into harbour. (By courtesy of Whitby RNLI)

City of Sheffield heading out of harbour on service in 1990. (Liam McKenna, by courtesy of Whitby Lifeboat Museum)

Chairman of the RNLI, Michael Vernon, was later presented to Coxswain/Mechanic Thomson and his crew in recognition of their efforts during this service and, in particular, the support they gave to their colleagues in the ILB.

On 6 May 1993 the lifeboat was involved in two services, both routine in nature. The first was to the fishing boat *Pride of Mansfield*, with seven people on board including a party of sea anglers, which got into difficulty off Whitby after striking a submerged object which smashed her rudder. *City of Sheffield* slipped her moorings at 8.37am and headed out into calm seas and a light north-westerly breeze, reaching the casualty at 9am. The disabled boat was taken in tow stern first, so as to minimise the effect of the smashed rudder, and brought into harbour half an hour later.

The second service was during the early evening, with the lifeboat putting to sea at 7.09pm to go to the motor boat *Tebble B*, with two people on board, which was reported to have broken down five miles north-west of Whitby. The lifeboat reached the casualty's reported position at 7.30pm, but the lifeboatmen found nothing. They began a search using the direction finder, but reception from the casualty was very poor. The Coastguard were asked to check the boat's position and they confirmed that it was, in fact, north-east of Whitby, not north-west, so the lifeboat proceeded to the new position at 7.45pm. She then found the casualty, a tow-line was rigged,

and the boat was towed back to harbour an hour and a half later.

On 14 June 1993 *City of Sheffield* went to a fishing boat that was on fire. She put to sea at 4.10pm to go to the fishing vessel *Ina B*, which was ablaze sixteen miles north-east of Whitby. An RAF helicopter, which was tasked to the burning vessel, winched three of the crew to safety and transferred them to the lifeboat as she headed for the scene at full speed, in choppy seas and an easterly wind. The fourth member of the vessel's crew refused to be winched off and was saved by another fishing vessel, which put him onto

Keith Stuart served as Coxswain from 1993 to 2002 having joined the crew in 1978. A joiner by trade, he was first Coxswain of George and Mary Webb. (By courtesy of Whitby RNLI)

the lifeboat. When *City of Sheffield* reached the casualty at 5.50pm, two lifeboatmen boarded it to seal off the area of the fire and secure a tow line. They remained on board as the lifeboat towed the fishing vessel back to harbour, where she was berthed at the Fish Quay. The fire brigade then boarded the vessel, and the lifeboat returned to her moorings at 8.48pm.

During 1994 *City of Sheffield* had another busy year, launching several times during the first three months to fishing vessels in difficulty. On the afternoon of 7 June 1994 she was launched to the motor cruiser *Lorna L*, with three people on board, which had broken down four miles north of Whitby. The lifeboat put to sea at 3.13pm and, once on scene, the lifeboatmen rigged a tow line to the bows of the disabled boat. The lifeboat began the tow towards harbour, but the casualty proved very difficult to tow as her bows were repeatedly digging into the water. The boat was therefore hauled to the lifeboat and lashed alongside, and both boats safely reached harbour at 5.45pm.

Less than a month later, *City of Sheffield* was launched to the same craft while on service to another vessel. In dense fog at about midday on 3 July 1994, she went to the cabin cruiser *Soup Dragon*, with two people on board, which had broken down nearly thirteen miles off Whitby. The lifeboat, which put out at 12.18pm, found the casualty an hour and a half later using the VHF direction finder and radar.

City of Sheffield leaving harbour on service to stand by fishing vessels returning to harbour. (By courtesy of Whitby Lifeboat Museum)

City of Sheffield returning to harbour in January 1994. (By courtesy of Whitby Lifeboat Museum)

City of Sheffield at speed in the harbour during the station's annual lifeboat day in 1993. (By courtesy of Whitby Lifeboat Museum)

City of Sheffield exercising with an RAF helicopter in the harbour during lifeboat day. (By courtesy of Whitby Lifeboat Museum)

A tow line was secured and the lifeboat began towing the disabled boat towards Whitby harbour. During the passage, a radio message from *Lorna L* was received requesting assistance. The four crew on board the motor cruiser were in difficulties off Whitby High Light, where they dropped anchor.

At first, they were asked to wait until the lifeboat had towed *Soup Dragon* into harbour, but, on checking the position of *Lorna L* by radar, it became clear to the lifeboatmen that the cruiser was in a dangerous position, less than half-a-mile offshore, in shallow water and on a falling tide. Coxswain Keith Stuart contacted Barry Sneddon, a former lifeboatman and owner of the old lifeboat *Mary Ann Hepworth* which was used a trip boat, and he agreed to take over the towing of *Soup Dragon* at the harbour entrance. The inshore lifeboat D-369 was also

City of Sheffield in the mooring pen next to the Fish Quay, February 1995. (Nicholas Leach)

City of Sheffield at her moorings in the harbour, February 1995. (Nicholas Leach)

launched and stood by until the tow had been transferred to the former lifeboat, which brought *Soup Dragon* safely into harbour. *City of Sheffield* and D-369 then proceeded to *Lorna L,* which was taken in tow by the offshore lifeboat and then also brought safely into harbour.

The Famous Grouse relief lifeboat was on station towards the end of 1994 when *City of Sheffield* went to Leggett's Boatyard, Grimsby, for survey. *City of Sheffield* returned to station on 18 December 1994 and within a week was called out on service. She slipped her moorings at 8.10am on Christmas Eve to go to the aid of the fishing vessel *Kingfisher,* which was disabled with a fouled propeller a mile north of Whitby harbour. A crew of four were on the disabled boat which was in difficulty in choppy seas and a fresh south-westerly wind. The lifeboat quickly reached the boat and towed it back to harbour, returning to station at 9am.

The last full year that *City of Sheffield* was on station, 1995, proved to be another

busy one. During the first three months of the year she was out regularly to assist local fishing vessels that had got into difficulty, including helping two vessels on 15 January. One of them, *Natalie B,* was more than twenty miles away and in force eight winds the lifeboat was at sea for five hours getting the vessel and her six crew to harbour. On 1 April, *City of Sheffield* went out in very choppy seas and a strong westerly wind to the yacht *Thavma,* with three people on board, which was unable to make progress against the flood tide a mile and a half south-east of Whitby. The lifeboat took the yacht in tow and brought her into harbour.

The most unusual service of the year took place on 2 June after a woman trainee, who was an epileptic, was taken ill on board the sail training vessel *Black Diamond.* The woman was drifting in and out of consciousness so the captain radioed for medical assistance. *City of Sheffield* put to sea at 11.20am and headed out at full speed and, fifteen minutes later, reached the training vessel eight miles north of the station. Accompanied by a team leader, the sick woman was transferred to the lifeboat, which rushed her ashore. An ambulance was waiting at Scotch Head and, as soon as the lifeboat had moored, paramedics went aboard to attend to the woman. She was subsequently taken to hospital, with the lifeboat returning to her moorings.

On 5 August *City of Sheffield* had to help the station's inshore lifeboat.

D-369 had launched at 9.04pm after several people had been reported to be cut off by the tide, three and a half miles south-east of Whitby harbour. The ILB was beached, but as the people had managed to scramble to safety unaided the lifeboat crew prepared to refloat their boat. However, very heavy ground swell prevented the ILB getting clear of the beach so the all-weather lifeboat was called. *City of Sheffield* put to sea at 10pm and, once on scene, the crew fired a rocket line over the ILB which was used to pull the boat through the surf. Once the ILB reached deeper water, the line was released and *City of Sheffield* escorted the inflatable back to harbour.

Both lifeboats were again involved in a service together on 1 October. At 11.45am, as D-369 was returning to the harbour following a routine exercise, her crew spotted the 35ft yacht *Tsimshian*, with three people on board, outside the harbour drifting towards the East Pier. The ILB went alongside and her crew advised the skipper to lower the sails and then pass a tow line across, but the skipper did neither. Helmsman Welham then used the ILB to push the yacht away from the pier, but the skipper continued to head towards the gap in the East Pier, where the yacht would almost certainly go aground. Eventually, the skipper did lower his sails and the crew of the ILB managed to get a line secured to a cleat on the yacht, by means of which they were able to keep the yacht clear of the pier until *City of Sheffield* arrived on scene. The tow line was then transferred to the offshore lifeboat which brought the yacht safely into harbour.

City of Sheffield was involved in a medical evacuation on 14 October after her assistance was requested by the fishing vessel *Deep Harmony*. A crewman on board the fishing vessel had been taken ill and was reported to be suffering from hypothermia. *City of Sheffield* put to sea at 1.25pm and met the fishing vessel north of Whitby, where the sick man was transferred across, given hot drinks and wrapped in blankets. He was landed at Scotch Head from where he was taken to hospital by ambulance. The lifeboat was out again later the same day, going to the motor boat *Lorna L*, with three people on board, which had broken down eight miles north-west of Whitby. The disabled boat was towed back to harbour and the lifeboat returned to station, reaching her moorings at 6.22pm.

The final services by *City of Sheffield*, undertaken during the first four months

City of Sheffield returning to harbour.

City of Sheffield, carrying a TV camera crew, leads her successor George and Mary Webb into harbour. (Tony Denton)

City of Sheffield in the pen at Fish Pier with Staithes Atlantic 21 ILB alongside and her successor, 14m Trent George and Mary Webb, after the new boat had arrived on station for the first time. (Tony Denton)

of 1996, were all straightforward. On 30 January 1996 she launched to the fishing vessel *Provider*, which had broken down in moderate seas, and on 14 February went to another fishing boat, *Radiant Morn*, which had a fouled propeller. On 24 March, both *City of Sheffield* and the ILB were tasked to the rigid inflatable *C2 Diver*, which had broken down and was being carried by the tide into broken water. As the lifeboats were already on exercise, they diverted to help the casualty, which was towed safely to harbour.

City of Sheffield was called out for what proved to be the last time while at Whitby at 9.26am on 10 April 1996, when she went out to the small motor boat *Pippin*, with one man on board, which was in difficulty a mile and a half from harbour. The lifeboat towed the motor boat in at 10.05am. During the evening of the same day, the station's new lifeboat was placed on service. *City of Sheffield* left Whitby on 16 April 1996 and went to the RNLI Depot at Poole via overnight stops at Lowestoft and Ramsgate. She was subsequently used as a relief lifeboat until being allocated to Hartlepool, where she served for three years. Since September 2001 she has been stationed at Poole.

George and Mary Webb

Whitby's next new lifeboat was allocated to the station in April 1994. It was a 14m Trent class self-righter, powered by twin 800hp MAN D2840 diesel engines, giving a top speed of twenty-five knots. The Trent was developed during the early 1990s, together with the larger 17m Severn, to replace the Waveney and Arun classes, designs used at stations where the lifeboat was moored afloat. The new designs were developed in-house by the RNLI, a process which involved extensive tank testing of scale models during the design process. Following the testing, a hard chine hull form was adopted, with the hull for the smaller 14m Trent a scaled down version of the 17m Severn. Both designs were self-righting by virtue of the watertight wheelhouse. The engine room was positioned aft, and the Trent's engines staggered so one powered a U-drive and the other a conventional straight drive.

Capable of reaching speeds up to twenty-five knots, much faster than the Tyne, the new boats reduced the time taken to reach a casualty by nearly thirty per cent and had a fully enclosed, heated wheelhouse. The Trent's deckhouse contained permanent seating for six crew, with a seat for a seventh who is usually a doctor when needed, together with provision for one stretcher in the wheelhouse and another in the forecabin. The hull was subdivided by five bulkheads into six compartments: a fore peak, fore store, forecabin/survivor cabin, tank space, machinery space and an aft peak steering compartment.

With a hull of moulded fibre-reinforced composite by Green Marine at Lymington, the new lifeboat for Whitby was fitted out by Souter Shipyard, at Cowes, between February and December 1995. During mid-December 1995 she was taken on her forty-hour trial via overnight stops at Fowey, Plymouth, Torbay and Weymouth

George and Mary Webb on speed trials shortly after she had been built. (By courtesy of the RNLI)

George and Mary Webb in build at Souter's Shipyard, Cowes, on 23 August 1995, with the stern of Trent lifeboat ON.1210 (14-12) destined for Exmouth visible. (Tony Denton)

before returning to the RNLI Depot at Poole on 15 December.

She arrived at Whitby on 2 April 1996 after a passage from Poole via Newhaven, Lowestoft and Scarborough. On board were Divisional Inspector Tom Nutman (his last passage before retirement), District Engineer Nick Day, Coxswain Keith Stuart, Mechanic Glenn Goodberry, Second Coxswain Keith Elliott, and crew members Nick Botham and John Pearson. They had spent a week at Poole undergoing training and familiarisation on the new boat during March 1996, before bringing the boat home. Built at a cost of £1,103,008, she was provided out of a gift from The Mary Webb Trust and was named *George and Mary Webb*.

The day after her arrival, 3 April, the new lifeboat went to sea for a series of radio checks with RNLI engineers and officials on board. When four and a half miles south-east of Whitby, the lifeboatmen heard on the radio that the Dutch barge *Jodie* was taking in water and in need of assistance. They informed the Coastguard that they were proceeding to the casualty and would put a pump on board. The pump was transferred at 1.35pm and the barge was escorted to Whitby. However, as the lifeboat and barge headed towards harbour, it became apparent that the pump could not cope with the water coming aboard the barge and so, at 2.23pm, *City of Sheffield* put to sea and three lifeboatmen and another pump were transferred onto the barge, which then reached harbour safely and was beached near Tate Hill Pier at 4pm.

The new lifeboat was officially placed on service on 10 April 1996, and just over a week later she was called out for a first service as the Whitby lifeboat. On 18 April she launched at 12.30pm to the 12m fishing vessel *Cadonga Two* which had lost a bilge keel and was taking on water. The Staithes & Runswick Atlantic 21 ILB had also launched and was standing by when *George and Mary Webb* arrived on scene. The all-weather lifeboat escorted the vessel towards Whitby and the port was reached without further incident.

On 4 May 1996, the all-weather lifeboat

George and Mary Webb heads out to sea from the RNLI Depot at Poole during crew training, March 1996. (Jeff Morris)

City of Sheffield leads
the new 14m Trent
George and Mary Webb
to Whitby, 2 April 1996,
as she arrives on station
for the first time. (By
courtesy of Steve Dutton)

George and Mary Webb
is escorted home by the
station's D class ILB and
Staithes & Runswick's
Atlantic 21 lifeboat.
(Tony Denton)

The new 14m Trent
George and Mary Webb
shows her speed off
Whitby, 2 April 1996,
as she arrives on
station. (By courtesy
of Steve Dutton)

was on hand to assist in a service which was particularly testing for the ILB. D-369 was launched at 5.13pm after two youths were swept out to sea by heavy surf at Sandsend, with one managing to get back to shore to raise the alarm. As the ILB cleared Whitby harbour, Helmsman John Pearson realised just how bad conditions were and so radioed for assistance from the all-weather lifeboat, while the Atlantic 21 from Staithes & Runswick was also tasked along with an RAF helicopter.

On arrival in the area, the ILB crew were told that the missing youth had been swept further to the north-west off the end of the sea wall at Sandsend. The ILB was taken into the very heavy surf and headed for the reported position, but nothing was found. Helmsman Pearson then had to take the ILB back out through the surf, as the boat was being swept dangerously near to the sea wall and keeping control of it was very difficult in the broken, confused seas so close inshore.

Several times Pearson took the ILB back into the surf, as the three lifeboatmen in the ILB scanned the waves, looking for the missing youth. Several times the

The new 14m Trent George and Mary Webb arrives at Whitby for the first time, 2 April 1996.

After arriving on station on 2 April 1996, George and Mary Webb puts out later that day with crew members and station personnel who had not been to sea on her.

ILB hit the bottom in very shallow water. No further sightings of the youth were reported by the Coastguard and, with the all-weather lifeboat and Staithes & Runswick ILB now on scene helping with the search, Helmsman Pearson turned the ILB to run out through the heavy surf.

However, unexpectedly, an exceptionally heavy sea struck the all-weather lifeboat, sweeping right over her flying bridge, drenching the lifeboatmen on deck. All the crew were clipped on by safety lines and, fortunately, no one was injured. The ILB was then hit by this enormous wave, which stopped the boat dead in the water. As the ILB cleared the wave, the boat filled with water and Helmsman Pearson struggled to maintain control. He then realised that he had hardly any feeling in his left arm and very little control with his left hand of the engine controls, but he managed to take the ILB clear of the surf.

He had severely strained his left arm and so decided that it would be putting his two colleagues at risk if he tried to continue. He therefore informed Coxswain Keith Stuart on the all-weather lifeboat and took the ILB back to the lifeboat station. His place was taken by Mike Russell, another experienced Helmsman, while the other two crew, Carl Welham and Anthony Morley, stayed on board to return to the scene, despite the terrific battering that they had already received.

D-369 put to sea again at 7.08pm and continued to help in the search for the missing youth. On at least two further occasions, the ILB was hit by extremely heavy seas, one of which knocked Anthony Morley across the boat injuring his right hand. But the battered and bruised ILB crew continued until the search was called off, and the two Whitby lifeboats returned to station at 8.40pm. A Letter of Thanks, signed by the RNLI's Chief of Operations,

George and Mary Webb leaves harbour for a training exercise on 21 April 1996, passing former lifeboat Mary Ann Hepworth inbound at the entrance. (Nicholas Leach)

George and Mary Webb returns to harbour after her training exercise on 21 April 1996. (Nicholas Leach)

The scene at Scotch Head during the naming ceremony of George and Mary Webb on 12 June 1996, after which the lifeboat went to sea for a short trip with the invited guests. (Jeff Morris)

Commodore George Cooper, was later sent to Helmsmen John Pearson and Mike Russell, and crew members Carl Welham and Anthony Morley, in recognition of their tenacity and seamanship in the hazardous conditions.

Both of Whitby's lifeboats put to sea again at first light the following morning, to resume the search, with the helicopter also returning to help. Unfortunately no trace was found of the missing youth. However, at 7.40am, the lifeboatmen received another call for help and so, with the agreement of the Coastguard, the search was called off and *George and Mary Webb* proceeded to the fishing vessel *Tamara*, with a crew of three, which had broken down two and a half miles southeast of Robin Hood's Bay. The disabled boat was towed to harbour at 10.15am and the new lifeboat returned to her moorings.

The naming ceremony of the new Trent lifeboat took place on the afternoon of 12 June 1996 in front of a very large crowd of supporters and well-wishers who packed every vantage point around the harbour. The lifeboat was formally handed over to the RNLI by Mrs Cherry Nash and Mrs Jacqueline Fancett, daughters of the late Mr and Mrs Webb. The boat was accepted by the Chairman of the RNLI, Michael Vernon. He in turn passed the boat into the care of the Whitby station and she was accepted by Honorary Secretary Arnold Harper. After a service of dedication

Relief D class inflatable D-469 sets off on exercise, 21 April 1996. (Nicholas Leach)

conducted by the Rev Michael Aisbitt, Rector of Whitby and lifeboat chaplain, HRH The Duchess of Kent formally christened the lifeboat *George and Mary Webb*. The Duchess then boarded the boat to meet Coxswain Keith Stuart and his crew, and went for a trip out to sea.

Following her formal christening *George and Mary Webb* performed a series of routine services during the remainder of the year. On 19 July she put out at 9.54am after the small powerboat *Lager II*, with two people on board, had broken down a mile north-east of Sandsend. The disabled boat was towed safely to Whitby harbour at 10.55am. Four days later, in a force four northerly wind and heavy swell, the cabin cruiser *Lady Helen*, with two people on board, broke down off the harbour. *George*

Relief D class inflatable D-469 in the launching trolley on the slipway of the 1919-built boathouse. The house was used for the offshore lifeboat until 1974, and then in the mid-1970s the ILB was moved here. During the early 1980s the door was altered with the building being re-sheeted in corrugated iron at the same time. Floors were put in above the door to create a crew space and the windows were changed to make them more practical. (Nicholas Leach)

and *Mary Webb* slipped her moorings at 12.11pm and towed the casualty in.

Between 14 August and 26 September 1996 the relief Waveney lifeboat *Connel Elizabeth Cargill* was on station and she performed three services during her stint. On 20 August, she put out at 5.50pm to escort a speedboat to safety, and was assisted by the ILB. While assisting the speedboat, she was tasked to go to another vessel, the power boat *Sea Ranger*, which was lost in the fog. The casualty was located and escorted back to harbour.

George and Mary Webb returned from Amble Boat Co in Northumberland on 26 September 1996 after various hull repairs and completed four more services during the remainder of the year. On 3 October she launched at 12.46pm to the yacht *Butterfly* in a force nine south-westerly gale, with moderate seas. The yacht was in difficulty a mile north of the harbour after its outboard engine had failed. Once on scene, the lifeboatmen found that the casualty's sail had blown out, so a tow was rigged and the boat was brought in.

During 1997 the all-weather lifeboat had another busy year, launching on 22 January to the fishing vessel *Radiant Morn* and on 16 February to the local fishing vessel *Opportune*, putting out at 1.18am to the latter vessel, which had suffered mechanical failure. The vessel was being towed by another vessel, *Jacqueline Louise,*

toward Whitby but the casualty's jammed rudder was making progress difficult. The lifeboat took over the tow, and brought the vessel into harbour. On approaching the pier ends, the tow was shortened and during this operation the casualty surged up on the lifeboat. Although the rope became entangled in one of the lifeboat's propellers, the rope was cut and fell clear, enabling both lifeboat and fishing vessel to enter harbour.

On 15 April 1997 *George and Mary Webb* was launched to the local fishing fleet after several vessels had been caught out by a sudden change in conditions. She put out at 12.50pm as it was going to be difficult for some of the smaller craft to enter harbour safely. The lifeboat proceeded to escort in about ten vessels, which were those most at risk, and then stood by while the larger vessels came into harbour.

For the 1997 season, starting in March, the relief inshore lifeboat D-428 *St Vincent Amazon* was on station as the survey on station boat D-369 had not been completed. In fact, D-369 never returned to Whitby and D-428 remained on station until July. The relief ILB attended a number of minor incidents, and on 10 June 1997 was launched to help with the removal of a dead body from a car at the foot of cliffs at Saltwick Nab. The car had been driven off the cliff with one occupant inside. The all-weather lifeboat

Inshore lifeboat D-521 OEM Stone II on the trolley at the head of the slipway. She was placed on station at Whitby in July 1997. (Arnold Taylor)

was also launched and took firemen with cutting equipment to the scene. The firemen were ferried to the cliffs by the ILB, which then stood by while the body was cut free. The body, as well as the doctor who had attended the incident, was then taken by the ILB to *George and Mary Webb,* which landed both body and doctor at Scotch Head before returning to the scene to pick up other helpers and bring them back to harbour.

On 30 June 1997, *George and Mary Webb* had the unusual duty of escorting into harbour the station's previous lifeboat, *City of Sheffield.* The boat was heading north on her way to Hartlepool, where she had been allocated for further service, but she was behind her passage schedule due to bad weather so the Whitby crew agreed to meet her and escort her in. They launched into rough seas and north-westerly force six winds at 6.45pm and reached the lifeboat five minutes later, guiding her and her crew safely through the harbour entrance.

In July 1997 D-428 was replaced by a new inshore lifeboat, D-521, which was officially placed on station on 23 July. Provided from the gift of Miss Olive Emma May Stone, the new boat was named *OEM Stone II* after the donor. The formal naming and dedication ceremony was held on 6 December 1997 at the lifeboat house on Fish Pier, with the new ILB being formally handed over to the RNLI by the donor. After a service of dedication conducted by Rev M. Asbitt, assisted by Rev Taylor of the Mission to Seamen, Miss Stone named the new ILB.

During 1997 the relief Trent lifeboat *Henry Heys Duckworth* was on station, spending two short periods standing in for *George and Mary Webb.* The first was for a month from mid-April to mid-May, and the second from August to October. She came in August after the station boat had been damaged, and one of the relief boat's first duties was to escort *George and Mary Webb* up part way to Amble, leaving just after 8am and returning at 11.26am.

George and Mary Webb heads out through heavy swell at the harbour entrance to go to the aid of the passenger vessel Coronia on 6 September 2000. (By courtesy of the RNLI)

On 31 August, *Henry Heys Duckworth* was involved in a search for missing divers, together with the new ILB. She launched at 2.25pm and arrived on scene twenty minutes later to search for two missing divers from a dive boat. Staithes & Runswick Atlantic 21 and the diving centre's motor boat *Whitby Diver* were also involved, with the latter locating the missing men at 2.57pm. The search was then called off, with the lifeboat escorting the vessels involved back to harbour.

In October 1997 *George and Mary Webb* was back on station after repairs to her had been completed. For the next few months she was involved in assisting fishing vessels in difficulty, and on three separate occasions went to the same one, *Sarah Thinnesen*. On 20 October 1997 she launched at 4.35 to the vessel after its steering gear had failed. On 30 January 1998 she went out again to the vessel, launching at 11.16pm after it had broken down eleven miles off Whitby. And on 12 February 1998 *George and Mary Webb* was again asked to help the vessel, which this time had a fouled rudder after running into its own fishing gear. It was initially suggested that the vessel ask another fishing boat for a tow, but at 12.57pm the lifeboat put out as no other vessel was available and the tide was suitable for the vessel to enter harbour.

Relief 14m Trent Edward Duke of Windsor arrives at Whitby on 8 August 1998, ready for a stint on duty, manned by a passage crew from Amble Boat Co. (Arnold Taylor)

Relief 14m Trent Edward Duke of Windsor is brought alongside George and Mary Webb near the Fish Market on 8 August 1998. The station lifeboat was later taken to Amble Boat Co for refit. (Arnold Taylor)

On 6 March 1998 *George and Mary Webb* stood by the Dutch tanker *Dutch Glory*, which had suffered engine failure in rough seas and force seven south-easterly winds off Whitby High Light. The lifeboat launched at 6.20pm and attended the vessel, which was at anchor and being swept by heavy seas, ready to take off the crew should the situation deteriorate. But the engineers on the tanker managed to eventually restore power, and the lifeboat then escorted the vessel into deeper water. Once the vessel had reached her normal speed and was on her way, the lifeboat returned to station at about 8.30pm, standing by two Whitby trawlers which were entering harbour.

On 27 April 1998 *George and Mary Webb* was involved in a very long search after the Belize-registered motor vessel *Rema* sunk about twenty miles from Whitby. A very brief mayday had been received from the casualty and at 3.55am the lifeboat put out, reaching the scene an hour later. Four lifeboats were involved, together with a rescue helicopter and other passing vessels rendered assistance. The Whitby lifeboat was designated on-scene commander. The

search continued for most of the day and a small amount of flotsam was found, but no trace of the vessel. The search was called off at 9.20pm as the light was fading, and the lifeboat returned to station after almost nineteen hours at sea.

During the latter half of 1998 the relief Trent lifeboat *Edward Duke of Windsor* was on station, arriving on 8 August and staying until 15 November, while *George and Mary Webb* went to Amble Boat Co for repairs and maintenance. The relief

George and Mary Webb returned from refit at Amble in the RNLI's new livery and colours, with the operational number 14-14 on the bow. (Nicholas Leach)

George and Mary Webb moored in the pen at Fish Pier by the ILB house. (Nicholas Leach)

Relief Trent lifeboat Earl and Countess Mountbatten of Burma setting off to help the dredger Sandsend on 1 March 2002 after the vessel got into difficulties at the entrance to the harbour. (Peter Thomson)

lifeboat performed twelve services while at Whitby, the first on 23 August 1998 when she launched at 1.45am to the yacht *Flying Fox* which had suffered engine failure and her sails were torn in force four westerly winds. The 24ft yacht was drifting four and a half miles north-west of Whitby while on passage from Scarborough to Amble. The lifeboat located the casualty and towed it back to Whitby.

George and Mary Webb returned to Whitby on 15 November 1998 and during 1999 performed a number of services, launching mostly to fishing vessels and pleasure craft. On 14 July 1999 she was involved in a long service to the 18m

fishing vessel *Venus* in force four to five winds. The vessel was taking on water thirty-two miles north of Whitby, with another fishing boat, *Star Award*, and a rig stand-by vessel also on scene. Tynemouth lifeboat and an RAF rescue helicopter were also assisting. The helicopter lowered a pump to the casualty and some of the crew were advised to leave the vessel and board *Star Award*. Whitby lifeboat put out at 10.27am and reached the scene at 12.10pm. Meanwhile, the water level on the casualty had reduced sufficiently for the engine to be started and the vessel then headed for Whitby. *George and Mary Webb* escorted the boat back to harbour and returned to station at 5.45pm after what had been a long service.

The last services of 1999 were all to fishing vessels, with the final one on 13 December after the fishing vessel *Sarah Thinnesen* got into difficulty with a fouled propeller eight miles north of the harbour. *George and Mary Webb* launched at 6.35pm and reached the casualty fifteen minutes later. As conditions at the harbour entrance were too dangerous, Coxswain Keith Stuart decided to head north, to the Tees. Tees Port Control was not happy about accepting the vessel, so Teesmouth lifeboat, the 47ft Tyne *Phil Mead*, was launched to take over the tow, and brought the vessel into Hartlepool. Whitby lifeboat returned to station at 10pm.

Further services to the fishing fleet were undertaken during 2000. On 21 January, *George and Mary Webb* was launched to stand by fishing vessels at the harbour entrance where heavy swell was making conditions difficult. One of the vessels had actually collided with the pier end, so the lifeboat stood by while the other vessels safely entered harbour. On 14 February, the relief Trent lifeboat *Earl and Countess Mountbatten of Burma*, which was on passage from Eastbourne to Sunderland, went to the assistance of another fishing vessel, *Dipper I*, four miles north-west of Whitby. The vessel had broken down so the lifeboat took it in tow, and passed the tow to *George and Mary Webb*.

Some other services during the year included a launch on 12 April 2000 to the 70m dredger *Sand Kite*, which had an injured seaman on board. The vessel was seven miles north-east of Whitby, and the lifeboat was quickly on scene. However, conditions were so bad, with force seven winds and rough seas, that a transfer was too dangerous. A helicopter from RAF Leconfield was tasked, winched the man off and airlifted him to Scarborough Hospital. On 30 June 2000, both *George and Mary Webb* and the ILB were involved in helping an injured person from the foot of the cliffs at Sandsend, with the patient, strapped into a stretcher, being transferred by the ILB to the lifeboat.

September 2000 proved to be a busy month for *George and Mary Webb*. On 2 September, she launched just after midday to the trimaran *Sis* which was being overwhelmed by heavy seas in Runswick Bay. The Runswick Bay Rescue Boat and Staithes & Runswick ILB were already on scene but were not powerful enough to pull the vessel clear, so *George and Mary Webb* attached a tow-line. With lifeboatmen from both Staithes and Whitby on board the yacht assisting the elderly owner, the lifeboat pulled the vessel clear and then headed for Scarborough as Whitby harbour entrance was too dangerous to pass through in the force six to seven winds blowing and the rough seas. The tow was passed to the Scarborough lifeboat and *George and Mary Webb* returned to station at 4pm. The lifeboat launched on 20 and 23 September to the same vessel, with the service on 20

The pilot boat St Hilda tows in the small pleasure boat Amy Lou on 23 January 2003. The pilot boat was built as a 44ft Waveney lifeboat named Margaret Graham, similar to The White Rose of Yorkshire, and served at Harwich and Amble before being sold out of service in 1999. (By courtesy of Whitby RNLI)

D class inflatable D-521 OEM Stone II shows her speed during the station's annual lifeboat day demonstrations. (By courtesy of Whitby RNLI)

September undertaken in easterly force eight winds and rough seas.

Three days later, the lifeboat was again in action, putting out at 2.50pm, five minutes after the call for help had been received, and arriving at the casualty just fourteen minutes later. The fishing vessel *Emmy Leigh* was sinking five miles north of Whitby and the sole occupant had taken to the life-raft. When the lifeboat reached the scene, crew members Mike Russell and Nick Botham went aboard the fishing boat with a salvage pump while the owner, in a state of shock in his life-raft, was transferred to the lifeboat. The crew managed to save the vessel with the pump, and it was towed back to Whitby. If the lifeboat had arrived any later, *Emmy Leigh* would have sunk.

The following day, 6 September, *George and Mary Webb* was out again, launching at 1.15pm to the Scarborough pleasure boat *Coronia* in rough seas and force six to seven north-westerly winds. The boat was on her weekly trip to Whitby with seventy-one people on board and requested lifeboat assistance because conditions at the entrance to the harbour were so bad. When the lifeboat arrived on scene, Second Coxswain Keith Elliott, who was in command, decided trying to enter Whitby harbour would be too dangerous

for *Coronia*, and so the lifeboat escorted the vessel back towards Scarborough.

On 30 October 2000 *George and Mary Webb* was launched at 10.28am in horrendous conditions, with a force eleven north-westerly wind whipping up heavy seas and six-metre swells. The coble *Mary Ann* had broken down half-a-mile off Runswick Bay and was being driven towards the shore in the terrible conditions. As the lifeboat left harbour, the radar failed and, with visibility down to a few yards because of driving rain and spray, the lifeboat crew's task was made more difficult. The rough seas and wind gusting up to 60mph made conditions very testing, but the lifeboat reached the casualty and took it in tow. Coxswain Keith Stuart decided that it was safer to enter Whitby harbour than run for Scarborough, and at about 12.15pm the two boats reached harbour safely. This difficult service was carried out in some of the worst conditions anyone at the station could recall, with Coxswain Stuart demonstrating excellent boat handling.

During May, June and part of July 2001, the relief Trent lifeboat *Corinne Whiteley* was on temporary duty. She only performed a couple of rescues during this time, including one on 11 July to the fishing vessel *Carol H*, which had an engine failure eighteen miles north of Whitby in force eight to nine south-westerly winds and rough seas. The lifeboat put out at 3.40am and found the casualty making slow progress with her engine overheating. The vessel was taken in tow and brought into harbour just before 7am. *George and Mary Webb* returned from refit on 22 July 2001.

On 2 January 2002 another relief Trent, *Earl and Countess Mountbatten of Burma*, was sent to the station and stayed until May, performing six services during this time, which included one false alarm, one to the dredger *Sandsend*, and one to a pleasure boat. The service to the dredger took place on 1 March with the lifeboat launching at 12.10pm after the laden dredger grounded at the harbour entrance between the pier extensions as it was heading out to sea. With conditions deteriorating and the dredger in danger of being washed towards the East Pier extension in the heavy swell, the lifeboat was launched to stand by. The dredger was stranded for nearly an hour until the lifeboat crew got a rope aboard and successfully pulled the vessel clear.

The service to the pleasure boat took place on 9 March 2002 when the cabin cruiser *Merryweather Bahamas*, with six persons on board, broke down, taking on water, in south-westerly force five winds two miles off Whitby. The lifeboat arrived on scene to find the situation was not as serious as first thought, and it proved to be a routine tow to harbour.

After *George and Mary Webb* returned to station on 22 May 2002, services during the second half of the year proved to be largely routine. On 26 August she towed the yacht *Kava* to harbour after its sole occupant became exhausted in rough seas and force five winds, three miles north of Whitby. An unusual incident occurred on 2 November after the Coastguard reported a vessel transmitting music on the emergency Channel 16. As the weather was poor, with force seven winds and rough seas, the lifeboat was tasked to find the vessel in question. She launched at 11.05pm, and was at sea for almost three hours but failed to find any vessel using the emergency channel, so returned to station as the music had stopped.

On 23 January 2003, the quick thinking of the lifeboat crew averted a possible tragedy just outside the harbour entrance. During the afternoon Mechanic Glenn Goodberry and some crewmembers who were in the lifeboat house saw the 17ft open fishing boat *Amy Lou*, with three men on board, heading out of the harbour to sea. The lifeboatmen watched the vessel going down the harbour and were concerned about the safety of the boat in the conditions when it came back because of the harbour entrance, where conditions were particularly bad. At 5pm, the relief inshore lifeboat D-491 *Cetrek* was launched to go to help the vessel.

By the time he was out at sea, the skipper of *Amy Lou* realised that the seas were too rough and attempted to return to

Lifeboat crew past and present pose in front of Robert and Ellen Robson after attending a service and wreath-laying in November 2004 to mark the ninetieth anniversary of the Rohilla disaster. Back row, left to right: Keith Stuart, Jeff Waters, Peter Thomson, Ron Frampton, Robert Harland, William Harland, Robert Pennock, James Pearson, Sonny Winspear, Dave Peart, George Paling, Lewis Breckon, Roy Weatherill. Front row, left to right: Mark Frankland, Steven Boocock, Mike Russell, Nick Botham, Geoff Hodgson, Mark Weatherill, Lee Harland, John Pearson, and Andrew Cass. (By courtesy of Whitby RNLI)

The fishing vessel Ocean Rose is assisted into harbour by George and Mary Webb in the early hours of 6 March 2004. (By courtesy of Whitby RNLI)

harbour, and at this point tragedy nearly struck. Heading back, the boat got caught by a steep sea coming from behind which broached the craft to port and nearly capsized it. The sea swamped the small boat's engine and killed it. The ILB sped to the boat, the lifeboat men pulled off the three men, and returned to harbour. The vessel was left adrift at sea, but was later towed in by the pilot boat.

In recognition of their work during this well-executed rescue, Mechanic Goodberry, and ILB crew members Stephen Boocock and Philip Webster received letters of appreciation from the RNLI. Helmsman John Pearson received a framed letter of thanks signed by the RNLI's Chairman. They were praised for their 'level-headed teamwork' and Helmsman Pearson for his seamanship.

On 6 March 2004 Humber Coastguard received a mayday distress call at about 1am from the 18m fishing boat *Ocean Rose*, of Whitby, with four crew on board, which had been hit by the 2,238-ton tanker *Reno*, of Lisbon, four miles north-east of Staithes. The fishing boat was badly damaged and in danger of capsizing, so *George and Mary Webb* was launched at 1.15am, together with Staithes & Runswick Atlantic 75 B-788 *Pride of Leicester,* and a rescue helicopter from RAF Boulmer was scrambled.

Substantial damage had been sustained by the fishing vessel and she was taking on water, while the tanker had only sustained superficial damage and continued on her way to Immingham. The fishing vessel's bilge pumps were working flat out to clear the water, and the lifeboats both transferred pumps which enabled the casualty to proceed under her own power towards Whitby. The vessel was brought to safety in the early hours of 6 March and *George and Mary Webb* returned to station just before 5am. Skipper of *Ocean Rose,* Richard Brewer, later thanked the lifeboat crews: 'I can't praise the lads from Whitby and Staithes enough. They were ultra quick in reaching us and reacted very professionally.'

Two weeks later the inshore lifeboat was in action after an urgent call was received from the dive boat *Grantham Flyer* that three canoeists, two adults and a twelve-year-old boy, were in need of assistance at the entrance to the harbour as the weather was worsening and they were unable to cope with the strong winds and heavy swell. The dive boat took all three on board and D-521 was launched to attend at 1.10pm, taking the casualties to Scotch Head. Here they were met by the Coastguard Rescue Team and an ambulance, which took them all to hospital, and the ILB returned to station.

During August 2004, two different relief Trent lifeboats were on station, with *John Neville Taylor* on duty for the station's annual lifeboat day. She performed one service during her short stay, launching at 1.43pm on 22 August to the fishing vessel *Brigand* which had broken down outside the harbour with two adults and a child on board. It was considered too dangerous to tow the boat into Whitby through the piers because of the weather conditions, so it was taken to Scarborough.

The following day, the relief Trent *Windsor Runner (Civil Service No.42)* arrived for a temporary spell and stayed for just over two months, launching ten times on service. She was tasked to help the inshore lifeboat on 25 September after a fisherman spotted a body in the sea off Sandsend just after 4pm. The ILB launched at 4.25pm and the all-weather boat put out five minutes later. Under the direction of a Coastguard team, the ILB, with John Pearson at the helm, manoeuvred through heavy swell until the body was located and pulled aboard by crew members Steve Boocock and Richard Dawson.

The body was transferred to the lifeboat, which had negotiated heavy waves crashing over her stern, and landed

at Whitby. Pulling dead bodies from the water is a difficult task for the crew, and former Coxswain Peter Thomson, as the station's press officer, commented after this incident: 'There is nothing good in picking dead bodies up. When there is a fatality it is not the same as a normal rescue. Everybody was feeling very flat.'

On 12 November 2004 *Windsor Runner (Civil Service No.42)* was launched to the fishing vessel *Capsa* which went aground on the beach west of the West Pier in very poor weather, force nine winds and very rough seas. The 36ft steel vessel, with two crew, lost power while attempting to enter harbour and drifted towards the beach. The crew radioed a mayday alert and the

Relief D class inflatable lifeboat D-470 Landlubber is put through her paces during the station's lifeboat day in August 2004. (By courtesy of Whitby RNLI)

George and Mary Webb putting out on 22 May 2004 in force six northerly winds to the motor boat St George. (Peter Thomson)

Relief lifeboat Windsor Runner (Civil Service No.42) at the entrance to the harbour after standing by the fishing boat Defiant, which is passing between the pier extensions, in force six winds and heavy seas on 24 September 2004. (Peter Thomson)

lifeboat was launched at 5.18pm. But she just stood by as the casualty grounded on the sand, and Coastguard and rescue teams on shore helped secure her, with her crew having to wait for an hour while the tide receded before being helped off. At one point, the lifeboat was operating in such shallow water that she had less than a metre clearance between her keel and the sea bed, but she did not touch the bottom. The two survivors were landed on the beach and taken to hospital for treatment.

Following this incident, Rob Parkin, Whitby Coastguard station officer, said: 'It was a very lucky escape. If they [Capsa's crew] had missed the harbour entrance and went on to the scar behind the East Pier there would have been a fatality that night. There was an extreme storm force, probably eight or nine, and the lifeboat would have had great difficulty making a

rescue. They were just fortunate that they ended up on the sand.'

During the service to Capsa, the lifeboat was damaged when large breaking seas smashed the aft rails and fractured two air intakes. The boat was taken off station and sent to Amble Boat Co for repairs and in her place came another relief boat, John Neville Taylor, which stayed until station boat George and Mary Webb eventually returned in March 2005.

During 2005, Whitby was statistically the busiest station in the RNLI's north division. Most services by the all-weather lifeboat involved getting to vessels in difficulty and towing them to safety after their engines had broken down or their propellers had been fouled. However, on 29 November 2005, both all-weather and inshore lifeboats were launched at 4.20pm after the fishing vessel Brian Hartley started sinking three and a half miles from Whitby in force four winds, and all the lifeboats could do was save those on board.

The vessel and her four crew were setting out on a three-day fishing trip when water started pouring into the engine room, and by the time the lifeboats reached the scene the casualty was well down at the stern. The four men were taken off two at a time by the ILB and transferred to George and Mary Webb, while the patrol vessel HMS Severn also

Relief Trent lifeboat Windsor Runner (Civil Service No.42) towing in the small fishing vessel Neptune Diver on 6 October 2004 after the vessel broke down with a fouled propeller a mile and a half from Whitby. (Peter Thomson)

In October 2006 a Whitby crew took the relief lifeboat Earl and Countess Mountbatten of Burma up the Manchester Ship Canal. The lifeboat was on display in Salford Quays from 9 to 15 October 2006 as part of a major fund-raising drive by the RNLI in the city. This was the first time an all-weather lifeboat had travelled via the Manchester Ship Canal into the heart of the city for the annual Lifeboat Week. The lifeboat was manned by a crew from Whitby made up of Coxswain Nick Botham, Mechanic Philip Webster, and crew members Richard Dawson, Mark Frankland and Eric Ambler. The boat was sailed from Ballyhack boatyard, near Waterford, leaving on 5 October, to Manchester via Arklow overnight and Conwy. From Conwy she was taken to Ellesmere Port for an overnight stop before making the passage up the Ship Canal during the morning of 9 October. Pilotage along the Mersey and the Canal was provided free by Mersey River as well as MSC pilots. (Nicholas Leach)

Relief lifeboat John Neville Taylor leaves harbour on service during 2007. This Trent, built in 2002, served in the Relief Fleet from then until May 2008, when she was placed on station at Dunbar. She served on relief at Whitby during 2004-05 and 2007. (Peter Thomson)

Relief lifeboat John Neville Taylor brings the small cabin cruiser Striker into harbour on 16 May 2007 after the vessel ran out of fuel. (Peter Thomson)

attended the incident. She stood by as *Brian Hartley* sank, at about 7.30pm, while the lifeboats landed the survivors by the bandstand and then returned to station.

New lifeboat station

Since the early 1990s the RNLI had been undertaking an extensive programme of modernising lifeboat stations and shore facilities, and not only were state-of-the-art lifeboats provided but new crew buildings and boathouses also built. Whitby benefited from this investment programme during 2005 to 2007 when a new lifeboat house and mooring berth were constructed at Fish Pier on the site of the boathouse which had been built in 1917-18 for the first motor lifeboat.

Proposals for a new lifeboat station were first presented in 2002, but were withdrawn after being deemed unsuitable for the locality. So the plans were changed and in July 2004 the local council gave the go-ahead for a new building. During 2005 preparations were made to ensure the lifeboat remained operational throughout the building work, and the all-weather lifeboat kit was moved out and the crew left the 1918-built boathouse for the last time on 21 September 2005. During September and October 2005, the building was demolished and piling work on the new structure began.

During the rebuilding, operations were moved to various sites around the harbour and two inshore lifeboats were operated, one at Coates Marina with access to the river four hours either side of high water, and the other at the Lifeboat Museum, which was refitted for the purpose. The main exhibit, former pulling lifeboat *Robert and Ellen Robson*, was moved into storage for the duration of the construction work. She was taken away in 2005 and returned to the Museum in November 2007, being kept in an old cargo shed on Endeavour Wharf during this time.

The ILB at the Museum, relief boat D-503 *Criddy and Tom*, was launched down the slipway and across the West Beach using a Land Rover. As launching from this slipway was dangerous and difficult during a northerly swell, the Marina ILB, D-521 *OEM Stone II*, was used primarily on service calls. The Coates Marine site afforded easier access

George and Mary Webb at temporary moorings while, behind her, dismantling work continues on the old lifeboat house and slipway, October 2005. (Nicholas Leach)

The temporary facility at Coates Marine housing inshore lifeboat D-521 OEM Stone II and the Honda quadbike used for launching. (Nicholas Leach)

The Lifeboat Museum was used for operational purposes once again, having not housed a lifeboat in service since 1958, with one of two D class inflatables using the building while the new lifeboat station was under construction. The relief D class inflatable D-503 occupied one half of the old boathouse, with the Land Rover used for launching, pictured in October 2005. (Nicholas Leach)

The Lifeboat Museum in 2007 when the north half (on right) was in operational service housing a Land Rover and D class inflatable. (Nicholas Leach)

and the crew began moving kit into the new building during July 2007. Not only was a new lifeboat station constructed, but a new inshore lifeboat, D-674 *OEM Stone III*, was sent to the station and placed in service on 15 May 2007. The ILB was of a new, improved type of inflatable designated the IB1. The main improvements over the previously used ILB were an increased speed from twenty to twenty-five knots, improved stowage and equipment, and easier maintenance.

The new lifeboat station, which had cost approximately £1.35 million to build, was officially opened on 7 September 2007 when the Duchess of Kent came to the town for a unique triple ceremony. Not only did she open the new lifeboat station, but she also unveiled a bust of Henry Freeman and named the new inshore lifeboat. The Duchess, who rarely made public appearances, agreed to perform the ceremony as she had a long affiliation with the Whitby lifeboat having named three of the station's previous lifeboats.

She arrived at Fish Pier, the site of the ceremony, on board *George and Mary Webb*, which picked up the guest of honour from the bandstand on the West Side and brought her across to the ceremony site. Chairman of the station,

with crew kit and quad bike on site, and a portacabin in the car park including a lock-up steel storage cabinet. *George and Mary Webb* was operated from a pontoon outside Shambles Wine Bar and reached by a Sillinger twin-engined boarding boat, which was also moored in Coates Marina.

The piling, support structure and new berth for the lifeboat were completed during the first half of 2006, and work on the ILB house and crew facility started in August 2006. This was completed in June 2007 by contractor Frank Brambles Ltd

George and Mary Webb returning from refit in July 2007 tows in the motor cruiser Belly Dancer, and her single occupant, from three miles north of the harbour at the end of her passage from Amble. (By courtesy of Whitby RNLI)

John Heselton, opened proceedings, and Mrs Margaret Gadsby, niece of Miss Olive E. M. Stone, handed over the new ILB to the RNLI. The boat was accepted by Michael Vlasto, RNLI Operations Director, and passed into the care of the station. It was accepted by Roy Weatherill, Lifeboat Operations Manager. A service of dedication then followed, conducted by the Rt Rev Robert S. Ladd, Bishop of Whitby, assisted by Canon David Smith, Rector of Whitby, and the Rev Terry Leathley, former Lifeboat Chaplain.

After the formalities, the Duchess unveiled a commemorative plaque to formally open the new station, and

Whitby lifeboat crew on board George and Mary Webb prior to the opening ceremony for the new lifeboat station. (Nicholas Leach)

The new lifeboat station built in 2007 on the site of the old boathouse adjacent to the Fish Pier. The new station consists of a boat hall to accommodate the new inshore lifeboat and changing facilities for both lifeboats on the ground floor. A large crew and training room upstairs has a kitchen area attached, as well as offices for the Lifeboat Operations Manager. (Nicholas Leach)

D class inflatable D-674 OEM Stone III is put through her paces in the harbour after her naming. (Nicholas Leach)

The scene on the Fish Pier during the naming and dedication of the new ILB and opening of the new lifeboat station. (Nicholas Leach)

then named the new inshore lifeboat by pouring champagne over the boat's bows. She assisted in the unveiling of the bronze bust of Henry Freeman, Whitby's most celebrated lifeboatman, which had been sculpted by artist Richard Sefton, and which was mounted on permanent display outside the boathouse (see page 29).

While the new station was under construction, it was business as usual on the operational side, and many services were undertaken from the temporary bases

during 2006 and 2007. Incidents during 2006 were generally routine in nature with the station's three lifeboats going to a mixture of fishing vessels, pleasure craft and people in difficulty. On 17 January 2006, the relief ILB based at the Museum, D-503 *Criddy and Tom*, was launched after a dog fell 100ft down the cliffs at Hawsker. The owners were walking the dog when it disappeared down the cliff, and so called the coastguard. The ILB was launched to search for the animal, and the crew eventually found it a third of the way up the cliff, trying to climb up. Rob Parkin, of Whitby Coastguard, abseiled down the cliff and was able to lead the dog down to the shore where the ILB took it to safety.

In June 2006 *George and Mary Webb* was out on consecutive days; on 16 June she went to the cabin cruiser *Shania* which had broken down off Robin Hood's Bay. The following day she launched at 10.10am to the fishing vessel *Challenger*, which was in difficulty with a rope around its propeller. Both vessels were towed to harbour. The lifeboat was in action almost a month later, on 15 July, when she towed in the cabin cruiser *Safari* and her two crew after the vessel ran out of fuel.

HRH The Duchess of Kent is introduced to the lifeboat crew by Coxswain Mike Russell (centre) prior to the naming of the new ILB and opening of the new lifeboat station, 7 September 2007. (By courtesy of Whitby RNLI)

The Duchess of Kent pours champagne over the bow of the new inshore lifeboat D-674 to christen the boat OEM Stone III, 7 September 2007. (By courtesy of Whitby RNLI)

D class inflatable D-674 OEM Stone III was bought from the legacy left by long-time RNLI supporter Miss Olive Emma May Stone, from Barnsley, South Yorkshire. Miss Stone donated Whitby's previous ILB, D-521 OEM Stone II. (Nicholas Leach)

Inshore lifeboat D-674 OEM Stone III lands two walkers who had become trapped by the tide at Saltwick Nab, along with their four dogs, on 13 June 2007. The ILB launched just after midday and was back on station within an hour. This was only the second service launch undertaken by the ILB D-674. (Peter Thomson)

On 16 August 2006, both inshore lifeboats, D-503 and D-521, and the all-weather lifeboat were involved in a long and ultimately tragic search for a teenage boy. The seventeen-year-old from Leeds was playing fully-clothed in the sea with his older brother on the West Cliff beach in the early evening when a large wave dragged him out to sea. Attempts were made by relatives to save him, but the water was too deep. Despite attempts by a surfer and a passer-by to effect a rescue, the teenager went under the water.

A large-scale rescue operation was mounted involving, as well as Whitby's lifeboats, Staithes & Runswick Atlantic 75, Runswick Bay Rescue Boat, and various private boats which searched for any sign of the missing boy. Coastguard teams from Whitby and Kettleness helped coordinate the operation from the beach. A Sea King helicopter was tasked from RAF Leconfield and arrived on scene at about 6.30pm to deploy its thermal imaging camera. Lifeboat volunteers and two off-duty lifeguards waded through breakers as the tide was falling, but all to no avail and the search was called off at 10pm as darkness fell. The boy's body was discovered the following day at 5.10am on the West Beach in front of the chalets.

The first service of 2007 was to escort the fishing vessel *Independence* on 27 January after the vessel's steering had failed half a mile from Whitby. Just over a week later, on 6 February, *George and Mary Webb* was launched at 10.15pm to the converted 16m trawler *Ile d'Yeu* which had collided with the tanker *Dutch Progress* two miles north-east of Whitby. Rough seas and snow showers reduced visibility, and when the lifeboat arrived on scene her crew found the casualty taking on water and sinking. Coxswain Mike Russell ordered that the trawler's crew launch their life-rafts as getting the lifeboat alongside was difficult in the conditions. From the life-rafts, the three survivors were taken on board the lifeboat and landed ashore, while their vessel eventually sank about a mile off Sandsend.

On 16 March 2007, *George and Mary Webb* went to the 30ft yacht *Suzi 4*, launching at 1.35pm to the vessel which was a mile and a half from Whitby. The yacht was on her way from Scarborough to Whitby when the weather worsened. With the wind gusting to thirty knots the lifeboat went to her and towed the vessel to harbour. Soon after this service, on 4 April 2007, *George and Mary Webb* went for refit and in her place came the relief lifeboat *John Neville Taylor*. The relief lifeboat launched eleven times on service, assisting a variety of yachts and fishing vessels, during her five-month stay.

On 28 April 2007, *John Neville Taylor* went to assist Staithes & Runswick

Atlantic 75 which had launched at 10.10am to assist a disabled yacht off Staithes. The yacht's skipper had contacted Humber Coastguard to report that he had no electrical power and could not start the engine or hoist the sails. With an onshore wind and a danger of the yacht blowing ashore, the lifeboats were called on. Staithes & Runswick ILB reached the

30ft vessel within seven minutes, began to pull it further offshore and made for Whitby. The tow was then transferred to Whitby lifeboat off Port Mulgrave at 10.50am and the yacht was safely taken into Whitby harbour.

On 8 July 2007, *John Neville Taylor* went to the fishing vessel *Sharmel*, with two people on board, which broke down off

George and Mary Webb on exercise off the harbour, with the famous Whitby Abbey silhouetted on the cliffs above the town. (Nicholas Leach)

Whitby lifeboat crew on board George and Mary Webb, March 2008, left to right: Adrian Blackburn, Jamie White, Nathan Jones, Philip Webster, Ben Laws, Coxswain Mike Russell and Second Coxswain Nick Botham. (Nicholas Leach)

Sandsend. The lifeboat launched just after 12.30pm and, after a tow lasting about four hours, the vessel was brought safely into harbour. Just over a week later, on 19 July, the relief lifeboat went to another small fishing boat, *Neptune Diver*, with two people on board, and towed the boat back to harbour. Its fishing gear had got entangled in its propeller resulting in the craft becoming disabled.

George and Mary Webb returned to station from her three-yearly refit on 29 August 2007, leaving Poole on 28 August and stopping overnight at Ramsgate to reach Whitby the following day. Towards

the end of the passage back to station, she towed the motor boat *Belly Dancer* into harbour. As the lifeboat was nearing Whitby, Humber Coastguard alerted her that the boat had suffered engine failure three miles north of the port. With the vessel in tow, the lifeboat returned home. During the next week, she was made ready for the opening of the new lifeboat station, as described above.

Before the end of 2007, a year notable for the opening of the new station, the lifeboat and crew were involved in a tragic incident which made national news headlines. On 23 November, the 22ft

George and Mary Webb batters her way through heavy seas as the crew pick up the bodies of two of the people lost when the cabin cruiser Last Call capsized in severe weather on 23 November 2007. (By courtesy of the Whitby Gazette)

George and Mary Webb returns to harbour to land the bodies of two people from the cabin cruiser Last Call on 23 November 2007 after one of the most tragic incidents in the history of the station. (By courtesy of the Whitby Gazette)

George and Mary Webb bringing in the fishing vessel Independence FR196 on 18 June 2008 after the vessel suffered gearbox failure two miles off Heyburn Wyke, south of Ravenscar. The lifeboat put out at 5.20pm and brought the 1977-built fishing vessel, owned by Eastern England Fishing Producers Organisation, back to harbour two and a half hours later, with the ILB in attendance after it was launched on a routine exercise. (Nicholas Leach)

cabin cruiser *Last Call*, with three people on board, headed out to sea despite a gale force eight warning being in place and its occupants evidently oblivious to the huge waves breaking at the harbour entrance. The pier had been sealed off earlier in the day because of high tides, but the severe conditions and attendant dangers seem to have been ignored by the three on board the boat, which got into difficulties as soon as it was out of the shelter of the harbour.

Lifeboat crew members watched as massive waves crashed into the boat as it tried to leave the harbour. They tried three times to radio the vessel to warn it to turn back, but were unable to make contact. It is believed the cruiser was attempting

to return to the harbour when it capsized 100 yards from the sea walls. *George and Mary Webb* was put out at 12.15pm to rescue the boat's occupants, who had been thrown into the sea, and battled through the heavy seas to get to the small boat. Sadly the lifeboat crew could do nothing as the conditions were too bad for anyone to survive in the water.

Two men and a woman were recovered by the lifeboat and an RAF rescue helicopter, which was tasked to the incident. One of the men and the woman died shortly after they were taken to hospital, while the second man was pronounced dead at the scene. Witnesses reported seeing one person wearing a

George and Mary Webb on exercise off Whitby in March 2008. (Nicholas Leach)

life-jacket, struggling in the water before drifting out to sea, while another was in the water between the sea walls. They were caught in swell between 20ft and 30ft high when they got into serious difficulties.

A North Yorkshire Police spokesman said: 'Witnesses have commented on the brave actions of the Whitby lifeboat crew and the helicopter crew, both operating in very challenging circumstances.' Roy Weatherill, Lifeboat Operations Manager, added his own praise for the Coxswain and crew, saying: 'The lifeboat launched very quickly and the crew did an absolutely magnificent job to recover the two people from the water.'

George and Mary Webb at the specially built pontoon berth, installed in 2007, on the East Side of the harbour, close to the Fish Pier. (Nicholas Leach)

George and Mary Webb on exercise with an RAF Rescue helicopter off the harbour for lifeboat day, 13 July 2008. This annual event, held to raise funds for the RNLI and publicise the work of the town's lifeboats, is a major event in the station's calendar and the neighbouring lifeboats from Staithes and Runswick are usually in attendance, with a helicopter exercise the main highlight of the rescue demonstrations. (Nicholas Leach)

In recognition of the efforts of all involved during this rescue, station personnel were presented in March 2008 with a framed Letter of Thanks by RNLI Chairman Sir Jock Slater, in recognition of the 'initiative, teamwork and professionalism' the crew displayed during the incident. Sir Jock concludes his letter: 'This was a service with a sad result but conducted in effective cooperation with all those involved and in the best traditions of the RNLI.' Roy Weatherill said: 'I am sure that none of us will ever forget this tragic incident, during which Whitby's RNLI crew, along with the RAF, air ambulance, coastguard and harbour staff, did everything they could to save the lives of these three people.'

The first service of 2008 took place on 13 January when the lifeboat, whilst on

At 3pm on Sunday 13 July 2008 the restored pulling lifeboat William Riley entered harbour on the last leg of her fundraising row from the Tyne to crown one of the best Lifeboat Weekends, with thousands of people lining the harbourside to welcome the vessel, which was escorted by former lifeboat Mary Ann Hepworth and current lifeboat George and Mary Webb. (Nicholas Leach)

exercise off Sandsend, was contacted by the 42ft pleasure fishing vessel *Demarok Argus*, with three persons on board, and informed that a rope was round the vessel's propeller. The lifeboat contacted the coastguard to make them aware of the situation and proceeded to the vessel. Once on scene, it was found that the rope was in fact her own anchor rope and that the vessel was in effect anchored to the sea bed via her propeller. The rope was inaccessible from the boat's deck, so a tow line was attached to the vessel's stern enabling the lifeboat to take the weight off the anchor rope, which was then cut free.

The casualty was able to return to harbour under her own power, with the lifeboat escorting her all the way.

Both this routine service and that undertaken in severe conditions a few weeks earlier at the end of November 2007 are typical of the kind of work which has been undertaken by the Whitby lifeboats and lifeboat crews for more than 200 years. Today, with a modern lifeboat, inshore lifeboat and lifeboat station, the volunteer crews of Whitby are better equipped than ever to help those in peril on the sea and continue the town's long and proud tradition of sea rescue.

Appendices

Appendix 1: Lifeboat Summary

No.1 Station (West Side)

Years on station	Built ON	Name Donor	Dimension Type	Launches/ lives saved
1802 – c.1817	1802 —	Not named Local Committee.	30' North Country	unknown
1822 – 1859	1822 —	Not named (to No.2 station) Whitby Lifeboat Association.	26'6" x 9'3" North Country	at least 8/50
1860 – 1861	1860 —	Not named Whitby Lifeboat Association.	30' x 8'9" North Country	5/26
1861 – 1870	1861 —	**Lucy** Legacy of A. W. Jaffray, London.	32' x 7'10" Peake self-righter	10/53
1870 – 1881	1869 —	**Lucy**/ 1871– **Robert Whitworth** As above/ 1871– Manchester Branch.	32' x 7'7" Self-righter	14/79
1881 – 1909	1881 180	**Robert and Mary Ellis** Legacy of Miss Mary Ann Ellis, Harrogate.	34' x 8' Self-righter	37/43
1909 – 1934	1908 588	**Robert and Mary Ellis** Legacy of Miss Mary Ann Ellis, Harrogate.	35' x 8'6" Self-righter	15/11

Fishermen's Lifeboat

Years on station	Built ON	Name Donor	Dimension Type	Launches/ lives saved
1861 – 1889	1822 —	**Fishermen's Friend** [from West Side] 1859– Fishermen's Committee.	26'6" x 9'3" NC	

No.2 Station (East Side)

Years on station	Built ON	Name Donor	Dimension Type	Launches/ lives saved
1822 – 1871	1822 —	Un-named/ 1863– **Petrel**/ 1871– **Gertrude** Whitby Lifeboat Association.	26'6" x 9'3" North Country	at least 12/68
1872 – 1879	1864 —	**Harriott Forteath** Legacy of Mrs H. Forteath, Nottingham.	30' x 7'3" Peake self-righter	9/34
1879 – 1881	1866 —	**Harriott Forteath** Legacy of Mrs H. Forteath, Nottingham.	32' x 7'6" Self-righter	4/6
1881 – 1887	1869 —	**Harriott Forteath** [transferred from No.1 station] Legacy of Mrs H. Forteath, Nottingham.	32' x 7'7" Self-righter	4/5
1887 – 1895	1887 114	**Christopher** Anonymous gift.	34' x 7'6" Self-righter	2/0

Years on station	Built ON	Name Donor	Dimension Type	Launches/ lives saved
1895 – 1914	1895 379	**John Fielden** Gift of John A. Fielden, London.	34' x 7'9" Self-righter	40/62
1914 – 1919	1900 455	**Forester** (Reserve 4) Ancient Order of Foresters.	34' x 8' Rubie self-righter	35/98
1919 – 1931	1909 594	**William Riley of Leamington and Birmingham** Legacy of William Riley, Leamington.	34' x 8' Rubie self-righter	31/10
1931 – 1938	1907 580	**John and Rachel Valentine** Legacy of Samuel Valentine, Brixton.	34' x 8' Rubie self-righter	14/19
1938 – 1947	1904 522	**John and Rachel Valentine** Legacy of Samuel Valentine, Brixton.	34' x 8' Rubie self-righter	5/0
1947 – 1957	1918 669	**Robert and Ellen Robson** Legacy of Robert Robson.	34' x 8' Rubie self-righter	15/0

Motor lifeboats

Years on station	Built ON	Name Donor	Dimension Type	Launches/ lives saved
1919 – 1938	1918 667	**Margaret Harker-Smith** Legacy of Miss M. Harker-Smith, Sheffield.	40' x 10'6" Motor self-righter	117/86
1938 – 1974	1938 808	**Mary Ann Hepworth** Gift of Mr W. Hepworth, Hull.	41' x 11'8" Watson motor	372/201
1974 – 1988	1974 1033	**The White Rose of Yorkshire** Anonymous gift (Miss Gwynaeth Milburn).	44' x 12'8" Waveney	237/51
1988 – 1996	1988 1131	**City of Sheffield** City of Sheffield Appeal, bequest of Mrs Mary Walker.	47' x 15' Tyne	239/88
1996 –	1995 1212	**George and Mary Webb** The Mary Webb Trust.	14.26m x 4.53m Trent	

Inshore lifeboats

Years on station	ON	Name (if any) Donor	Dimensions Type
5.1966 – 10.1970	D-84	— —	15'6" x 6'4" RFD PB16
3.1971 – 1977	D-193	— South Kirby (Emsall) Round Table.	15'6" x 6'4" RFD PB16
3.1978 – 1988	D-260	**Gwynaeth** Gift Miss G. M. G. Milburn.	15'6" Zodiac Mk.II
10.8.1988 – 7.1997	D-369	— Legacy of Mr J. Wilson.	16'3" x 6'7" Avon EA16
23.7.1997 – 5.2007	D-521	**OEM Stone II** Gift of Miss Olive Stone.	16'3" x 6'7" Avon EA16
15.5.2007 –	D-674	**OEM Stone III** Gift of Miss Olive Stone.	4.95m x 2m IB1

Upgang Station

Years on station	Built ON	Name Donor	Dimension Type	Launches/ lives saved
7.1865 – 7.1879	1860 —	**William Watson**/1878– **Joseph Sykes** Gift of Dr H. W. Watson, Derby/ 1878– Legacy of Mrs A. E. Sykes, How Grasmere.	30' x 7'4" Self-righter	0/0
7.1879 – 8.1885	1879 —	**Joseph Sykes** Legacy of Mrs A. E. Sykes, How Grasmere.	32' x 7'6" Self-righter	2/0
8.1885 – 11.1900	1882 184	**Joseph Sykes** Legacy of Mrs A. E. Sykes, How Grasmere.	32' x 7'6" Self-righter	0/0
11.1890 – 6.1908	1890 292	**Upgang** (named 1892) Anonymous gift.	34' x 7'6" Self-righter	6/8
6.1908 – 7.1909	1890 275	**James and Caroline** (Reserve 7) Legacy of James Goss, Stratford Green.	34' x 7'6" Self-righter	1/1
27.7.1909 – 11.1919	1909 594	**William Riley of Leamington and Birmingham** Legacy Mr William Riley, Leamington.	34' x 8' Rubie self-righter	2/0

Robin Hood's Bay Station

Years on station	Built ON	Name Donor	Dimension Type	Launches/ lives saved
1830 – c.1843	1830 —	[Not named] Coastguard	 Coble	Unknown
1839 – 1881	1839 —	[Not named]	26' x 10' North County	Unknown
26.9.1881 – 11.1902	1881 234	**Ephraim and Hannah Fox** Children of Mr and Mrs Fox, Dewsbury.	32' x 8' Self-righter	11/24
6.11.1902 – 30.4.1931	1902 499	**Mary Ann Lockwood** Legacy of Thomas Lockwood, Harrogate.	34' x 8' Self-righter	35/58

Crew of the Robin Hood's Bay lifeboat Mary Ann Lockwood outside the lifeboat house. (By courtesy of Whitby Lifeboat Museum)

Appendix 2: Lifeboat details

First lifeboat

ON STATION 1802 – 1817

RECORD At least one launch

DONOR Local Collections through Francis Gibson, plus contribution from Lloyds

DIMENSIONS 30ft

CLASS North Country, ten-oared

YEAR 1802

COST £160

BUILDER Henry Greathead, South Shields

DISPOSAL Reported as 'quite unserviceable', 1817

Fishermen's Friend (named 1861)

ON STATION No.1 station (West Side Lifeboat) 1822 – December 1859; Fishermen 1861 – 1889

RECORD 1822–59: at least 8 launches, 50 lives saved

DONOR Whitby Lifeboat Association.

DIMENSIONS 26ft 6in x 9ft 3in

CLASS North Country, ten-oared

YEAR 1822

BUILDER William Wake, Bishopswearmouth, Sunderland

COST £100

NOTES Condemned December 1859, bought by a group of fishermen for £3 3s 10d, repaired and used as an independent lifeboat

DISPOSAL Sold 1889

Not named/ 1861– Petrel/ 1871– Gertrude

ON STATION No.2 station (East Side Lifeboat) 1822 – 1871

RECORD At least 12 launches, 68 lives saved

DONOR Whitby Lifeboat Association, 1861– taken over by RNLI

DIMENSIONS 26ft x 9ft 3in

CLASS North Country, ten-oared

YEAR 1822

BUILDER Christopher Gale, Church Street, Whitby

COST £100

NOTES Hung from davits on the side of Tate Hill Pier; known as 'the Green boat' until 1863 when altered and improved 1863

DISPOSAL Broken up 1872

Not named

ON STATION No.1 station (West Side Lifeboat) September 1860 – February 1861

RECORD no launches

DONOR Whitby Lifeboat Association

DIMENSIONS 30ft x 8ft 9in

CLASS North Country

YEAR 1860

BUILDER William Falkingbridge, Church Street, Whitby

COST £130

NOTES Capsized and wrecked on service, 9 February 1861, 12 of 13 crew on board lost

DISPOSAL Sold to builder for £2 and broken up 1861

Lucy

ON STATION No.1 station (West Side) 12 April 1861 – January 1870

RECORD 9 launches, 53 lives saved

DONOR Legacy of Mr A. W. Jaffray, London.

DIMENSIONS 32ft x 7ft10in

CLASS Peake self-righter, ten-oared

YEAR 1861

COST £195 14s 2d

BUILDER Forrestt, Limehouse

DISPOSAL Broken up 1870

Lucy/ 1871– Robert Whitworth/ 1881– Harriott Forteath

ON STATION No.1 station (West Side) 1870 – 1881, No.2 station (East Side) 1881 – 1887

RECORD 1870–71: 1 launch, 4 lives saved; 1871–81: 21 launches, 126 lives saved; 1881–87: 4 launches, 5 lives saved

DONOR Legacy of A. J. Jaffray, London; 1871 appropriated to gift of Manchester Branch; 1881 appropriated to legacy of Mrs H. Forteath, Nottingham.

DIMENSIONS 32ft x 7ft 7in

CLASS Self-righter, ten-oared

BUILD 1869, Forrestt, Limehouse

COST £248 7s 6d

NOTES Transferred from No.1 to No.2 station in December 1881

DISPOSAL Sold 1887

Harriott Forteath

ON STATION No.2 station 1872 – 1879

RECORD 9 launches, 34 lives saved

DONOR Legacy of Mrs Forteath, Nottingham

DIMENSIONS 30ft x 7ft 3in x 3ft 7in

CLASS Self-righter, eight-oared

YEAR 1864

BUILDER Forrestt & Son Ltd, Limehouse

COST £216

NOTES Built as Dorinda and Barbara and served at Theddlethorpe 1864- 71, launching 4 time and saving 41 lives; renamed Harriott Forteath in 1872; capsized on service 9.1.1877

DISPOSAL Broken up 1880

Harriott Forteath

ON STATION No.2 station July 1879 – August 1881

RECORD 4 launches, 6 lives saved

DONOR Legacy of Mrs Forteath, Nottingham

DIMENSIONS 32ft x 7ft 6in x 3ft 10in

CLASS Self-righter, ten-oared

YEAR 1866,

COST £242

BUILDER Forrestt, Limehouse

NOTES Originally stationed at Wexford; described as 'unfit' in 1878, so renovated and sent to Whitby

DISPOSAL Returned to London 1881

Robert and Mary Ellis

ON STATION No.1 station November 1881 – December 1908

RECORD 37 launches, 43 lives saved

DONOR Legacy of Miss M. A. Ellis, 3 Prospect Place, Harrogate, Yorks

OFFICIAL NUMBER 180

DIMENSIONS 34ft x 8ft x 4ft

CLASS Self-righter, ten-oared

WEIGHT 3 tons 12 cwt

YEAR 1881, Woolfe, Shadwell, yard no.W147

COST £363 0s 0d

NOTES Fitted with six relieving tubes, two standing lugs and jib; harbour trial 13 October 1887, sent to station 29 November 1881

DISPOSAL Condemned May 1909, broken up July 1909

Christopher

ON STATION No.2 station, August 1887 – March 1895

RECORD 2 launches, 0 lives saved

DONOR Anonymous gift

OFFICIAL NUMBER 114

DIMENSIONS 34ft x 7ft 6in x 4ft

CLASS Self-righter, ten-oared

WEIGHT 3 tons 6 cwt

YEAR 1887

COST £325 7s 0d

BUILDER Forrestt, Limehouse, yard no.F34

NOTES Fitted with six relieving tubes, two standing lugs and jib

DISPOSAL Broken up November 1895

John Fielden

ON STATION No.2 station, 20 November 1895 – October 1914

RECORD 40 launches, 62 lives saved

DONOR Gift of John A. Fielden, London.

OFFICIAL NUMBER 379

DIMENSIONS 34ft x 7ft 9in x 3ft 10in

CLASS Self-righter, ten-oared

WEIGHT 2 tons 17 cwt 16 qtrs 22 lbs

YEAR 1895

BUILDER Waterman Bros, Cremyll, Plymouth, yard no.WN7

COST £305

NOTES Fitted with two water ballast tanks, six relieving tubes

DISPOSAL Damaged beyond repair on service to HMHS Rohilla, October 1914, and broken up

Robert and Mary Ellis

ON STATION No.1 station, 9 December 1908 – March 1934

RECORD 15 launches, 11 lives saved

DONOR Legacy of Miss Mary Ann Ellis, Harrogate, York

OFFICIAL NUMBER 588

DIMENSIONS 35ft x 8ft 6in x 4ft

CLASS Self-righter, ten-oared

WEIGHT 3 tons 15 cwt 1 qtr 0 lbs

YEAR 1908

COST £887 0s 8d

BUILDER Thames Ironworks, Blackwall, yard no.TL29

NOTES Harbour trial 10 November 1908, fitted with No.1 rig

DISPOSAL Sold out of service March 1934 to Captain W. Milburn

Forester (Reserve No.4)

ON STATION No.2 station, 3 November 1914 – November 1919

RECORD 35 launches, 89 lives saved

DONOR Ancient Order of Foresters

OFFICIAL NUMBER 455

DIMENSIONS 34ft x 8ft 6in x 3ft 6in

CLASS Rubie self-righter, ten-oared

WEIGHT 2 tons 6 cwt

BUILD 1900, Thames Ironworks, Blackwall, yard no.TL61

COST £712

NOTES Harbour trial 14.11.1900 at RNLI storeyard

DISPOSAL Dismantled and sold July 1920 to Multi-Lowler SB Co.

William Riley of Birmingham and Leamington

ON STATION Upgang July 1909 – 13 November 1919, No.2 station 13 November 1919 – February 1931

RECORD 31 launches, 10 lives saved

DONOR Legacy of Mr William Riley, Leamington

NAMING CEREMONY 23 August 1909

OFFICIAL NUMBER 594

DIMENSIONS 34ft x 8ft x 3ft 6in

CLASS Rubie self-righter, ten-oared

WEIGHT 2 tons 6 cwt

BUILT 1909, Thames Ironworks, Blackwall, yard no.TL.37

COST £722 9s 1d

NOTES No masts or sails, harbour trial 18 June 1909

DISPOSAL Sold out of service November 1931 to B. Greenstreet, 4 Muller Road, Hoe Street, Walthamstow, London E17

Richard/ 1941– Jacob and Rachel Vallentine

ON STATION No.2 station, 14 February 1931 – March 1938

RECORD 15 launches, 19 lives saved

DONOR Appropriated to legacy of Samuel Vallentine, London

OFFICIAL NUMBER 580

DIMENSIONS 34ft x 8ft x 3ft 6in

CLASS Rubie self-righter, ten-oared

WEIGHT 2 tons 5 cwt 1 qtr 9 lbs

BUILT 1907, Thames Ironworks, Blackwall, yard no.TL20

COST £730 7s 2d

NOTES Fitted with small mizen mast after bulkhead; at Happisburgh 11.1907–4.1926 and Palling No.1 4.1926–10.1930, transferred to storeyard 29.10.1930, before being reallocated to Whitby No.2

DISPOSAL Sold out of service 11 February 1938 to Charles Fleming, 105A Cheyne Walk, London; subsequent whereabouts unknown

Jacob and Rachel Vallentine

ON STATION No.2 station, March 1938 – May 1947

RECORD 5 launches, no lives saved

DONOR Legacy of Mr Samuel Vallentine, Brixton, London

OFFICIAL NUMBER 522

DIMENSIONS 34ft x 8ft x 3ft 6in

CLASS Rubie self-righter, ten-oared

WEIGHT 2 tons 6 cwt

BUILT 1904, Thames Ironworks, Blackwall, yard no.TK52

COST £665 8s 2d

NOTES Carried no masts or sails, fitted with one water ballast tank;

originally named Richard, funded from the gift of Miss A. Dixon, West Caistor, and stationed at Donna Nook 1904-31 and Reserve 1931-38; renamed 1938 and reappropriated to legacy of Samuel Valentine when reallocated to No.2 station

DISPOSAL Sold out of service 1 July 1947 to Whitby Boatbuilding Co and converted into a yacht named Janderval, fitted with a six-cylinder petrol engine

Robert and Ellen Robson

ON STATION No.2 station, 30 May 1947 – 14 November 1957
RECORD 15 launches, no lives saved
DONOR Legacy of Mr Robert Robson
OFFICIAL NUMBER 669
DIMENSIONS 34ft x 8ft x 3ft 5in
CLASS Rubie self-righter, ten-oared
WEIGHT 2 tons 6 cwt 2 qtrs 0 lbs
BUILD 1918, S. E. Saunders Ltd, Cowes, yard no.S29
COST £1,615 10s 11d
NOTES Stationed at Tramore 1918–1923, Aberdeen No.2 1924–1939 and 1943–1947, before being transferred to Whitby in May 1947
DISPOSAL After being taken out of operational service, she was exhibited at Whitby Lifeboat Museum from 26 July 1958; also displayed at Plymouth in 1974 during RNLI's 150th anniversary celebrations; in storage 2005–07 while new lifeboat house built

Margaret Harker-Smith

ON STATION June 1919 – April 1938
RECORD 117 launches, 86 lives saved
DONOR Legacy of Miss M. Harker-Smith, Sheffield
NAMING CEREMONY Inaugurated 28 June 1919, named by Miss Jenkyn-Brown, Sheffield, a close relative of the donor, the late Miss Harker-Smith
OFFICIAL NUMBER 667
DIMENSIONS 40ft x 10ft 6in x 5ft 9in
CLASS Motor self-righter
WEIGHT 10 tons 18 cwt
BUILD 1918, S. E. Saunders Ltd, Cowes, yard no.S23
ENGINE Single 40h Tylor C.2 four-cylinder petrol
COST £5,022 15s 11d
NOTES Fitted with No.1 rig modified
DISPOSAL Sold out of service in April 1938 to Chelsea Yacht & Boat Co, of Cheyne Walk, London; subsequent whereabouts known

Mary Ann Hepworth

ON STATION 12 April 1938 – November 1974
RECORD 372 launches, 201 lives saved
DONOR Gift of Walter W. Hepworth, Hessel, Hull
NAMING CEREMONY Named 27 June 1938 at Whitby by the Marchioness of Normanby.
OFFICIAL NUMBER 808
DIMENSIONS 41ft x 11ft 8in
CLASS Watson motor
WEIGHT 14 tons 2 cwt
YEAR 1938
ENGINES Twin 35hp Weyburn AE.6 six-cylinder petrol engines; re-engined 1963 with two 47hp Parsons Porbeagle diesels

COST £6575 10s 3d
BUILDER Groves & Guttridge, Cowes, yard no.G&G 228
DISPOSAL Sold out of service in July 1974 for £6,750 plus £1,687 to W. J. Aldiss, of Sparrow Hill, Hindringham, Fakenham, Norfolk

The White Rose of Yorkshire

ON STATION 24 November 1974 – December 1988
RECORD 239 launches, 51 lives saved
DONOR Gift of Miss Gwynaeth Milburn, Harrogate
NAMING CEREMONY Named 21 May 1975 at Whitby by HRH The Duchess of Kent, wife of the RNLI President
OFFICIAL NUMBER 1033 (operational number 44-012)
DIMENSIONS 44ft 10in x 12ft 8in
CLASS Waveney fast afloat lifeboat
WEIGHT 19 tons 2 cwt
YEAR 1974
ENGINES Twin 260hp General Motors 8V-53 eight-cylinder diesels
COST £79,018
BUILDER Groves & Guttridge, Cowes
DISPOSAL Sold out of service on 15 March 1999 to the Canadian Lifeboat Institution, based at Roberts Bank, near Vancouver, after being shipped from Sheerness across the Atlantic

City of Sheffield

ON STATION 12 December 1988 – April 1996
RECORD 239 launches, 88 lives saved
DONOR The City of Sheffield Lifeboat Appeal with the bequest of Mrs Mary Mabel Walker, and other gifts and legacies
NAMING CEREMONY Named 28.7.1989 by HRH The Duchess of Kent at Whitby
YEAR 1988
BUILDER Hull by Wright, Derby; fitted out by Souter Shipyard, Cowes
OFFICIAL NUMBER 1131 (operational number 47-023)
DIMENSIONS 47ft x 15ft
CLASS Tyne fast slipway lifeboat
WEIGHT 25 tons 2 cwt
ENGINES Twin 425hp General Motors 6V-92-TA diesels; re-engined 1997 with twin 565hp General Motors D-DEC diesels
COST £566,000
NOTES Transferred to Ramsgate 1996, Hartepool in 1997 and stationed at Poole from September 2001

George and Mary Webb

ON STATION 10 April 1996 –
DONOR The Mary Webb Trust
NAMING CEREMONY Named 12.6.1996 by HRH The Duchess of Kent at Scotch Head, Whitby
YEAR 1996
BUILDER Hull by Green Marine, Lymington; fitted out by Souter Shipyard, Cowes
OFFICIAL NUMBER 1212 (operational number 14-14)
DIMENSIONS 14.26m x 4.90m x 2.55m
CLASS Trent fast afloat lifeboat
DISPLACEMENT 25.5 tonnes
ENGINES Twin 810hp MAN D2840 LE40 diesels
COST £1,103,008

Appendix 3: Service summary

Pre-RNLI Lifeboats

1802 lifeboat

1802	Nov 30	Sloop Edinburgh, of Sunderland, saved crew
1807	Nov	Fly, saved crew
1811	June 30	Edinburgh Packet, of Leith, saved crew
1813	Oct 28	Sloop Mars, of Whitby, saved crew of 2 persons

Lifeboats of 1822

1822	Feb 28	Brig Barnevelt, of Sunderland, saved crew
		Elizabeth, of Newcastle, saved crew
1823	Jan 16	Lyon, of Sunderland, saved crew
		Acorn, of Wells, saved crew
	Feb 3	Hoop, of Sandwich, saved crew
		Neutral Fisher, of Yarmouth, saved crew
	Oct 26	Autumn, of Sunderland, assisted to saved vessel
1824	Oct 11	Ships Fortitude, Friendship, Henry, Larj and Liberty, all of Sunderland, saved crews
	Nov 2	Sloop Friends, of Whitby, assisted
		Sloop Friends, of Whitby, reboarded crew
		Sloop Jemma, of Sunderland, saved vessel
1827	Feb 17	Oak, of Whitby, saved crew
		Comet, of Whitby, saved crew
		Henry and Mary, of Whitby, saved crew
		Traveller, of Sunderland, saved crew
		Ann, of Stockton, saved crew
1828	Sep 15	Local cobles, attempted rescue
1830	Jan 20	Brig Smales, of Whitby, saved 10
		Coastguard gig, saved 5
1830	Jan 25	Schooner William and George, of Dundee, saved 5
		Schooner Catherine and Ann, of Dundee, saved 5
1834	Apr 29	Schooner William, of Newcastle, landed 2 and assisted to save vessel
1835	July 1	Brig Thales, of Sunderland, saved 12
1837		Schooner Matilda, of Leith, saved crew
	Oct 29	Brig Ivanhoe, saved 8
	Dec 21	Brig Middlesbrough, of Newcastle, saved 8
1838	Feb	Brig Derwent, of Sunderland, saved crew
		Brig Betsy, of Sunderland, saved crew
	Oct 29	Brig Jupiter, of Whitby, saved 10
1839	Dec	Brilliant, saved crew
		John and Anne, saved crew
1841	Oct 6	Two yawls, saved 9
1849	Sep 30	Brig Wrancez (?), saved crew
		Brig Black Diamond, saved crew
1850	Jan 14	Brig Vina, of Bristol, saved 1
1851	Mar	Barque Saxon Maid, of Sunderland, saved crew
1852		Susan King, assisted
1857	Jan	Poll, assisted
1861	Feb 9	Brig Tribune, saved crew
	10	Brig Memnon, of Shields, saved crew

Falkingbridge Lifeboat of 1860

1860	Oct 3	Schooner KITTY (or KELTY) of Whitby, saved 3
1861	Feb 9	Schooner GAMMA, of Newcastle, saved 4
		Brig CLARA, of Memel, saved 12
		Brig UTILITY, of London, saved 5 or 6
		Schooner ROE, of Dundee, saved 4

Fishermen's Friend Lifeboat

1862	Mar	Steamship Deptford, of Shields, saved vessel
1866	Dec 30	Two pilot cobles of Hartlepool, escorted

NB This list of pre-RNLI rescues is not necessarily complete

RNLI No.1 Lifeboats

Lucy Lifeboat

1862	Dec 22	Steamship Alice, of Leith, assisted to save vessel and 12
1865	Apr 19	Steamship Ocean Queen, of Newcastle, saved 15
	May 9	Barque Maria Somes, of London, saved 19
	Oct 19	Schooner Elizabeth, of Goole, rendered assistance
1866	Dec 31	Schooner Lion, of Goole, saved 5
1867	Oct 1	Schooner Comet, of Whitby, saved 4
1868	Jan 2	Steam tug Swan, of Middlesborough, saved 2
		Sloop Industry, of Whitby, saved 2
		Sloop Mulgrave, of Whitby, saved 2
1869	Dec 27	Brigantine Lutha, of Leith, saved 6

Lucy (second) Lifeboat

1870	July 26	Brigantine Mary and Jane, of Sunderland, assisted to save vessel and 4

This Lifeboat renamed Robert Whitworth

1871	Oct 2	Schooner Dispatch, of Whitby, saved 3
	3	Schooner Dispatch, of Whitby, reboarded crew
	Dec 6	Four fishing cobles, of Whitby, saved 12
1875	Oct 18	Barque Teazer, of Whitby, saved 9
1876	May 24	Four fishing cobles, of Whitby, saved (with No.2 lifeboat) 12
1877	Feb 23	Fishing coble Ann Elizabeth, of Whitby, landed 3
	Mar 1	Boat of brig Christopher Hansteen, of Norway, saved 8
1878	Jan 5	Steamship Oscar, of Leith, saved 22
	6	Steamship Oscar, of Leith, reboarded Captain to save papers and instruments
	May 8	Fishing cobles Eliza and James & Sarah, of Scarborough, assisted to save 1 coble and 4
	Sep 12	Fishing vessels in the Roads, boarded crews and stood by
		Fishing coble Welcome, of Hartlepool, saved 2
1879	Mar 12	Steamship Lorentzen, of London, saved 17
1880	Oct 28	Schooner Reaper, of Douglas, saved 4
		Fishing yawl Good Intent, of Staithes, saved 8
		Schooner Robert Snell, of Great Yarmouth, saved 5
1881	Jan 19	Brig Visitor, of Whitby, saved 6

Robert and Mary Ellis Lifeboat

1882	Sep 20	Schooner William, of Denmark, stood by and gave help
	Dec 6	Brig Star of Hope, of Newcastle, saved 6
1883	Apr 20	Three fishing cobles, of Whitby, gave help
1892	Oct 8	Fishing coble Palm Beach, of Whitby, saved 3
1895	Jan 11	Fishing cobles Rosa Marion and William, of Whitby, saved cobles and 6
1896	Aug 1-2	Steamship Lady Gray, of West Hartlepool, assisted to save vessel
1898	Feb 21	Fishing coble R.W. Jackson, assisted to save coble and 3
		Fishing coble Tranquil, saved 3
		Fishing coble Martha Dryden, saved 2
1899	Aug 19	Pilot coble Robert, stood by
	Nov 25	Fishing cobles, stood by
1901	Mar 18	Fishing cobles, stood by
1902	Feb 7	Cobles Thomas and Richard and Lady Morris, landed 6
	May 5	Fishing cobles, stood by
1903	Nov 28	Three fishing cobles, stood by
1904	Jan 21	Steamship Cayo Bonito, of London, gave help
	Apr 15	Fishing coble Lady Morris, of Whitby, saved 3
		Six fishing cobles, of Whitby, landed 1 and stood by
	June 10	Three fishing cobles, of Whitby, stood by
1905	Mar 24	Fishing coble May Blossom, of Whitby, stood by
	Apr 25	Six fishing cobles, of Whitby, stood by

	May 20	Steamship Cogent, of Sunderland, assisted to save vessel
1906	May 14	Fishing coble William and Tom, of Whitby, landed 3
		Fishing coble Jane and Mary, saved 3
	June 28	Two cobles, of Whitby, stood by
	Dec 7	Steamship Isle of Iona, of Newcastle, saved 11
1907	Mar 23	Fishing coble Robert and Mary, of Whitby, stood by
	Apr 3	Fishing cobles, of Whitby, stood by
	5	Three fishing cobles, of Whitby, stood by
	Oct 28	Three fishing cobles, of Whitby, stood by
1908	Feb 10	Fishing coble Robert and Mary, of Whitby, stood by
	Apr 2	Fifteen fishing cobles, of Whitby, stood by
	22	Five fishing cobles, of Whitby, stood by
	July 15	Fishing cobles, of Whitby, landed 3 and stood by
	Sep 9	Fishing coble Salmo, of Whitby, saved coble and 3
	Nov 27	Nine fishing cobles, of Whitby, stood by

Robert and Mary Ellis (second) Lifeboat

1909	Feb 15	Ketch Gem of the Ocean, of Whitby, saved 1
	May 15	Fishing coble Robert and Mary, of Whitby, stood by
1913	Mar 9	Fishing coble Eliza Jane, of Whitby, saved coble and 3
1915	Dec 23	Steamship Skane, of Helsingborg, saved 7
1916	Nov 20	Steam trawler Eagle, of Grimsby, landed 9
	21	Steam trawler Eagle, assisted to save vessel
1919	July 15	Schooner Fern, of Hull, landed 3
1922	July 19	Fishing coble May Blossom, of Whitby, escorted

RNLI No.2 Lifeboats

Petrel Lifeboat

1862	Dec 21	Barque Royal Rose, of Whitby, saved 12
1871	Dec 6	Two fishing cobles, of Whitby, saved 6

Harriott Forteath Lifeboat

1874	Feb 14	Five fishing cobles, of Whitby, saved
	Dec 9	Schooner Pride, of Southampton, saved 2
	16	Salvage party from Schooner Pride, saved 8
1875	Oct 22	Swedish Barque Svadsfare, assisted to save barque and 16
1876	May 24	Four fishing cobles, of Whitby, saved (with No.1 lifeboat) 12
1878	Sep 12	Fishing vessels in the Roads, boarded crews and stood by

Harriott Forteath (second) Lifeboat

1879	Dec 2	Four fishing cobles, of Whitby, stood by
1880	Apr 15	Two fishing cobles, of Whitby, gave help and stood by
	Oct 1	Fishing boat Matchless, reboarded crew
		Fishing coble, of Whitby, landed 1
	28	Schooner Elizabeth Austin, or Rye, saved 5
1885	May 3	Sloop Wear, of Sunderland, saved 2
	Aug 20	Fishing coble Robert and Henry, of Whitby, saved 3
1886	Jan 28	Five fishing cobles, of Whitby, stood by and stood by
	Oct 5	Fishing cobles Lady Morris and Anne Elizabeth, of Whitby, stood by and gave help

Christopher Lifeboat

1895	Feb 6	Fishing cobles, of Whitby, stood by

Reserve Lifeboat

1895	Aug 9	Fishing coble Eliza Jane, of Whitby, landed 3
		Fishing cobles, stood by

John Fielden Lifeboat

1896	Jan 15	Fishing coble Secret, of Whitby, saved 4
	Feb 13	Fishing cobles, of Whitby, warned cobles
	July 27	Fishing cobles Star of Peace and Mary Ann, of Whitby, escorted vessels

	Aug 1-2	Steamship Lady Gray, of West Hartlepool, assisted to save vsl
	Sep 3	Fishing cobles, stood by
	Nov 10	Fishing cobles, stood by
1897	Mar 12	Fishing coble Mary Alice, of Whitby, assisted to save coble
		Fishing coble Tranquil, of Whitby, stood by
	Sep 21-2	Fishing cobles, stood by
1898	Apr 16	Fishing cobles, stood by
	28	Fishing cobles, stood by
1900	Feb 12	Fishing cobles, stood by
	Nov 8	Fishing coble Victoria, of Whitby, saved coble and 2
1901	Sep 17	Fishing cobles, stood by
	Nov 19-20	Steamship Cygnet, of London, stood by and gave help
1902	June 2	Three-masted schooner Frier, of Poole, stood by and gave help
1905	May 10	Steamship Cogent, of Sunderland, assisted to save vessel
1906	Dec 7	Steamship Isle of Iona, of Newcastle, saved 6
1907	Jan 22	Fishing coble Margaret, of Filey, saved 4
		Fishing coble Jane and Priscilla, of Filey, saved 4
1908	Dec 26	Fishing coble Robert and Mary, of Whitby, stood by
1909	Apr 15	Seven fishing cobles, of Whitby, stood by
	Sep 12-3	Nine fishing cobles, of Whitby, stood by
1910	Apr 6	Seven fishing cobles, of Whitby, stood by
	22	Fishing coble Robert and Mary, of Whitby, saved 4
		Fishing coble Brotherly Love, of Whitby, saved 3
	Oct 19	Fishing coble Rose of Sharon, of Whitby, stood by
	Dec 9	Eight fishing cobles, of Whitby, stood by
1911	Apr 17	Fourteen fishing cobles, of Whitby, stood by
	May 1	Six fishing cobles, of Whitby, stood by
	Nov 30	Steamship Vostizza, of Andros, stood by
1912	Dec 3	Eleven fishing cobles, of Whitby, stood by
1913	Mar 17	Two fishing cobles, of Whitby, stood by
1914	Mar 16	Five fishing cobles, of Whitby, stood by
	Oct 30-Nov 1	Government Hospital Ship Rohilla, saved (in two trips) 35

Forester Reserve Lifeboat

1914	Nov 25	Steamship Ingrid II, of Christiania, saved vessel and 16
	Dec 24-7	Steamship Fane, of Bergen, assisted to save vessel
	25	Coble Harvest Home, of Whitby, saved coble and 1
	30	Steamship Peveril, of Leith, assisted to save vessel
1915	Mar 18	Twelve cobles and a motor fishing boat, of Whitby, stood by
	Dec 1	Steamship Skane, of Helsingborg, saved 10
		Steamship Skane (second trip), saved 2
		Steamship Skane (third trip), saved 8
1916	Dec 11-2	Steamship Hedworth, of Sunderland, stood by
1917	Feb 20	Steamship Braeside, of Sunderland, assisted to save vessel
	Oct 8-9	Steamship Carlotta, of Chevant (four launches), stood by and saved 19
	Dec 9	Steamship Venetia, of Glasgow, saved 8
1918	Jan 23	Steamship Portaferry, of Glasgow, saved 8
	Feb 14	Steamship Spurt, of Christiania, saved 3
	Mar 25	Steamship Nordstrand, of London, saved 23

William Riley of Leamington and Birmingham Lifeboat

1919	Dec 19	Steamship Mojave, of Tacoma, stood by
1920	Jan 21	Steamship Dorothy Talbot, of London, landed 11
	Mar 3	Steam tug St Keyne, of London, rendered assistance
	Apr 21	Schooner Mathilda, saved 1
	30	Six fishing cobles, of Whitby, escorted
1921	Jan 27	Six fishing cobles, of Whitby, landed 7 and escorted
1922	May 12	Fishing cobles Emma, May Blossom, Helen and Brotherly Love, of Whitby, escorted
	Oct 27	Motor fishing boat Welcome Home, of Whitby, saved boat and 5
1923	Nov 7	Five motor fishing boats, of Whitby, escorted
1925	Mar 25	Fishing coble Jean and Alice, of Whitby, escorted
	Apr 19	Motor vessel Mimi Selmer, of Hamburg, stood by
	Dec 22	Sloop barge Mary Bridge, of Hull, saved 4

1926	July 27	Fishing coble Elsie, of Whitby, landed an unconscious man
		Six fishing cobles, of Whitby, landed 3 and stood by
	Dec 14	Nine motor fishing boats, of Whitby, stood by
1927	May 30	Fishing coble Mary Elizabeth, of Whitby, stood by
	Nov 7	Motor fishing boat Remembrance, of Whitby, escorted
	Dec 7	Fishing fleet, of Whitby, stood by and gave help
1928	Nov 5	Motor fishing boat Mary Rose, of Whitby, escorted
	27	Motor fishing boats Pilot Me and Remembrance, of Whitby, escorted
1929	Jan 1	Six motor fishing boats, of Whitby, escorted
	Feb 1	Four fishing boats, of Whitby, stood by
	Apr 23	Motor fishing boat Faith, of Whitby, stood by
	June 27	Fishing cobles John Wray, Lady Lee and Doris, of Whitby, stood by
		Fishing coble Silvester, of Whitby, saved coble
	Oct 27	Steam trawler Earl Haig, of Hull, rendered assistance

Jacob and Rachel Vallentine Lifeboat

1931	Mar 1	Motor coble Topsy, of Whitby, escorted
	Sep 4	People trapped in houses by floods, saved 5
1932	Aug 22	Thirteen fishing cobles, of Whitby, escorted
1934	Jan 19	Motor fishing boats Pilot Me and Royal Empire, escorted
	Feb 21	Motor fishing boat Royal Empire, of Whitby, escorted
1935	Jan 13	Small boat, of Whitby, saved 3
	Mar 2	Fishing boats Lady Mary, Royal Empire and Louise Mary, esc'd
1936	Jan 25	Steam trawler Andri, of Eskifjarder, saved 11
	Mar 10	Steamship Ardgantock, of Greenock, stood by
	Apr 19	Motor fishing coble Lily, of Whitby, escorted
	Dec 2	Motor fishing boats Provider, Success and Pilot Me, of Whitby, escorted
1937	Apr 25	Motor fishing boat Enterprize, of Whitby, escorted
	Dec 6	Motor fishing boats Pilot Me, Provider and Success, stood by

Jacob and Rachel Vallentine (second) Lifeboat

1939	Nov 13	Fishing boat Royal Empire, of Whitby, escorted
1941	June 13	Fishing boats Silver Line, Rosamond, Cutty Sark and Brighter Hope, of Whitby, escorted
1946	May 16	Five fishing boats, of Whitby, escorted
1947	Apr 8	Ten fishing boats, of Whitby, stood by
	May 2	Motor fishing boats Floral Queen and Royal Empire, stood by
		Seven motor fishing boats, of Whitby, stood by

Robert and Ellen Robson Lifeboat

1947	Dec 4	Fishing cobles Silver Line, Good Faith, Floral Queen and Effort, of Whitby, escorted
1948	Apr 20	Motor fishing boat Provider, of Whitby, escorted
1949	Oct 5	Persons cut off by the tide, landed 16
1952	Apr 2	Fishing cobles Floral Queen, Silver Line, Little Lady and Margaret, of Whitby, escorted
	Sep 4	Motor fishing boats Gem and Whitby Lass, of Whitby, esc'd
	21	Motor launches Lady Margaret and Georgina II, of Middlesborough, and Pandora B, of Whitby, stood by
1953	Mar 31	Fishing coble Little Lady, of Whitby, escorted
	June 5	Fishing cobles Galilee, Venus, Pilot Me, Progress and Lead Us, of Whitby, escorted
1955	Nov 23	Four fishing boats, of Whitby, escorted
	24	Fishing boat Pilot Me, of Whitby, escorted

Motor Lifeboats
No.3 Station 1919–34, No.1 Station 1934–57

Margaret Harker-Smith Lifeboat

1919	Oct 24	HM ML.292, assisted to save vessel and 11
	Nov 5	Steamship Bratto, of Newcastle, assisted to save vessel

	Dec 19	Steamship Mojave, of Tacoma, stood by
	31	Four motor fishing boats, of Whitby, escorted
1920	Mar 3	Steam tug St Keyne, of London, gave help
	Jul 27	Motor boat Edward Henry, of Bolton, saved boat and 4
	Nov 15	Five-masted schooner Cap Palos, of Vancouver, saved 16
1922	Aug 9	Fishing boats May Blossom, Faith and Remembrance, of Whitby, stood by
	Oct 27	Fishing cobles Dorothy, Friendship and Four Sisters, of Runswick, escorted
	Dec 22	Steam trawler Northern King, of Grimsby, stood by
1923	Jan 13	Steamship Spero, of Newcastle, with Lifeboat Hesther Rothschild, of Runswick, assisted
	Feb 26	Fishing coble of Staithes, escorted
		Motor fishing boat Remembrance, of Whitby, escorted
	Aug 24	Fishing coble Pansy, of Whitby, saved 2
		Cobles Providence and Maria, of Whitby, stood by
	Nov 9	Motor fishing boat Mizpah, of Whitby, escorted
1924	Feb 18	Motor fishing boats Remembrance and Fortuna, of Whitby, stood by
	Jun 12	Steamship Redhall, of Aberdeen, stood by
1925	Jan 9	Motor fishing boats Pilot Me and Remembrance, of Whitby, stood by
	Feb 16	Motor fishing boats Fortuna, Mizpah, Pilot Me, Noel and Remembrance, of Whitby, escorted
	Mar 2	Motor fishing boats Fortuna, Eva, Pilot Me, Remembrance, and Welcome Home, of Whitby, escorted
	Apr 1	Motor fishing boats Fortuna and Mizpah, of Whitby, escorted
	Sep 10	Motor fishing boat Pilot Me, of Whitby, stood by
	Dec 11	Motor fishing boats Comet, Noel, Remembrance, Diligence, Pilot Me, and Irene, of Whitby, escorted
	21	Motor fishing boat Pilot Me, of Whitby, stood by
	22	Motor fishing boats Remembrance, Pilot Me and Irene, of Whitby, escorted
1926	Feb 5	Motor fishing boats Radiance, Diligence, Pilot Me, Irene and Remembrance, of Whitby, escorted
	Mar 10	Motor fishing boat Pilot Me, of Whitby, stood by
	22	Motor fishing boats Diligence, Fortuna, Irene, Remembrance, Noel, Pilot Me and Comet, of Whitby, stood by
	Apr 28	Motor fishing coble Gratitude, of Whitby, escorted
	July 6	Motor fishing boats Pilot Me and Irene, of Whitby, stood by
	Oct 12	Motor fishing boats Mizpah, Pilot Me, Remembrance and Excelsior, of Whitby, escorted
	Dec 14	Fishing coble Francis, of Whitby, escorted
	29	Motor fishing boat Pilot Me, of Whitby, stood by
1927	Mar 26	Fishing cobles John Ray, Unity and Mary, of Whitby, stood by
	June 22	Fishing coble Francis, of Whitby, escorted
	Nov 9	Mtr fishing boats Faith, Mizpah, Irene, Pilot Me and Guide Me, of Whitby, escorted
	Dec 14	Twelve motor fishing boats, of Whitby, escorted
1928	Jan 6	Motor fishing boats Remembrance, Irene and Faith, of Whitby, escorted
	17	Motor fishing boats Irene, Faith, Diligence, Remembrance and Lady Kitchener, of Whitby, escorted
		Motor fishing boats Fortuna and Guide Me, of Whitby, saved boats and 9
	Apr 18	Motor fishing boats Pilot Me and Guide Me, of Whitby, esc'd
	20	Motor fishing boats Guide Me, Pilot Me and Remembrance, of Whitby, escorted
	Dec 11	Motor fishing boats Noel, Irene, Diligence, Fortuna, Guiding Star, Guide Me, Remembrance, Pilot Me and Faith, of Whitby, escorted
	13	Motor fishing boats Remembrance and Guide Me, of Whitby, escorted
	20	Six fishing boats, of Whitby, escorted
	28	Motor fishing boat Diligence, of Whitby, escorted
1929	Jan 25	Motor fishing boats Remembrance and Guide Me, of Whitby, escorted
	Feb 1	Five fishing boats, of Whitby, escorted

	Apr 23	Motor fishing coble Sybil, of Whitby, stood by
		Motor fishing cobles Jennie and Freda, of Staithes, stood by
		Fishing coble Florence, of Runswick, stood by
	Dec 22	Fishing coble W. H. Gladstone, of Whitby, stood by
	24	Motor fishing boat Pilot Me, of Whitby, stood by
1930	Feb 3	Motor fishing boats Pilot Me and Fortuna, of Whitby, stood by
	6	Motor fishing coble Topsy, of Whitby, escorted
		Steamship Brandon, of London, landed a sick man
		One coble and eight motor fishing boats, escorted
	June 3	Fishing cobles St Hilda, Faith and Irene, of Whitby, escorted
	Oct 1	Motor fishing boats Faith and Irene, of Whitby, escorted
	Dec 25	Steamship Lucy, of Helsingborg, saved 18
1931	Feb 27	Fishing boat Brethren, of Whitby, escorted
		Fishing boats Guiding Star and Noel, of Whitby, escorted
		Fishing boats Lady Kitchener, Guide Me and Radiance, of Whitby, escorted
		Fishing boats Pilot Me and Irene, of Whitby, escorted
		Fishing boats Faith and Fortunus, of Whitby, escorted
	Oct 20	Fishing boats Golden Gate, Faith, Irene and Noel II, of Whitby, escorted
	Dec 15	Fishing coble Lilian, of Whitby, escorted
		Motor fishing boats Irene and Faith, of Whitby, escorted
1932	Jan 8	Fishing boats Fortunatus and (in tow) Remembrance, of Whitby, escorted
	Feb 29	Fishing boats Fortunatus and Pilot Me, of Whitby, escorted
	Mar 11	Motor fishing boats Noel and Irene, of Whitby, escorted
		Motor fishing boat Progress, of Scarborough, escorted
	Apr 8	Motor fishing boat Pilot Me, of Whitby, gave help
	May 3	Motor fishing boat Fortunatus, of Whitby, gave help
	Oct 18	Motor fishing boats Pilot Me and Venus, of Whitby, escorted
	Dec 5	Motor fishing coble Primrose, of Whitby, saved coble and 3
		Ten fishing boats, of Whitby, stood by
1933	Feb 3	Three cobles and eleven motor fishing boats, of Whitby, escorted
	10	Fishing boats Fortunatus, Noel II and Venus, of Whitby, esc'd
		Fishing boat Pilot Me, of Whitby, escorted
	17	Fishing boat Pilot Me, of Whitby, escorted
	21	Fishing boats Fortunatus and Pilot Me, of Whitby, escorted
	Mar 4	Motor fishing boats Galilee, Fortunatus, Mizpah, Pilot Me, Noel and Venus, of Whitby, escorted
	Oct 28	Steamship Comitas, of Genoa, stood by and gave help
	Dec 29	Motor fishing boats Success, Venus, Pilot Me and Galilee, of Whitby, escorted
1934	Apr 7	Motor fishing boats Brethren and Gratitude, of Whitby, esc'd
		Motor fishing boat Curlew, of Whitby, gave help
	Oct 30	Motor fishing boat Pilot Me, of Whitby, escorted
	Dec 5	Motor fishing boats Pilot Me and Success, of Whitby, escorted
1935	Feb 4	Motor fishing boats Noel II, Golden Gate, Venus, Galilee, Lady Kitchener, Pilot Me and Success, of Whitby, escorted
	Mar 2	Two cobles and seven motor fishing boats, of Whitby, esc'd
	July 21	Motor yacht Maroc, escorted
	Nov 4	Three cobles and eleven motor fishing boats, of Whitby, esc'd
	21	Motor fishing boat Provider, of Whitby, escorted
	Dec 2	Eleven motor fishing boats, of Whitby, escorted
1936	Jan 13	Motor fishing boat Provider, of Whitby, escorted
	Feb 10	Motor fishing boat Provider, of Whitby, escorted
	24	Motor fishing boats Success and Pilot Me, of Whitby, and two RAF motor launches, escorted
	Apr 15	Motor fishing boats Prosperity, Progress, Endeavour, Flying Spray and Success, of Whitby, escorted
	22	Motor fishing boats Endeavour, Noel, Venus, Prosperity, Progress, Flying Spray, Success and Easter Morn, of Whitby, escorted
	May 6	Seven fishing boats, of Whitby, escorted
	28	Motor fishing boats Galilee, Progress, Endeavour, Noel II, Provider and Venus, of Whitby, escorted
	Dec 4	Motor fishing cobles Mayflower, of Whitby, escorted
	5	Motor fishing boats Venus, Easter Morn, Provider, Galilee, Endeavour and Success, of Whitby, escorted

1937	Jan 19	Motor fishing boats Pilot Me, Provider, Venus, Galilee, Progress and two others, of Whitby, escorted
	27	Motor fishing boat Pilot Me, of Whitby, escorted
	Mar 3	Motor fishing boat Provider, of Whitby, escorted
	11	Motor fishing boats Galilee, Victoria and Provider, of Whitby, escorted vessels
	Aug 20	Motor fishing boats Galilee and Venus, of Whitby, stood by and escorted
	Nov 15	Motor fishing boats Noel II, Venus, Galilee, Pilot Me and Success, of Whitby, escorted
1938	Feb 12	Motor fishing boats. Endeavour, Pilot Me and Success, of Whitby, escorted
	Apr 8	Motor fishing boats Pilot Me and Provider, of Whitby, esc'd

Mary Ann Hepworth Lifeboat

1938	Apr 18	Motor fishing boats Pilot Me and Success, of Whitby, escorted
	29	Motor fishing boat Noel II, of Whitby, saved boat and 5
		Motor fishing boats Venus, Success, Galilee, Provider and Easter Morn, of Whitby, escorted
	May 30	Fishing coble Rawleigh, of Whitby, escorted
	Sep 19	Fishing cobles Comrade and Royal Empire, of Whitby, escorted
	Dec 23	Seven motor fishing boats, of Whitby, escorted
1939	Jan 2	Fourteen fishing boats, of Whitby, escorted
	19	Four motor fishing boats, of Whitby, escorted
	23	Motor fishing boat Pilot Me, of Whitby, escorted
	Feb 18	Motor fishing boats Endeavour, Progress, Easter Morn, Venus, Pilot Me, Prosperity, Galilee, Success and Provider, of Whitby, escorted
	Mar 15	Fishing boats Venus, Galilee, Success, Pilot Me and Provider, of Whitby, escorted
	Apr 22	Fishing cobles Ramleh, Royal Empire, Sarah, Guide Me and Margaret, of Whitby, escorted
	May 16	Fishing cobles Royal Empire, Silver Line and fishing boat Galilee, of Whitby, escorted
	Nov 12	HM Minesweeper Cape Cormorin, saved 18
	17	Fishing boat Pride, and two cobles, of Scarborough, escorted
1940	Feb 28	Fishing boats Success and Provider, of Whitby, escorted
	Mar 30	Motor vessel Frederick, of Zwartsluis, stood by
	Apr 19	Fishing boats Success, Provider and Venus, of Whitby, escorted
	29	Steamship Whiteoft, of Middlesbrough, saved 15
	May 7	Fishing boat Propserity, of Whitby, saved boat and 5
	Oct 9	Fishing cobles Rosamond, Royal Empire and Britannia, of Whitby, escorted
	Dec 24	Fishing boat Proficient, of Lowestoft, saved 5
1941	Feb 13	Steamship Westcliffe Hall, of Montreal, gave help
	15	Steamship Paris, of London, saved 22
	Apr 4	Six fishing cobles and a pulling boat, of Whitby, escorted
	June 12	Fishing cobles Guide Me, Brighter Hope, Silver Line, Rosamond, Freda, Margaret and Cutty Sark, of Whitby, escorted vessels
	July 16	HM Minesweeper Lord Darling, saved 21
	Oct 10	Fishing cobles Freda, Brighter Hope, Dorothy and Enterprise, of Whitby, escorted
	22	Fishing cobles Ramleh, Freda and Rosamond, of Whitby, esc'd
	Nov 24	Fishing coble Spray, of Whitby, saved coble and 4
	Dec 23	Fishing cobles Zephyr, of Whitby, saved coble and 3
1942	Mar 25	British aircraft, saved an inflatable dinghy and 4
	July 18	Motor fishing coble Freda, of Whitby, saved coble and 3
	Dec 1	Fishing cobles Freda, Silver Line and Margaret, and seven fishing boats, of Whitby, escorted
1943	Dec 21	Motor fishing coble Hilda, of Scarborough, saved coble and 3
1944	Mar 1	Motor fishing boat North Star, of Whitby, escorted
	Aug 28	Motor fishing coble Silver Line, of Whitby, escorted
	Nov 26	Harbour Defence Motor Launch D.421049, escorted
1945	Jan 27	Motor fishing boat North Star, of Whitby, escorted
	Dec 11	Motor fishing boat Gem, of Hull, escorted

1946	Feb 11	Motor fishing boats Easter Morn, Gem, Pilot Me, Jessie Ann and Mona, of Whitby, escorted
	23	Fishing boat Easter Morn, and seven others, of Whitby, escorted boats and saved 1
	Mar 13	Danish motor fishing boat Ole Knude, escorted
	Apr 10	Fishing boat Provider, of Whitby, escorted
	Aug 30	Rowing boats Dorothy II and Howdale, of Whitby, saved boats and 5
	Sep 18	Fifteen fishing boats, escorted
	29	Steamship Torni, of Liverpool, landed 1
	30	Steamship Torni, of Liverpool, landed 11
	Nov 14	Four motor fishing boats, of Whitby, escorted
	19	Motor fishing boat Success, of Whitby, escorted
	20	Motor fishing boats Provider, Pilot Me and Gem, of Whitby, escorted
	Dec 4	Motor fishing boat Pilot Me, of Whitby, escorted
	28	Motor fishing coble Jane and Ann, of Whitby, escorted
	29	Steamship Fosdyke Trader, of London, gave help
1947	Feb 19	Motor fishing boats Pilot Me and Gem, of Whitby, escorted
	28	Motor fishing boats Provider, Galilee and Pilot Me, of Whitby, escorted
	Mar 24	Six motor fishing boats, of Whitby, escorted
	Apr 8	Motor fishing boat North Star, of Whitby, escorted
	30	Motor fishing boat Prosperity, of Whitby, escorted
	Nov 14	Motor fishing boat Pilot Me, of Whitby, gave help
	15	Motor fishing boat Pilot Me, of Whitby, gave help
	28	Motor fishing boat Gem, of Whitby, escorted
	29	Motor fishing boat Venus, of Whitby, gave help
	Dec 17	Motor fishing boat Gem, of Whitby, escorted
		Motor trawler Tut, of Esbjerg, escorted
1948	May 20	Motor fishing boat Success, of Whitby, escorted
		Motor fishing boat Galilee, of Whitby, escorted
	June 13	Steamship Cerne, of London, gave help
	Sep 15	Motor fishing coble Helena, of Whitby, escorted
	Nov 1	Motor fishing boat Provider, of Whitby, gave help
1949	Jan 2	Motor fishing boat Providence, of Whitby, saved boat and 5
	8	Motor fishing boat Pilot Me II, of Whitby, escorted
	Apr 8	Motor fishing boat Pilot Me II, of Whitby, escorted
	26	Motor fishing boats Provider A, Easter Morn, Gem, Venus and Enterprise, of Whitby, escorted
	May 7	Motor yacht Red Rover, of Southwold, in tow of motor fishing boat Prosperity, of Whitby, escorted
		Four motor fishing boats, of Whitby, escorted
	12	Motor vessel Arbroath, of Dundee, in tow of steamship Anna Maria Nurminen, escorted
		Motor vessel Arbroath, reboarded crew, stood by and esc'd
	Dec 17	Four fishing cobles, of Whitby, escorted
	18	Motor fishing boat Gem, of Whitby, escorted
1950	Jan 27	Motor fishing coble Resolution, of Whitby, escorted
	Feb 24	Motor fishing boats Galilee, Provider A, Venus, Success, Pilot Me II and Express, of Whitby, escorted
	25	Motor fishing boats Pilot Me II and Success, of Whitby, esc'd
	Mar 13	Motor fishing boats Success, Provider A and Pilot Me II, of Whitby, escorted
	Apr 2	Fishing coble Jean and Valerie, of Whitby, escorted
	19	Steamship Durhambrook, of London, stood by
	Sep 26	Fishing boats, of Scottish ports, escorted
	Nov 29	Fishing boats Foxglove and Forth Star, of Whitby, gave help
		Motor fishing boats, escorted
	Dec 7	Motor fishing coble Enterprize II, of Whitby, and others, esc'd
1951	Mar 8	Motor fishing boats Success, Gem, Provider A and Lead Us, of Whitby, escorted
	Apr 10	Motor fishing boats Provider A and Lead Us, of Whitby, esc'd
	May 8	Motor fishing boats Pilot Me II and Lead Us, of Whitby, esc'd
	13	Motor fishing boat Lead Us, of Whitby, escorted
	June 23	Motor vessel Dagny, of Groningen, saved vessel and 7
	Aug 13	Barge Cornelia, of Hull, gave help
	Sep 28	Motor fishing vessel Elizabeth Taylor, of Hull, gave help
		Motor fishing vessel Incentive, of Fraserburgh, gave help
	Oct 22	Steamship Gripfast, of Newcastle, stood by
	Nov 4	Motor vessel Gezina, of Rotterdam. gave help
		Motor fishing boat Courage, of Scarborough, gave help
	5	Motor vessel Gezina, of Rotterdam, gave help
	26	Fishing boats Galilee, Success, Provider A, Progress, Venus and Pilot Me, of Whitby, gave help
		Motor fishing vessel Girl Ann, of Fraserburgh, gave help
	Dec 10	Fishing boats Pilot Me II, Success, Progress, Provider A and Lead Us, of Whitby, escorted
1952	Jan 26	Motor fishing boat Pilot Me II, of Whitby, escorted
	Feb 4	Motor fishing boat Lead Us, of Whitby, escorted
	Mar 7	Fishing boats Endeavour, Faith Star, Progress, Venus, Success, Lead Us, Provider A and Pilot Me II, of Whitby, escorted
	28	Fishing boats Lead Us and Pilot Me II, of Whitby, escorted
	31	Twelve fishing boats, of Whitby, escorted
		Lifeboat The Cuttle, of Filey, escorted
	July 20	RAF Meteor Aircraft, landed a body from HM Trawler
	Sep 3	Fishing boat Provider A, of Whitby, gave help
	11	Fishing cobles Silver Line, Floral Queen, Little Lady, Gem, Victory Rose and Enterprise II, of Whitby, escorted
	18	Fishing boats Acorn, Golden Arrow and Elm, of Scotland, and Pilot Me, of Whitby, escorted
	30	Five fishing boats, of Whitby, escorted
	Oct 1	Ten fishing boats, of Whitby, escorted
	10	Fishing boats Lead Us and Pilot Me, of Whitby, escorted
	11	Fourteen fishing boats, escorted
	Nov 11	Fishing boats Pilot Me II, Provider A and Lead Us, of Whitby, escorted
	24	Fishing boats Success I, Faith Star, Pilot Me II, Provider A and Lead Us, of Whitby, escorted
	Dec 17	Fishing boats Faith Star, Progress, Success, Galilee, Provider A, Lead Us and Pilot Me II, of Whitby, escorted
1953	Jan 3	Fishing boats Enterprise II, Galilee, Faith Star, Success II, Lead Us and Pilot Me II, of Whitby, escorted
	31	Fishing boats Enterprise II, Galilee, Faith Star, Success II, and Pilot Me II, of Whitby, escorted
	Feb 4	Fishing boats Provider A, Pilot Me II, Venus, Lead Us and Progress, of Whitby, escorted
	10	Fishing boats Galilee, Provider A, Success and Lead Us, of Whitby, escorted
	Apr 14	Fishing boat Lead Us, of Whitby, escorted
	June 15	Motor vessel C.648, of London, stood by
		Steamship Libra, of Panama, stood by, landed an injured man
	Aug 13	Motor vessel Regency Belle, of Guernsey, put pilot on board
	Sep 22	Trawler Patriot, of Rostock, landed a sick man
1954	Jan 15	Fishing boats Whitby Lass, Foxglove, and others, escorted
	17	Steamship Durward, of Grangemouth, escorted and gave help
	Feb 19	Steamship City of York, of London, landed a sick man
	Mar 4	Fishing boats Lead Us and Falth Star, of Whitby, escorted
	10	Steamship Guildford, of London, saved 18
	24	Sick cobles and twelve motor fishing boats, of Whitby, esc'd
	Apr 15	Fishing boats, of Whitby, escorted
		Fishing boat Foxglove, of Whitby, saved 4
	Oct 25	Fishing boats, of Whitby, escorted
	28	Steamship Pass of Glenogle, of London, landed a body
	Nov 4	Motor fishing boat Venus, of Whitby, saved boat and 5
	15	Five fishing boats, of Whitby, escorted
	Dec 8	Motor fishing boats Pilot Me II, and others, of Whitby, also Motor fishing boat Courage, of Scarborough, escorted
1955	Jan 16	Fishing boat Provider A, of Whitby, escorted boat
	Feb 10	Three fishing boats, of Whitby, escorted boats
	17	Five fishing boats, of Whitby, escorted boats
	Mar 17	Three fishing boats, of Whitby, escorted boats
	26	Motor vessel Lea, of Groningen, landed 4 and stood by

J. W. Archer Reserve Lifeboat
[on station 18.5–1.6.1955]

May 19	Fishing boat Pilot Me, of Whitby, escorted
21	Fishing cobles Three Brothers, Victory Rose and Gem, of Whitby, escorted
	Fishing boats Lead Us, Pilot Me, Faith Star, Venus, Galilee, Progress, Prosperity and Easter Morn, escorted

Mary Ann Hepworth Lifeboat

	Oct 30	Fishing boats Gem and Progress, of Whitby, escorted
	Nov 13	Trawler Erich Honnecker, of Rostock, gave help
	23	Fishing boats, of Whitby, escorted
		Fishing boat Progress, of Whitby, saved boat and 5
	Dec 18	Fishing boat Lead Us, of Whitby, escorted
	30	Fishing boats Pilot Me, Success, Provider A, and Lead Us, of Whitby, escorted
1956	Jan 18	Fishing boats Faith Star, Galilee, Provider A, Lead Us, Success, and Pilot Me, of Whitby, escorted
	Jun 8	Motor fishing coble Enterprise, of Whitby, escorted
	Aug 30	Fishing boat Dorothy, of Whitby, gave help
	31	Fishing boats, of Whitby, and from Scotland, gave help
	Oct 5	Fishing boat Galilee, of Whitby, saved boat and 5
		Three fishing boats, of Whitby, escorted
	Nov 2	Motor fishing boat Lead Us, of Whitby, escorted
	3	Motor fishing boats Lead Us and Provider A, of Whitby, escorted
	14	Fishing boats Success, Lead Us and Pilot Me, of Whitby, escorted
1957	Jul 16	Motor vessel Spontaniety, of London, landed a sick man
	27	Rowing dinghy, saved dinghy and 2
	Sep 14	Six fishing boats, of Whitby, escorted
	Nov 22	Five fishing boats, of Whitby, escorted
	Dec 18	Steamship Thrift, of Aberdeen, stood by
		Steamship Thrift, of Aberdeen, stood by
1958	Feb 17	Fishing boats Provider A and Pilot Me, of Whitby, escorted
	Mar 7	Fishing boat Success, of Whitby, stood by
	Jun 27	Fishing boat Our Confidence, of Bridlington, gave help
	Jul 6	Fishing boat Dorothy, of Whitby, gave help
	Dec 5	Fishing boat Whitby Rose, of Whitby, gave help
1959	Jan 22	Fishing boats Stokesley Rose, Success, Pilot Me and Lead Us, of Whitby, escorted
	Apr 18	Fishing boats Prosperity, Progress, Pilot Me, Lead Us, Easter Morn, Whitby Rose and Stokesley Rose, of Whitby, esc'd
	May 18	Fishing boat Remembrance, of Whitby, stood by
	Sep 3	Steamship Valga, of Leningrad, landed and later reboarded an injured man
	Dec 10	Five fishing boats, of Whitby, escorted
1960	Jan 16	Five fishing boats, of Whitby, escorted
	Feb 16	Three fishing boats, of Whitby, escorted
	Mar 9	Four fishing boats, of Whitby, escorted
	Apr 4	Eight fishing cobles, of Whitby, escorted
	Jul 22	Fishing boat Success, of Whitby, escorted
1961	Jan 6	Eight fishing boats, of Whitby, escorted
	Mar 27	Six fishing boats, of Whitby, escorted
	Oct 17	Fishing fleet, of Whitby, escorted
	Dec 7	Seven fishing boats, of Whitby, escorted
	29	Eight fishing boats, of Whitby, escorted
1962	Mar 2	Motor fishing boats Lead Us and Success, of Whitby, escorted
	Apr 13	Fishing cobles Little Lady and Guide Me, of Whitby, escorted
	May 31	Motor fishing boat Pilot Me, of Whitby, stood by
	July 3	Three fishing boats, of Whitby, stood by
	Sep 12	Five fishing boats, of Whitby, escorted
	Oct 26	Five fishing boats, of Whitby, escorted
	Nov 9	Seven fishing boats, of Whitby, stood by
	Dec 12	Three fishing boats, of Whitby, escorted
1963	Jan 16	Six fishing vessels, of Whitby, gave help and escorted
		RNLB J. G. Graves of Sheffield, of Scarborough, escorted
	Apr 6	Motor fishing vessels, escorted vessels

Rosa Woodd and Phyllis Lunn Reserve Lifeboat
[on station 1.7–30.11.1963]

Jul 5	Motor fishing vessel Wakeful, of Whitby, gave help
Aug 17	Auxiliary yacht Marika II, of Blyth, escorted boat
Nov 20	Seven motor fishing vessels, escorted vessels
26	Motor vessel Eminence, of Rochester, landed a sick man thereby saving a life

Mary Ann Hepworth Lifeboat

1964	Feb 27	Missing children, gave help
	Mar 13	Three fishing boats, of Whitby, escorted
	Apr 25	Local fishing cobles, stood by
	June 1	Motor fishing boat Venus II, of Whitby, gave help
	3	Four fishing boats, of Whitby, escorted
	Sep 25	Fishing boat Ann Elizabeth, of Whitby, saved boat and 3
	Oct 2	Steamship Queensgate, of Goole, stood by
	3	Steamship Queensgate, of Goole, stood by
	23	Fishing boats Ocean Venture and Lead Us, of Whitby, escorted
	25	Motor fishing boat Golden Hope, of Whitby, gave help
1965	Jan 16	Coble Venture, of Whitby, escorted
	27	Five fishing boats, of Whitby, escorted
	Feb 26	Five fishing boats, of Whitby, escorted
		Motor fishing boat Success, of Whitby, escorted
	Apr 19	Eight fishing boats, of Whitby, escorted
	June 7	Motor yacht Seline, of Sandsend (Whitby), gave help
	26	Motor cruiser Dolores, gave help and landed 2
	27	Motor coble Mary, of Whitby, saved coble and 3
	Aug 13	Steamship Cardiganbrook, of London, landed an injured man
	20	Boy cut off by tide, saved 1
	Oct 19	Boy fallen from cliff, gave help
	Nov 13	Fishing coble William and Martha, of Whitby, escorted
	16	Fishing cobles Venture and William and Martha, of Whitby, escorted
	18	Motor fishing boat Ocean Venture, of Whitby, stood by
	22	Fishing boats Ocean Venture, Success and Lead Us, of Whitby, escorted
	25	Fishing boats Wakeful, Success and Provider, of Whitby, esc'd
	27	Motor vessel Fred Everard, of Lodnon, saved 14
		Motor vessel Fred Everard, gave help
	Dec 9	Fishing boats Ocean Venture, Endeavour and Lead Us, of Whitby, escorted
1966	Jan 3	Motor fishing boats Easter Morn and Galilee, of Whitby, esc'd
	5	Steam trawler Arctic Brigand, of Hull, took out doctor and landed a body
	Feb 8	Fishing boats Lead Us and Ocean Venture, of Whitby, esc'd
	Mar 12	Fishing coble William and Martha, of Whitby, escorted
	13	Motor vessel Olna Firth, of Newcastle, landed a sick man
	18	Four fishing boats, of Whitby, escorted
	29	Three fishing boats, of Whitby, escorted
	Apr 10	Fishing boat Golden Hope, escorted
	11	Eight fishing boats, of Whitby, escorted
	May 24	Fishing coble William and Martha, of Whitby, escorted
		Five fishing boats, of Whitby, escorted
	June 8	Fishing boat Provider, of Whitby, gave help
	July 21	Motor vessel Taurus, of Panama, stood by
	Aug 30	Yacht Kalispera, escorted
	Oct 8	Motor cruiser Marigella, gave help
	Nov 21	Fishing boats Lead Us, Wakeful and Ocean Venture, of Whitby, escorted
1967	Jan 5	Fishing boats Ocean Venture, Lead Us and Wakeful, of Whitby, escorted
	24	Motor vessel Egton, of Whitby, stood by
	Apr 5	Fishing coble Dorothy Hughes, of Whitby, escorted
	18	Fishing cobles Provider, Ocean Venture and Success, of Whitby, escorted
	May 15	Fishing boat Success, of Whitby, stood by
	Jun 25	Motor cruiser Mandy, escorted
	27	Fishing boat Summer Rose, of Whitby, gave help

	Oct 1	Yacht Merlin, and others, escorted
	17	Fishing boat Ocean Venture, of Whitby, escorted
	Dec 6	Fishing boats Ocean Venture and Success, of Whitby, stood by
	10	Fishing boat Ocean Venture, of Whitby, stood by
	16	Fishing boats Golden Hope and Ocean Venture, of Whitby, escorted
1968	Jan 3	Four fishing boats, of Whitby, stood by
	Mar 27	Fishing boat Summer Rose, of Whitby, gave help
	Apr 4	Four fishing boats, of Whitby, escorted
	5	Two fishing boats, of Whitby, escorted
	May 28	Fishing boat Endeavour, in tow of fishing boat Achieve, esc'd
	Jun 8	Injured man on the beach, gave help
	Jul 25	Fishing cobles Mary, Sea Harvest and Sea Breeze, of Whitby, escorted
	Oct 6	Converted ship's boat Craigdoon, gave help
1969	May 3	Fishing boat Golden Hope, of Whitby, escorted
	Sep 9	Motor vessel Sustina, of San Francisco, took out doctor and gave help, saving 1

Rosa Woodd and Phyllis Lunn Reserve Lifeboat
[on station 27.9–1.11.1969]

1969	Oct 1	Fishing boat Fairmorn, of Whitby, saved boat and 1

Mary Ann Hepworth Lifeboat

1970	Jan 15	Eight fishing boats, of Whitby, escorted
	31	Fishing boat Jaceena, of Hull, gave help
	Feb 9	Children cut off by the tide, saved 4
	16	Fishing boat Lead Us II, of Whitby, escorted
	Mar 31	Fishing coble Ocean Wonder, of Whitby, escorted
	May 19	Fishing coble David and Amanda, of Whitby, gave help
	Jun 18	Steam trawler Northern Jewel, of Grimsby, landed a sick man
	30	Motor boat Marina, gave help
		Motor fishing boat Ocean Wonder, of Whitby, gave help
	Jul 15	Motor fishing boat Gannet, saved 2
	Aug 1	Motor trawler Ross Tern, of Grimsby, landed a sick man
	17	Rowing boat, saved 1
	23	Dinghy, landed 1
	Sep 1	Motor boat Wave Crest, landed 4 and a dog from Belgian trawler
	13	Motor vessel W. J. H. Wood, of London, landed a sick man
	Nov 3	Fishing boat Golden Hope, of Whitby, escorted
	5	Fishing coble Ocean Wonder, of Whitby, escorted
1971	June 6	Thirteen yachts, stood by
		Yacht Shotgun II, escorted
	27	Motor yacht Philander, of Hull, landed 14 from motor vessel Lady Sorcha, of Rochester
	July 16	Fishing boat Galilee, of Whitby, gave help
	Aug 24	Fishing coble Francis Mary, of Whitby, gave help
	Sep 2	Fishing coble Dorothy Hughes, of Whitby, gave help
	26	Yacht Merlin, escorted
	Oct 3	Cabin cruiser Banjo, gave help
	31	Cabin cruiser Day Go, gave help
1972	Apr 27	Motor fishing boat Golden Hope, of Whitby, escorted
	May 4	Motor cruiser Susie G, saved 2
	July 26	Fishing coble Marianess, of Whitby, saved coble and 3
	Aug 17	Motor trawler Viron 8, landed a sick man
	24	Motor vessel Martina, of Haren-Ems, saved (also a dog) 3
	Oct 27	Persons cut off by tide, gave help
	Nov 7	Fishing coble Renown, of Whitby, gave help
	Dec 18	Fishing boat Golden Hope, of Whitby, gave help
1973	Apr 2	Fishing boat Golden Hope, of Whitby, escorted
	May 29	Trawler Jean Roxane, of Boulogne, landed a sick man
	Sep 9	Coble Sea Fisher, gave help
	16	Cabin cruiser Nicholas, gave help
	Oct 3	Landed a body from the sea
	10	Coble M.A.S., escorted
	Nov 10	Motor vessel Lady Sarita, of Rochester, gave help

1974	Jan 11	Fishing coble Serene, of Whitby, gave help
	16	Two cobles Sunroyd Viper and Friendship, of Whitby, escorted
	Feb 6	Motor fishing vessel Iolite under tow, gave help
	Apr 23	Catamaran Sis, gave help
	May 6	Motor fishing vessel Golden Hope, in tow of fishing boat Whitby Light, of Whitby, escorted
	July 8	Cabin cruiser Mayfly, gave help
	Sep 24	Trimaran Kalu Kun, saved boat and 4
	30	Motor fishing vessel Sea Fisher, gave help

The White Rose of Yorkshire Lifeboat
[on station 24.11.1974]

1974	Dec 12	Three motor fishing vessels, escorted vessels
	21	Motor fishing vessel Golden Hope, gave help
	23	Dutch motor vessel Mercurius, of Spaarndam, landed a sick man
	25	Cabin cruiser Care Free, gave help
1975	Jan 12	Outboard dinghy, gave help
	31	Injured man on board motor fishing vessel Eskglen, landed injured man
	Feb 12	Motor vessel Actuality, of London, stood by boat
	Mar 20	Converted ship's lifeboat, gave help
	21	Motor fishing vessel Resolution, saved boat and 2
	26	Two motor fishing vessels Golden Hope and Lead Us, escorted boats
	Apr 4	Three fishing cobles Sea Fisher, Advance and Lead Us, of Whitby, escorted
	13	Seven cobles Deep Harmony, Endurance, Brighter Dawn, Sea Breeze, Amanda D, Endeavour and Sally Lunn, escorted
	26	Sick man on board motor vessel Queensland, of London, landed sick man
	May 14	Coble Advance and keelboats Success and Ocean Venture, escorted boats
	21	Coble Advance, gave help
	22	Three motor fishing vessels Lead Us, Success and Success II, escorted
	June 3	Motor fishing vessel Success, escorted boat
	July 15	Motor fishing vessel George Weatherill, gave help
	Aug 10	Fishing coble Silver Spray, gave help
	17	Fishing coble Faith L, gave help
	30	Motor boat Terry Ann, saved boat and 5
	Sep 9	Cabin cruiser Joan, in tow of cabin cruiser Galante, escorted
	29	Motor fishing vessel Golden Hope, gave help
	Oct 3	Fishing coble Gillian and Richard, escorted boat
	25	Coble Elliott Duke, gave help
	Dec 18	Motor fishing vessel Pacem In Terris, saved vessel and 3
1976	Jan 20	Coble Sundryd Viper, escorted
	Feb 4	Fishing boat Geaorge Weatherill, in tow of coble Success, escorted
	5	Motor vessel Collhusen, of Hamburg, gave help
	27	HMS Brereton, in collision with fishing boat Cyrano, of Esbjerg, gave help
	Mar 12	Coble Wardley, gave help
	21	Rubber dinghy, saved dinghy and 2
	24	Fishing boat Ocean Venture, landed a sick man

44-001 Relief Lifeboat

	Apr 16	Motor boat Snow Goose, gave help
	May 13	Cobles Ocean Venture, Golden Hope and Whitby Light, escorted
	30	Cabin cruiser Tonique, saved cruiser and 6

The White Rose of Yorkshire Lifeboat

	June 3	Fishing boat George Weatherill, landed an injured man
	Sep 2	Fishing boat George Weatherill, gave help
	21	Fishing boat Anmara, gave help

William and Mary Durham Relief Lifeboat
[on station 20.9–10.1976]

Sep 30   Fishing boat Admiral Van Tromp, of Leith, landed 1

The White Rose of Yorkshire Lifeboat

	Dec 5	Cobles Alliance and Sharmalie, escorted
1977	Jan 17	Motor fishing vessel Carol Ann, gave help
	25	Fishing boat Conquest, escorted to Scarborough
	Mar 27	Fishing cobles Friendship, Revenge and Endeavour A, escorted
	Apr 13	Motor fishing vessel George Weatherill, in tow of fishing coble Scorseby, escorted
	May 14	Cabin cruiser Yorkist II, gave help
	June 16	Motor fishing vessel Golden Hope, saved vessel and 3
	July 19	Fishing coble Advance, saved boat and 3
	Sep 13	Yacht Cumulus, gave help

Edian Courtauld Relief Lifeboat

1977   Oct 8   Various motor boats, escorted boats

The White Rose of Yorkshire Lifeboat

	Dec 4	Fishing coble Bay of Islands, of Whitby, gave help
	6	Motor fishing vessels Our Heritage, Our Rachel, Casamanda and Independence, of Scarborough, escorted vessels
1978	Jan 11	Fishing cobles Michaela Christopher, Rachel Claire, C.K.S. and Wakeful, of Whitby, escorted
	18	Motor fishing vessel Deevale, of Aberdeen, stood by

Edian Courtauld Relief Lifeboat
[on station 6.10.1977–21.4.1978]

Mar 20   Fishing coble Hannah Mary, gave help

The White Rose of Yorkshire Lifeboat

	Apr 10	Motor fishing vessels Golden Hope and C.K.S., escorted
	May 25	Fishing coble Karen D, escorted boat
	June 10	Sick man on board motor fishing vessel Prince Igor, took out doctor and landed a sick man
	July 10	Motor fishing vessel Esk Glen, gave help
	11	Injured man on board fishing vessel Ocean Venture, took out doctor and landed injured man
1979	Jan 2	Cabin cruiser Manora, gave help
	Feb 8	Motor fishing vessel Wakeful, of Whitby, stood by

T. G. B. Relief Lifeboat
[on station 6.4–29.6.1979]

Apr 15   Fishing coble Brighter Dawn, of Whitby, gave help
May 1   Fishing coble Gaidan, escorted boat

The White Rose of Yorkshire Lifeboat

	Sep 13	Motor fishing boat Cragievaar, in tow of fishing vessel Success, escorted vessels
	Oct 13	Fishing coble, gave help
	Nov 10	Sick man on board trawler Jean Helene, landed sick man
	Dec 11	Fishing boats, escorted boats
	14	Fishing boats Guide Me and Golden Hope, escorted boats
1980	Jan 25	Fishing cobles, escorted boats
	31	Fishing boats, escorted boats
	Mar 25	Injured man on motor fishing boat Clee, landed injured man
	Apr 2	Twenty persons cut off by tide, gave help
	8	Fishing cobles, escorted boats
	26	Persons cut off by tide, gave help

T. G. B. Relief Lifeboat
[on station 13.6–15.9.1980]

No services

The White Rose of Yorkshire Lifeboat

	Sep 20	Fishing cobles Rose of England and Lady Jacqueline, escorted boats
	21	Yacht Karlee, escorted boat
	Nov 25	Fishing vessels, escorted vessels
	Dec 2	Fishing vessels, escorted vessels
	16	Injured man on board cargo vessel Helen Schulte, took out doctor and landed injured man
1981	Feb 10	Three canoes, saved 2
	Mar 22	Fishing vessel Rachel Clare, saved vessel and 4
	May 1	Fishing coble Karen D, escorted boat
	26	Sick man on board motor fishing vessel Carlo, took out doctor and landed a sick man
	June 21	Motor boat Sundance II, gave help
	July 23	Fishing coble Royal Sovereign, gave help
		Fishing cobles, escorted boats

T. G. B. Relief Lifeboat
[on station 9.8–12.9.1981]

No services

The White Rose of Yorkshire Lifeboat

	Oct 4	Yachts, escorted boats
		Motor boats, escorted boats
	8	Sick man on board motor boat Joseph Conrad, took out doctor
	11	Motor fishing vessel Rachel Claire, in tow of motor fishing vessel Golden Hope, escorted
	18	Injured man on board motor fishing vessel Venus, took out doctor and landed an injured man
	25	Fishing coble Mistral, gave help
	Nov 23	Fishing vessels, escorted vessels
	Dec 18	Fishing boats, escorted boats
1982	Feb 12	Fishing coble Endurence, of Whitby, landed 3
	18	Motor fishing vessel Golden Hope, of Whitby, saved vessel and 3
	Mar 3	Fishing coble Repus, of Whitby, saved boat and 2
	Apr 2	Fishing vessel Golden Hope, of Whitby, gave help
	8	Fishing vessel Rayella, of Grimsby, gave help
	July 17	Rowing boat George Nasher, in tow of fishing boat Howdale, escorted
	Aug 7	Speed boat Surf Red, saved boat and 3
	10	Fishing vessel Fairwind, of Ballantrae, landed 3 and saved vessel
	29	Fishing coble Elliot Duke, gave help
	Oct 24	Fishing coble Companion, in tow of fishing boat Gina St Belle, escorted
	Nov 28	Fishing vessel Linda Louise, escorted vessel
	Dec 29	Man cut off by tide, stood by
1983	Jan 31	Motor fishing vessel Sonjan, of Peterhead, escorted vessel
	Feb 10	Fishing coble Guide Me, of Whitby, escorted boat
	Mar 23	Fishing boats, escorted boats
	June 23	Motor fishing vessel Pentland Wave, gave help

Wavy Line Relief Lifeboat
[on station 24.6–13.9.1983]

July 5	Speedboat, saved boat
9	Motor boat Golden Days, escorted boat
28	Motor cruiser Pentland Wave, saved boat and 10
Aug 15	Injured man on board fishing vessel Nichola Suzanne, landed injured man
28	Speedboat, recovered wreckage
31	Cabin cruiser Osprey, escorted boat

The White Rose of Yorkshire Lifeboat

	Sep 12	Cargo vessel Renate S, recovered wreckage
	13	Rubber dinghy, saved boat
	28	Yacht Serenade, saved boat and 6
	Oct 18	Fishing coble Karen D, in tow of motor fishing vessel George Weatherill, escorted
	Nov 15	Fishing coble Mark D, escorted boat
		Trawlers, escorted vessels
	Dec 21	Aircraft of USA, gave help
1984	Jan 18	Pilot launch, escorted boat
	Mar 9	Fishing vessel Navell, of Grimsby, stood by vessel
	Apr 6	Pilot launch, gave help
	May 4	Cabin cruiser Marina, gave help
	26	Cabin cruiser Moon Rake, gave help
	June 6	Motor fishing vessel George Weatherill, of Kirkwall, landed 5
		Motor fishing vessel George Weatherill, of Kirkwall, (second service) gave help
	22	Yacht Highfly, gave help
	July 18	Cabin cruiser Fairwater, gave help
	29	Dinghy Hunky Dory, gave help
	Aug 11	Injured man on board motor fishing vessel Prince Bernhardt, landed injured man
	23	Yacht Blyth Andora, escorted boat
	24	Fishing vessel Trudella, gave help
	Sep 4	Motor fishing vessels Venus, Lead Us, and Scoresby, escorted
	23	Yacht Rosie III, of Hartlepool, escorted boat
	Oct 20	Yacht Blue Streak, of Scarborough, saved boat and 3
	Nov 15	Six fishing cobles, escorted boats
	16	Motor fishing vessel Golden Hope, escorted vessel
		Fishing coble Deep Harmony, escorted boat
		Motor fishing vessels Three Boys and Clavis, escorted vessels
	Dec 16	Fishing coble All My Suns, of Whitby, gave help
	26	Motor cruiser Sundance II, of Whitby, gave help
1985	Jan 24	Motor fishing vessel Shulamit, of Blyth, escorted vessel

Wavy Line Relief Lifeboat
[on station 10.3–25.7.1985]

	Mar 19	Thirty persons cut off by tide, gave help
	Apr 9	Fishing coble Merlin, of Whitby, escorted boat
	27	Fishing vessel Helga Maria, escorted vessel
	July 3	Fishing coble Pilot Me, gave help
	22	Fishing coble Amanda D, of Whitby, gave help

The White Rose of Yorkshire Lifeboat

	July 25	Fishing coble Redemption, of Whitby, saved 2
	27	Yacht Taal, gave help
	Aug 25	Woman overboard from yacht Floozie, saved boat and 1
	26	Sick man on board fishing vessel North Star, of Whitby, landed a sick man
	31	Yacht Escapade, of Whitby, gave help
	Sep 2	Motor fishing vessel Dominator, of Whitby, gave help
	Oct 28	Fishing vessel Radiant Morn, of Whitby, gave help
	Nov 8	Motor cruiser Crescendo, gave help
	26	Fishing vessel Resolution, of Whitby, gave help
	27	Fishing vessel Alliance, of Whitby, escorted vessel
		Fishing vessel Harvester, of Whitby, in tow of fishing vessel Saxon Lady, escorted
	30	Fishing vessel Swan, escorted vessel
	Dec 1	Fishing vessel Resolution A, gave help
	6	Fishing cobles Michaela Christopher and Harvester, escorted
1986	Feb 25	Fishing vessel Scoresby and Gemma Fidelis, escorted vessels
	Mar 16	Fishing vessel Dark Island, of Whitby, saved vessel and 3
	Apr 22	Fishing vessel Emulate, took out RN Bomb Disposal Unit and gave help
	June 5	Fishing vessels, escorted vessels
	28	Motor boat, saved boat and 2

	July 28	Yacht Golden Dolphin, gave help
	Aug 20	Injured man on board fishing vessel Kirkella, of Hull, landed an injured man
	Sep 3	Cobles, escorted boats

Wavy Line Relief Lifeboat
[on station 20.9.1986–19.2.87]

	Sep 23	Fishing vessel Our Heritage, of Whitby, escorted vessel
	Oct 4	Twn persons cut off by tide, gave help
	Nov 1	Coble Mark D, escorted boat
	11	Cabin cruiser Astgood, gave help
	24	Coble Karen D, gave help
	25	Coble Christina Mary, gave help
1987	Jan 21	Fishing boat, of Whitby, landed 1
	26	Fishing coble, escorted vessel
	28	Cobles, escorted boats
		Fishing vessels Sardia Louise and Golden Hope, of Whitby, escorted vessels

The White Rose of Yorkshire Lifeboat

	Apr 12	Fishing boat Rose Marie, of Whitby, landed 2
	20	Fishing vessel Kelly, of Whitby, escorted and saved vessel
	May 20	Eight cobles, escorted boats
	27	Cabin cruiser Lucy, gave help
	June 24	Coble Wendy Ann, of Whitby, gave help
	July 13	Injured man on board fishing vessel Emulate, of Whitby, landed an injured man
	21	Two cobles, escorted boats
		Fishing coble Michaela Christopher, escorted boat
	25	Fishing coble Michaela Christopher, escorted boat
	Nov 18	Fishing vessel Arie Dirk, of Barrow, gave help
	25-6	Fishing vessel Mary Allison, gave help and escorted vessel
1988	Feb 3	Fishing vessel Talisman, escorted vessel
	23	Fishing vessels Provider, Kelly and Venus, escorted vessels
	23	Fishing coble Michaela Christopher, escorted boat
	Mar 10	Sailing dinghy, saved boat and 1
	11	Injured man on board fishing vessel Sarah Thinneson, of Grimsby, landed an injured man
	Apr 4	Fishing vessel Libby, of Whitby, gave help
	9	Yacht Cymba, saved 1
		Cobles Alliance and Progress, of Whitby, escorted boats
	26	Coble Amanda D, gave help
	May 2	Yacht Aligandy, gave help
	June 4	Fishing vessel Sea Ranger, of Whitby, escorted boat

Khami Relief Lifeboat
[on station 11.6–13.9.1988]

	June 12	Fishing vessel Karen D, in tow of fishing vessel Golden HOPE, escorted
	19	Fishing vessel Karen D, of Whitby, gave help
	29	Fishing vessel Inger, of Grimsby, gave help
	July 3	Motor boat How Much, gave help
	25	Fishing vessel Nicola Faith, of Whitby, gave help
	Aug 7	Cabin cruiser Barry Andrew, saved boat and 7
	14	Fishing vessel Tancho, of Hartlepool, saved vessel
	22	Yachts tender, recovered boat
	25	Catamaran Chefren, of Amble, gave help

The White Rose of Yorkshire Lifeboat

	Oct 10	Inshore Lifeboat D-369, of Whitby, saved boat
	19	Fishing coble Michaela Christopher, of Whitby, escorted
		Coble Nicola Faith, of Whitby, escorted
	Nov 2	Fishing boat Nova Venture, of Whitby, escorted
	27	Fishing vessel O. B. J., of Whitby, craft brought in – gave help
	Dec 1	Motor fishing vessel Eventide, of Whitby, , escorted

City of Sheffield Lifeboat
[on station 12.12.1988]

1989	Jan 22	Cabin cruiser Billy B II, gave help
	Feb 27	Mine, took out RN Bomb Disposal Unit
		RN Bomb Disposal Unit inflatable, saved boat and 4
	Mar 19	Fishing coble Pride of Mansfield, of Whitby, gave help
	Apr 9	Cabin cruiser Weather or Knot, gave help
	26	Passenger vessel Regal Lady, gave help
	May 1	Fishing vessel Caro-Sal, gave help
	2	Motor boat Barry Andrew, with coble Amanda D in tow, gave help
	11	Mine, took out RN Bomb Disposal Unit
	12	Fishing vessel Golden Hope, gave help
	28	Yacht Magna, gave help
	30	Fishing vessels Dominator A and Blenheim, escorted
	June 1	Yacht Karoline, saved vessel and 5
	21	Ten cobles, escorted boats
		Yacht Blue Hawk, escorted
		Yacht Duck, saved boat and 2
	29	Fishing vessel Scoresby, in tow of fishing vessel Lead Us, gave help
	July 1	Fishing vessel Andromeda, gave help
	9	Fishing vessel Nova Venture, gave help
	15	Fishing vessel Rose of Sharon, gave help
	19	Fishing vessel Solitaire, of Whitby, gave help
	22	Yacht Blue Hope, gave help
	31	Fishing vessel Indomitable, of Whitby, gave help
	Aug 5	Cabin cruiser Suzals 3, gave help
	8	Motor boat Kingfisher, gave help
	24	Sail Training vessel James Cook, of Newcastle, gave help
	28	Two persons cut off by the tide, gave help
	Oct 5	Fishing vessel Golden Hope, of Whitby, gave help

Owen and Anne Aisher Relief Lifeboat
[on station 21.10.1989–20.7.90]

	Nov 2	Fishing coble Yorkshire Rose, gave help
	6	Injured man on fishing vessel Ina B, landed an injured man
1990	Jan 25	Fishing coble Guide Me, gave help
	Feb 19	Fishing coble Yorkshire Rose, gave help
	21	Fishing vessel B. M. Melnic, gave help
	Apr 1	Motor boat Gemma Lee Ann, escorted boat
		Motor boat Lucky Me, escorted boat
	3	Fishing vessel Nova Venture, stood by
		Fishing vessel George Wetherill, stood by
		Fishing vessel Sophie Louise, gave help
	June 1	Fishing coble My Pal, gave help
	7	Fishing vessel Blenheim A, escorted vessel
	12	Fishing vessel Scoresby, gave help
	July 3	Sick man on fishing vessel Guide Me, landed a sick man
	15	Yacht Humberella, gave help

City of Sheffield Lifeboat

	July 23	Yacht Karen Kelly, gave help
	25	Sick man on board motor boat Heather of Burnham, landed a sick man
	31	Motor boat Lady Tine, saved boat and 2
	Sep 6	Took out fire brigade personnel and equipment to fire at Kettleness
	8	Sick man on board fishing vessel Dirk Dirk, landed a sick man
	Oct 6	Fishing vessel Ocean Venture, gave help
	26	Fishing coble Solitaire, gave help
	Nov 2	Fishing vessels Margreta M and Pioneer, escorted vessels
	7	Fishing coble Pride of Mansfield, saved boat and 2
	30	Fishing vessel Nova Venture, gave help
1991	Jan 18	Fishing vessel Harvester, gave help
	Feb 16	Fishing vessel Nicola Faith, saved vessel and 4
	17	Fishing vessel Kelly, stood by

	18	Fishing vessel Nova Venture, saved vessel and 4
	27	Fishing vessel Resolution, gave help
	Mar 31	Fishing vessel North Star, gave help
	Apr 16	Six fishing vessels, escorted vessels
	18	Fishing vessel Silver Line W, escorted vessel
	30	Fishing vessel Guiding Star, gave help
	June 3	Fishing vessel Pride and Joy, gave help
	8	Yacht Merlin, gave help
	11	Fishing vessel Aurora, gave help
	July 10	Yacht Reyward T, gave help
	13	Fishing vessel Navicular, gave help
	21	Fishing boat Norseman, landed a sick man
	29	Fishing vessel Lilly B, gave help
	Aug 3	Sick man on board fishing boat Sea Roma, took out doctor and landed a sick man
	4	Injured man on board fishing vessel Nova Venture, landed an injured man
	11	Yacht Vedra, gave help – craft brought in
	15	Fishing vessel Portunus, gave help
	18	Fishing vessel Katy Jane, gave help
	Sep 3	Sick man on board fishing vessel Dirk Dirk, gave help
	28	Cargo vessel Kirsten, stood by
	29	Cargo vessel Vineta, stood by
	Oct 9	Fishing vessel Allegiance, gave help
	16	Fishing vessel Resolution A, gave help
	Nov 3	Fishing vessel Harvester, gave help
	5	RoRo cargo ferry Stora-Korsnas Link I, stood by
	27	Sick woman on board cargo vessel Bergen, took out doctor and landed a sick woman
	Dec 12	Fishing coble Endurance, gave help
1992	Jan 8	Fishing vessel Sarb J, in tow of fishing vessel Radiant Morn, gave help
	18	Cabin cruiser Coronet, saved boat and 2
	Feb 16	Fishing vessels Aurora and Pride and Joy, escorted vessels
	Mar 5	Fishing vessel Surdmaa, saved vessel and recovered liferaft
	Apr 5	Sick man on board fishing vessel Provider, landed a sick man
	14	Yacht Cheryl Claire, escorted boat
	18	Yacht Karlee, in tow of yacht Ladybird, gave help
	May 17	Rowing boat, saved boat
	20	Power boat, landed 1
		Power boat in tow of Whitby Inshore Lifeboat, escorted boats
		Fishing coble Jane Elizabeth, gave help
		Yacht Sylvia, escorted boat
	23	Yacht Summer Wine, gave help
	June 11	Motor boat Sea Urchin, gave help
	13	Cabin cruiser Lucky Bird, gave help
	15	Fishing vessel Margareta M, gave help
	21	Yacht Reynard T, gave help
	25	Motor boat My Pal, gave help
	26	Injured man on fishing vessel Aurora, landed an injured man
	30	Fishing vessel Provider, escorted vessel
	July 11	Fishing vessel My Pal, gave help
	21	Fishing vessel Harvester, gave help
	31	Cabin cruiser Saros, escorted boat
	Aug 9	Cabin cruiser Flying Dutchman, gave help
	Sep 14	Fishing vessel Jeulan, gave help
	23	Yacht Zelia B, gave help

Owen and Anne Aisher Relief Lifeboat
[on station 30.9–7.12.1992]

	Oct 11	Two persons cut off by tide and one person attempting the rescue thereof, stood by
		Fishing vessel Nova Venture, escorted vessel
	12	Fishing vessel Opportune, gave help
	13	Fishing vessel Margareta M, gave help
	26	Fishing vessel George Wetherill, gave help
	28	Fishing vessel Caro Sal, escorted vessel
	Nov 10	Fishing vessel Success, saved vessel and 4

City of Sheffield Lifeboat

	Dec 2	Fishing vessel Darren S, gave help
	18	Fishing vessel Lead Us Forth, gave help
	29	Fishing vessel Sea Dan, escorted vessel
1993	Jan 26	Fishing vessel Indomitable, saved boat and 3
	Feb 20	Rubber dinghy, assisted to save 1
	Mar 28	Motor boat Carol Ann, escorted boat
	May 6	Fishing vessel Pride of Mansfield, gave help
		Motor boat Trebble B, gave help
	9	Fishing vessel Nova Venture, saved vessel and 4
	19	Fishing vessel Lead Us Forth, gave help
	22	Yacht Aqua Venture, gave help
	23	Motor cruiser Puffin, gave help
	31	Fishing vessel Deep Harmony III, gave help
	June 14	Fishing vessel Ina B, landed 4 and saved vessel
	July 12	Fishing vessel Resolution A, gave help
		Yacht Poppea, gave help
	20	Yacht Tron, saved boat and 2
	31	Two skin divers, gave help
	Aug 5	Fishing vessel Success II, gave help
		Fishing cobles, escorted boats
		Fishing coble Guiding Star, gave help
	17	Cabin cruiser Box A Day, escorted boat
	22	Fishing vessel Radiant Morn, in tow of fishing vessel Kristian Jo, gave help
	28	Motor boat Tintoria, gave help
	31	Fishing vessel Osprey, gave help
	Sep 3	Dredger Sandsend, stood by
	23	Fishing vessel Nova Venture, gave help
		Fishing vessel Maid of Iron, gave help
	26	Fishing vessel Lead Us Forth, escorted
		Fishing vessel Kristianjo, escorted vessel
	Oct 2	Fishing vessel Kelly, in tow of fishing vessel Opportune, gave help
	3	Fishing vessel Sea Breeze, gave help
	6	Fishing vessel Silver Echo, gave help
	8	Fishing vessel Boy Tom, gave help
	13	Fishing vessel Kingfisher, escorted vessel
	26	Fishing vessel Kingfisher, gave help
	Nov 17	Injured man on board fishing vessel St Andrew, gave help
	22	Fishing vessel Nicola Faith, gave help
	25	Fishing vessel Shy Torque, gave help
	Dec 23	Fishing vessel Sarb J, stood by
1994	Jan 12	Fishing vessel Valdee, saved vessel and 3
	16	Fishing vessels Pride and Joy and Rose Ann, escorted vessels
	20	Fishing vessel Sarb J, stood by vessel
	Jan 24	Fishing vessel Selina Ann, four persons and craft brought in
	Feb 2	Fishing vessel St Leger, saved vessel and 4
	5	Sailboard, saved board
		Sailboard, saved board and 1
	9	Fishing vessel Selina Ann, stood by
	Mar 2	Fishing vessel Radiant Morn, in tow of fishing vessel Venus, saved boat and 4
	13	Fishing vessel St Leger, escorted vessel
	18	Fishing coble Charisma, escorted boat
		Fishing cobles, escorted boats
	Apr 30	Two persons cut off by the tide, gave help
	May 1	Yachts, escorted boats
		Motor boat, escorted boat
	4	Fishing vessel Provider, three persons and craft brought in
	12	Yacht Bonify, two persons and craft brought in
	27	Yacht Chenoa, gave help
	June 7	Motor cruiser Lorna L, three persons and craft brought in
	16	Missing diver, gave help
		Diver support craft Dive Action, gave help
	July 3	Motor cruiser Soup Dragon, gave help
		Motor cruiser Lorna L, saved boat and 4
	19	Fishing vessel Caro Sal, four persons and craft brought in

	26	Fishing vessel Nova Venture, saved vessel and 3
	27	Mine in sea, gave help
	29	Fishing vessel Boy Mike, three persons and craft brought in
	Aug 7	Ten persons cut off by tide, ten persons brought in – saved by another lifeboat
	27	Three divers, saved 3
	Sep 1	Runswick Rescue Boat, Staithes and Runswick ILB B-576 and Whitby ILB D-369, escorted

The Famous Grouse Relief Lifeboat
[on station 2.9–18.12.1994]

	21	Fishing vessel Deep Harmony III, escorted vessel
	27	Fishing vessel Selina Ann, escorted vessel
	Nov 26	Injured man onboard fishing vessel Clifford Noel, landed an injured man
	Dec 3	Fishing vessel Samantha, stood by vessel
	10	Fishing vessel Caro Sal, saved vessel and 4

City of Sheffield Lifeboat

	24	Fishing vessel Kingfisher, four persons and craft brought in
1995	Jan 7	Fishing vessel Selina Ann, saved boat and 2
	15	Fishing vessel Fiddlers Green, three and craft brought in
		Fishing vessel Natalie B, assisted to save vessel and 6
	16	Fishing vessel Natalie B, saved vessel and 6
	26	Fishing vessel Pride and Joy, escorted vessel
	Feb 8	Fishing vessel Heather of Burnham, three persons and craft brought in
	22	Fishing vessel Silver Line W, escorted vessel
	Mar 11	Fishing vessel Sara Maria, landed 5 and vessel saved
	31	Fishing coble Endurance, two persons and craft brought in
	Apr 1	Yacht Thavma, three persons and craft brought in
	9	Fishing vessel North Star, three persons and craft brought in
	May 13	Yacht Fir Grace, landed 3 and craft brought in
	18	Fishing vessel Anais, two persons and craft brought in
	21	Motor boat Exel in tow of motor boat At Last, two persons and craft brought in
	June 2	Sick woman onboard sail training vessel Black Diamond, landed a sick woman
	17	Fishing vessel Wakeful, four persons and craft brought in
	24	Fishing vessel Codonga Two, landed 2 and craft brought in
	July 5	Fishing coble Alliance, saved boat and 3
	20	Fishing vessel Venture, two persons and craft brought in
	22	Motor cruiser Lorna L, six persons and craft brought in
	23	Fishing vessel Valiant, one person and craft brought in
	25	Fishing vessel Girls Own, two persons and craft brought in
	29	Dinghy, craft brought in
		Motor cruiser Lorna L, saved boat and 3
	Aug 2	Fishing vessel Maid of Iron, three and craft brought in
	3	Fishing vessel Jacqueline Louise, four and craft brought in
	5	Whitby ILB D 369, saved boat and 3
	7	Yacht Let It Be, landed 2 and craft brought in
	12	Fishing vessel Osprey, three persons and craft brought in
	13	Yacht Petrafin, three persons and craft brought in
	29	Fishing vessel Steel Away, landed 2 and craft brought in
	Sep 3	Cabin cruiser Sea Spray, two persons and craft brought in
	10	Fishing vessel Radiant Morn, six persons and craft brought in
	30	Fishing vessel Patricia Barry, four persons and craft brought in
	Oct 1	Yacht Tsimshian, assisted to save boat and 3
	3	Fishing vessel Helen Claire, gave help
	9	Man fallen from cliffs, assisted to save 1
	14	Sick man on fishing vessel Deep Harmony, landed a sick man
		Motor cruiser Lorna L, three persons and craft brought in
	Nov 28	Fishing vessel Yorkshire Rose, two and craft brought in
	29	Fishing vessel Joshan, three persons and craft brought in
	Dec 3	Fishing vessel Ceedan, three persons and craft brought in
1996	Jan 30	Fishing vessel Provider, of Whitby, landed 3, craft brought in
	Feb 14	Fishing vessel Radiant Morn, of Whitby, five persons and craft brought in

Mar 24	Diver support craft C2 Diver, five persons and craft brought in
30	Fishing vessel Tamara, three persons and craft brought in
Apr 3	Barge Jodie, assisted to save craft and 3
10	Motor cruiser Pippin, one person and craft brought in

George and Mary Webb Lifeboat
[on station 10.4.1996]

Apr 18	Fishing vessel Cadonga Two, escorted craft
22	Fishing vessel Ocean Herald II, five and craft brought in
28	Fishing vessel Gannet with fishing vessel Never Can Tell in tow, escorted craft
May 5	Fishing vessel Tamara, three persons and craft brought in
13	Fishing vessel Good Intent, four persons and craft brought in
14	Cabin cruiser, three persons and craft brought in
July 2	Sixteen persons cut off by tide at Gunny Hole, landed 16
19	Motor boat Lager II, two persons and craft brought in
23	Cabin cruiser Lady Helen, two persons and craft brought in

Connel Elizabeth Cargill Relief Lifeboat
[on station 13.8–26.9.1996]

Aug 20	Speedboat, escorted craft
	Motor boat Sea Ranger, escorted craft
Sep 15	Fishing vessel Lord Halden, three persons and craft brought in

George and Mary Webb Lifeboat

Oct 3	Yacht Butterfly, saved craft and 2
30	Surfboard, assisted to save 1
Nov 2	Fishing vessel Silver Line W, three and craft brought in
6	Man fallen from Fish Quay, saved 1
1997 Jan 22	Fishing vessel Radiant Morn, four and craft brought in
Feb 16	Fishing vessel Opportune, four persons and craft brought in
Mar 9	Fishing vessel Anne Marie, escorted craft
16	Motor boat Shellron, escorted craft
Apr 2	Five persons cut off by the tide, assisted to save 5
15	Fishing vessels Silver Line W and Hunter II, escorted craft
	Fishing vessels Cadonger Too, Achetes, Yorkshire Rose, Dominator A, Quest and Pride and Joy, escorted craft
	Fishing vessels Steelaway and Christandale, escorted craft
20	Fishing vessel Gannet, three persons and craft brought in

Henry Heys Duckworth Relief Lifeboat
[on station 25.4–22.5.1997]

May 10	Motor cruiser Marina, four persons and craft brought in
20	Fishing vessel Embrace, two persons and craft brought in

George and Mary Webb Lifeboat

29	Rubber dinghy, three persons and craft brought in
June 10	Car over cliffs, landed a body
21	Cabin cruiser Up Yours, escorted craft
30	Relief lifeboat ON.1131, of Hartlepool, escorted craft
July 6	Injured woman on board motor boat Kismet, injured woman brought in
9	Yacht Gilla, one person and craft brought in

Henry Heys Duckworth Relief Lifeboat
[on station 2.8–18.10.1997]

Aug 6	Fishing vessel Yorkshire Rose, landed 2 and craft brought in
	Lifeboat ON.1212, of Whitby, escorted craft
10	Cabin cruiser Phoenix, two persons and craft brought in
12	Yacht Nadine, gave help
19	Yacht Quatro, gave help
31	Two divers, gave help
Sep 2	Fishing vessel Four Seasons, landed 3 and craft brought in
20	Fishing vessel Cadonga Too, four persons and craft brought in
21	Fishing vessel Sea Ranger, three persons and craft brought in

George and Mary Webb Lifeboat

Oct 20	Fishing vessel Sara Thinnesen, four and craft brought in
30	Fishing vessel Deep Harmony, landed 3 and craft brought in
Nov 3	Fishing vessel Regulus, four persons and craft brought in
23	Fishing vessel Tamara, three persons and craft brought in
26	Fishing vessel Pride and Joy, three and craft brought in
29	Fishing vessel Coamandel, gave help
Dec 14	Fishing vessel Eclipse, two persons and craft brought in
19	Fishing vessel Kristanjo, in tow of vessel Carisan, gave help
21	Fishing vessel Silver Line, of Whitby, three persons and craft brought in
1998 Jan 8	Fishing vessel Orion II, four persons and craft brought in
17	Fishing vessel Mary Ann, of Whitby, landed 3 and craft brought in
21	Fishing vessel Arrivain, Whitby, five and craft brought in
30	Fishing vessel Sarah Thinnesen, four persons and craft brought in
Feb 1	Sick man on board fishing vessel Enterprise, Whitby, sick man brought in
12	Fishing vessel Sarah Thinnesen, Whitby, five persons and craft brought in
20	Fishing vessel Tamara, escorted craft
Mar 6	Tanker Dutch Glory, escorted craft
	Two fishing vessels, escorted craft
15	Fishing vessel North Star, 12 persons and craft brought in
20	Fishing vessel Tamara, of Whitby, three persons and craft brought in
Apr 25	Cargo vessel Rema, recovered wreckage
May 22	Yacht Kosmipoliet, landed 2 and craft brought in
29	Fishing vessel Mimosa, two persons and craft brought in
	Fishing vessel Orion II, landed 4 and craft brought in
June 14	Fishing vessel Guiding Star, in tow of fishing vessel Star Award, escorted craft
	Fishing vessel Revenge, two persons and craft brought in
26	Trimaran Panderino, of Utrecht (Netherlands), two persons and craft brought in
28	Fishing vessel Regulus, escorted craft
July 2	Fishing vessel Sardius, Whitby, four persons and craft brought in
	Fishing vessel Venus, six persons and craft brought in
July 5	Inshore lifeboat D-521, of Whitby, escorted craft
11	Cabin cruiser Sea Chimp, escorted craft
	Diver support craft Attack, six persons and craft brought in

Edward Duke of Windsor Relief Lifeboat
[on station 8.8–15.11.1998]

Aug 23	Yacht Flying Fox, saved craft and 2
Sep 19	Yacht Butterfly, landed 2 and craft brought in
22	Fishing vessel Appin I in tow of fishing vessel Roseanne, escorted craft
26	Cabin cruiser Whoo, two persons and craft brought in
Oct 7	Fishing vessel Headway VI, gave help
15	Fishing vessel Mary Ann, landed 3 and craft brought in
Nov 2	Fishing vessel Crusader, one person and craft brought in
3	Fishing vessel Coromandel, escorted craft
7	Fishing vessel Regulus, two persons and craft brought in
12	Fishing vessel Sarah Thinnesen, gave help

George and Mary Webb Lifeboat

21	Two youths cut off by the tide, assisted to save 2
25	Fishing vessel Pride and Joy, escorted craft
1999 Jan 24	Powerboat Orca, three persons and craft brought in
Feb 17	Woman fallen from Whitby Cliffs, stood by
27	Fishing vessel Charisma, two persons and craft brought in
Mar 9	Fishing vessel Ocean May, gave help
26	Fishing vessel Ramara, escorted craft
30	Cabin cruiser Rickshaw, two persons and craft brought in

Apr 1   Fishing vessel Tamara, three persons and craft brought in
30   Fishing vessel Yorkshire Rose, escorted craft
May 2   Commercial angling vessel Katy Two, four persons and craft brought in
6   Sail training vessel Black Diamond, eight persons and craft brought in

Edward Duke of Windsor Relief Lifeboat

23   Fishing vessel Christendale, three and craft brought in

George and Mary Webb Lifeboat

29   Speedboat Orkney Flyer, two persons and craft brought in
30   Yacht Far La, two persons and craft brought in
June 6   Yacht Blue Dling, escorted craft
8   Yacht Ursula, escorted craft
19   Cabin cruiser Jo Lee, two persons and craft brought in
July 3   Fishing vessel Gemini, three persons and craft brought in
14   Fishing vessel Venus, escorted craft
Aug 11   Fishing vessel Challenger, three persons and craft brought in
26   Fishing vessel Sardius, three persons and craft brought in
28   Yacht Tio Lobo, three persons and craft brought in
Sep 5   Fishing vessel Emmy Leigh, three and craft brought in
22   Fishing vessel Tamara, four persons and craft brought in
Nov 22   Fishing vessel Challenger, three persons and craft brought in
Dec 13   Fishing vessel Sarah Thinnesen, three persons and craft brought in
2000   Jan 8   Fishing vessel Deep Harmony, two and craft brought in
21   Fishing vessels Rebecca, Orion, Christinanjo and Carrisan, escorted craft
Feb 14   Cabin cruiser Dipper I, two persons and craft brought in
26   Yacht Horizon Quest, two persons and craft brought in
May 16   Fishing vessel Quest, three persons and craft brought in
28   Fishing vessel Regulas, three persons and craft brought in
June 29   Powerboat Cerfin, landed 2 and craft brought in
30   Man fallen from cliff, three persons brought in
July 30   Fishing vessel Two Dogs, two persons and craft brought in
Aug 10   Yacht Aquilla, two persons and craft brought in
15   Fishing vessel Eady D, two persons and craft brought in
22   Fishing vessel Golden Days, two persons and craft brought in
28   Injured crewman on board fishing vessel Jan Maria, one person brought in
Sep 3   Trimaran Sis, assisted to save craft and 1
5   Fishing vessel Emmy Leigh, saved craft and 1
6   Passenger vessel Coronia, escorted craft
20   Trimaran Sis, assisted to save 1
23   Trimaran Sis, gave help
Oct 7   Fishing vessel Eddie-D, landed 3 and craft brought in
23   Fishing vessel Christy G, of Whitby, four persons and craft brought in
28   Fishing vessel Ocean Way, escorted craft
30   Fishing vessel Mary Ann, saved craft and 3
Nov 29   Fishing vessel Christie G, of Whitby, saved craft and 4
Dec 16   Yacht Gay Cygnet, escorted craft
2001   Jan 12   Fishing vessel Maise B, two persons and craft brought in
14   Angling vessel Sea Otter, landed 7 and craft brought in
16   Tug Goliath towing dredger, stood by
Feb 21   Angling craft Kandoo, six persons and craft brought in
Mar 4   Angling craft Kandoo, nine persons and craft brought in
7   Fishing vessel Star Award, three persons and craft brought in

Corinne Whiteley Relief Lifeboat
[on station 23.5–22.6.2001]

31   Fishing vessel Challenger, landed 2 and craft brought in
Apr 27   Yacht Maid of Kyrenia, landed 2 and craft brought in
May 2   Fishing vessel Sedulous, two persons and craft brought in
19   Powerboat Taboo, two persons and craft brought in

June 11   Barge Dutch Barge, two persons and craft brought in
21   Powerboat Jennifer Ann, two persons and craft brought in

George and Mary Webb Lifeboat

23   Fishing vessel Jacqueline Louise, of Whitby, three persons and craft brought in
24   Powerboat Blue Glass, two persons and craft brought in

Corinne Whiteley Relief Lifeboat
[on station 6–22.7.2001]

July 11   Fishing vessel Carol H, landed 4 and craft brought in

George and Mary Webb Lifeboat

Aug 3   Fishing vessel Olivia Rose, four persons and craft brought in
19   Yacht Kilpecon, two persons and craft brought in
26   Yacht Mrs Mouse, escorted craft
Nov 12   Fishing vessel Carol H, escorted craft
18   Pleasure craft Brigand, two persons and craft brought in
Dec 9   Cabin cruiser Vital Spark, two persons and craft brought in

Earl and Countess Mountbatten of Burma Relief Lifeboat
[on station 2.1–22.5.2002]

2002   Feb 28   Fishing vessel Sarah Thinnesen, landed 2
Fishing vessel Shaun Dawn, three and craft brought in
Mar 1   Dredger Sandsend, landed 3 and saved craft
9   Cabin cruiser Merryweather Bahamas, landed 6 and craft brought in
23   Fishing vessel Silver Line, three persons and craft brought in

George and Mary Webb Lifeboat

May 29   Pleasure craft Awd Rope, three persons and craft brought in
June 12   Yacht Nina, two persons and craft brought in
15   Sick man on board angling vessel Sea Otter, landed 1

Macquarie Relief Lifeboat
[on station 19–24.6.2002]

21   Yacht Jason, two persons and craft brought in
24   Yacht Capella Endeavour, four persons and craft brought in

George and Mary Webb Lifeboat

July 13   Speedboat, two persons and craft brought in
31   Yacht Wayward, escorted craft
Aug 13   Fishing vessel, seven persons and craft brought in
26   Yacht Kava, landed 1 and craft brought in
Nov 22   Fishing vessel, escorted
Dec 13   Fishing vessel, two persons and craft brought in
2003   Jan 8   Merchant vessel Trueburg, stood by
Feb 16   Fishing vessel Challenge, two persons and craft brought in
Mar 2   Fishing vessel Our Lass, escorted craft
23   Fishing vessel Fairwater, gave help
Apr 30   Fishing vessel Olivier Rose, three and craft brought in
May 8   Fishing vessel Abby Lee, four persons and craft brought in
24   Cabin cruiser Lorraine, two persons and craft brought in
June 4   Fishing vessel Radiant Morn, four and craft brought in
16   Yacht Spica, two persons and craft brought in
July 10   Fishing vessel Christina, three persons and craft brought in
12   Angling boat Super Leeds, three persons and craft brought in
22   Fishing vessel Sea Harvest, two persons and craft brought in
Aug 10   Speedboat That One, two persons and craft brought in
22   Catamaran Sea Flame 2, two persons and craft brought in
Sep 8   Cabin cruiser Malvina, three persons and craft brought in
30   Fishing vessel Bonny Bu, two persons and craft brought in
Oct 26   Fishing vessel Fulmar, three persons and craft brought in
Nov 10   Fishing vessel Neptune Diver, two and craft brought in
14   Fishing vessel Challenger, landed 2 and saved craft

	Dec 11	Fishing vessel Neptune Diver, two and craft brought in
	16	Fishing vessel Christina, escorted craft
2004	Feb 18	Injured man on research vessel CEFAS Endeavour, escorted
	Mar 6	Fishing vessel Ocean Rose, gave help
		Powered boat Freebooter, escorted craft
	14	Angling boat Achates, five people and craft brought in
	20	Canoes, saved craft
	21	Powered boat Codonger 2, escorted craft
	28	Powered boat Pisces, three people and craft brought in
	Apr 25	Powered boat Sam Jam, escorted craft
	25	Yacht Apollo, three people and craft brought in
	May 22	Powered boat Saint George, four people and craft brought in
	June 6	Fishing vessel Abbie Lee, four people and craft brought in
	8	Fishing vessel Golden Bells, two people and craft brought in
	19	Fishing vessel Kristanjo, escorted craft
	29	Fishing vessel Sea Otter, gave help – assessed situation

John Neville Taylor Relief Lifeboat

Aug 22	Powered boat Brigand, three people and craft brought in

Windsor Runner (C.S.No.42) Relief Lifeboat

24	Fishing vessel Shaun Dawn, three and craft brought in
Sep 24	Fishing vessel Defiant, stood by
25	Person in sea, assisted to save 1
29	Powered boat Belly Dance, one person and craft brought in
Oct 6	Fishing vessel Neptune Diver, two and craft brought in
8	Fishing vessel Nicola Faith, three people and craft brought in
19	Fishing vessel Good Intent, three people and craft brought in

John Neville Taylor Relief Lifeboat

	Nov 20	Fishing vessel Deep Harmony, escorted craft
	21	Angling vessel Sea Otter, stood by
2005	Jan 27	Fishing vessels Defiant, Copius and Rebe, stood by

George and Mary Webb Lifeboat

	Apr 11	Fishing vessel Challenger, gave help – completed tow
	May 6	Powered boat Vikingen, stood by
	June 25	Fishing vessel Copius, four people and craft brought in
	July 8	Fishing vessel Kristanjo under tow by fishing vessel Success,
		gave help – assisted with tow
	8	Fishing vessel Defiant, four people and craft brought in
	Aug 1	Fishing vessel Olivia Rose, four people and craft brought in
	4	Fishing vessel Olivia Rose, four people and craft brought in
	7	Yachts Peg and One Plus Two, escorted craft
	13	Rowing boat Emily Jane, two people and craft brought in
	14	Diver support craft Viking Diver, escorted craft
	17	Yacht Jolly Swagman, two people and craft brought in
	21	Yacht Zwerver, two people and craft brought in
	29	Rowing boat, craft brought in
	Sep 17	Yacht Ladybird, two people and craft brought in
	Oct 1	Powered boat Teddy B, four people and craft brought in
	9	Sick diver on board diver support craft My Clivey, gave help
		– transferred survivor to helicopter
	Nov 13	Fishing vessel Defiance, escorted craft
	29	Powered boat Brian Hartley, four people brought in
2006	Mar 27	Yacht Wild Duck, gave help – completed tow
	30	Yacht Inca, two people and craft brought in
	31	Fishing vessel Codonger Two, two and craft brought in
	Apr 1	Powered boat Avondale, three people and craft brought in
	28	Whitby inshore lifeboat, three people and craft brought in
	May 28	Powered boat Castaway, three people and craft brought in
	June 16	Powered boat Shania, two people and craft brought in
	17	Fishing vessel Challenger, two people and craft brought in
	July 15	Powered boat Safari, two people and craft brought in
	Aug 19	Yacht Katie Ann, two people and craft brought in
	27	Powered boat Castaway, four people and craft brought in
	28	Powered boat Poppy, escorted craft

	Sep 7	Yacht Sea Hawk 2, escorted craft
	8	Fishing vessel Shaun Dawn, stood by
	19	Person cut off by tide, stood by
	Oct 1	Fishing vessel Olivia Rose, three people and craft brought in
	13	Fishing vessel Resolute, escorted craft
	27	Fishing vessel Nicola Faith, escorted craft
	27	Fishing vessels Pride and Joy, Defiant, Codonger and
		Dominator, stood by vessels
	Nov 12	Fishing vessel Our Lass, escorted craft
2007	Jan 27	Fishing vessel Independence, escorted craft
	Feb 6	Powered boat Ill de Yeu, saved 3
	14	Powered boat Misty Blue, stood by
	15	Powered boat Merryweather, two persons and craft
		brought in
	23	Fishing vessel Nicholas M, gave help – moored craft
	26	Yacht Goshawk, gave help – transferred tow to Hartlepool
		lifeboat
	Mar 16	Yacht Suzi 4, one person and craft brought in
	Apr 8	Powered boat Osprey, two persons and craft brought in

John Neville Taylor Relief Lifeboat

28	Yacht Strider, gave help – took over tow from Staithes and
	Runswick lifeboat
May 5	Yacht Kantika, one person and craft brought in
16	Cabin cruiser Striker, one person and craft brought in
22	Fishing vessel Olivia Rose, three persons and craft brought in
27	Diver support craft My Clivey, four and craft brought in
June 29	Angling vessel Chieftain, 15 persons and craft brought in
July 8	Powered boat Sharmel, two people and craft brought in
19	Fishing vessel Neptune Diver, two and craft brought in
Aug 7	Powered boat Mallard, four persons and craft brought in
19	Catamaran Catawumpus, gave help
26	Powered boat Demorak Argus, seven persons and craft
	brought in

George and Mary Webb Lifeboat

	29	Powered boat Bellydancer, one person and craft brought in
	Sep 5	Yacht Gooseander, two people and craft brought in
	15	Angling vessel Tina Dawn, 12 people and craft brought in
	Nov 23	Powered boat Last Call, gave help
2008	Jan 13	Fishing vessel Demarok Argus, three and craft brought in
	28	Fishing vessel, gave help
	Feb 10	Fishing vessel, two persons and craft brought in
		Fishing vessel, two persons and craft brought in
	Apr 25	Persons cut off by tide, landed 5
	May 5	Ill person on board fishing vessel, gave assistance
	June 18	Fishing vessel Independence, craft brought in

Relief lifeboat John Neville Taylor escorts the catamaran Catawumpus into harbour on 19 August 2007. (By courtesy of Whitby RNLI)

Appendix 4: ILB service summary

D-84 inshore lifeboat

1966	July 30	Motor boat Jackie, gave help
1967	May 12	Motor boat, escorted
	25	Boy fallen from cliff, landed a body
	June 4	Yacht Allie, stood by
	Aug 27	Men stranded on Black Rock, saved 2
1968	June 8	Injured man on beach, gave help
	14	Bathing fatality, landed a body
	July 21	Motor boat, gave help
	Aug 18	Motor launch, saved (also a dog) 3
	22	Girls cut off by tide, saved 1
	Sep 9	Persons cut off by tide at Yellow Sands Bight, saved 2
1969	May 6	Motor cruiser in tow of work boat, escorted
	July 12	Motor boat Susan Ann, gave help
	19	Boys stranded on cliff, saved 1
	Aug 11	Three racing gigs, gave help and saved 1
	21	Motor boat, saved boat and 1
1970	May 26	Youths cut off by tide, saved 2
	June 6	Youths cut off by tide, stood by
	Aug 14	Sailing dinghy, saved dinghy and 3
	31	Girls cut off by tide, saved 2
	Sep 11	Sailing dinghy, gave help

D-193 inshore lifeboat

1971	June 27	Motor yacht Philander, of Hull, gave help
	July 7	Motor dinghy, saved dinghy and 3
	Aug 9	Persons cut off by tide, saved 2
	26	Persons cut off by tide, saved 2
	29	Motor boat, escorted
	Sep 4	Yacht Zostara, escorted
		Motor boat, escorted
	Oct 3	Cabin cruiser Banjo, gave help
1972	Apr 2	Persons cut off by tide, saved 4
	4	Anglers cut off by tide, saved 3
	May 9	Youth over cliff, landed 2 and a body
	28	Boys cut off by tide, saved 2
	June 2	Dinghy, saved dinghy and 2
	17	Fishing coble Silver Spray, of Whitby, gave help
	July 1	Persons cut off by tide, saved (also a dog) 4
	10	Wreckage, investigated and gave help
	Aug 24	Persons cut off by tide, saved 2
	25	Children cut off by tide, saved 4
	Sep 24	Motor boat, escorted
	Oct 25	Person fallen from cliff, recovered a body
1973	May 13	Cabin cruiser Masyplu, saved boat and 5

D-87 Relief inshore lifeboat

	July 1	Yacht Moon Eyed, saved 2
	Aug 27	Persons cut off by tide, saved 4
	Sep 1	Dinghy, gave help
	29	Sailing dinghy Running Wild, saved dinghy and 2

D-193 inshore lifeboat

1974	June 12	Dinghy, saved dinghy and 3
	July 5	Persons cut off by tide, gave help
	9	Persons cut off by tide, gave help
	Aug 2	Persons cut off by tide, gave help
	9	Fishing boat Orsinus, landed a sick man
	15	Fishing boat Vooran, landed an injured man
	23	Injured person under a cliff, gave help
	29	Persons trapped on rocks, gave help
	30	Persons cut off by tide, saved 2
	Sep 3	Inflatable dinghy and swimmer, saved dinghy and 1

1975	July 23	Dinghy, saved 1
	25	Stranded angler, saved 1
	Aug 5	Persons on cliff, gave help
	24	Persons stranded, landed 2
1976	June 2	Motor boat, gave help
	11	Persons cut off by tide, landed 2
	19	Cabin cruiser Moby Dick, gave help
	26	Cabin cruiser Mharani, gave help
	July 20	Person stranded on cliff, saved 1
	29	Coble Flora Jane, in tow of a coble, escorted vessels
	Aug 10	Persons cut off by tide, landed 2
	Sep 5	Persons cut off by tide, landed 2
		Cabin cruiser Irene, in tow of motor boat, escorted
	8	Fishing boat Kenlyn, in tow of yacht Galown, escorted
	30	Fishing boat Admiral van Tromp, saved 1
1977	Apr 16	Motor boat, saved 3
	30	Coble Marvalantha, gave help

D-114 Relief inshore lifeboat

	July 19	Persons cut off by tide, saved 2
	23	Speedboat Yabadabadoo, gave help
		Coble, escorted

D-260 Gwynaeth inshore lifeboat

1978	June 21	Man cut off by tide, saved 1
	Aug 25	Sailing dinghy, gave help
1979	Apr 14	Five persons cut off by the tide, saved 5
	June 10	Two canoes, saved one boat and 2
		Raft, landed 2
	July 4	Sick man on fishing coble Alliance, landed a sick man
	Sep 2	Sailing dinghy Puffin, escorted boat
1980	Apr 2	Twenty persons cut off by tide, saved 20

D-205 Relief inshore lifeboat

	6	Cabin cruiser Astgood, gave help
	26	Persons cut off by tide, gave help
	July 5	Motor launch Jennifer Margaret, stood by boat
	13	Boy cut off by tide, saved 1
	14	Rowing boat Janet, saved boat
	Aug 10	Two persons cut off by tide, gave help

D-260 Gwynaeth inshore lifeboat

	27	Two swimmers and lifeguard, saved 3
1981	Apr 8	Seven persons cut off by tide, landed 7
	May 6	Twelve persons cut off by tide,
	June 6	Rubber dinghy, gave help
	July 26	Two children cut off by tide, saved 2
	Aug 2	Two swimmers, landed 2
1982	Mar 27	Motor boat, saved boat and 4
	Apr 2	Fishing vessel, gave help
	25	Person fallen from cliff, gave help
	26	Yacht, craft brought in
	July 17	Person cut off by tide, saved 1
	26	Person cut off by tide, gave help
	Aug 5	Persons cut off by tide, saved 2
	8	Cabin cruiser, craft brought in
	30	Motor boat, landed 2
	Sep 2	Person cut off by tide, gave help
	26	Yacht, gave help
	Oct 30	Persons cut off by tide, saved 2
1983	Mar 31	Persons cut off by tide, saved 2
	Mar 29	Divers, saved 4
	June 8	Persons cut off by tide, saved 2

July 22	Persons cut off by tide, saved 2
23	Fishing vessel, craft brought in
Aug 14	Rubber dinghy, saved 1

D-224 Relief inshore lifeboat

Aug 28	Power boat, gave help
Sep 18	Sailboard, escorted
Oct 9	Persons cut off by tide, saved 2
23	Motor boat, craft brought in

D-260 Gwynaeth inshore lifeboat

1984	Apr 14	Persons cut off by tide, saved 2
	20	Persons cut off by tide, saved 2
	June 16	Persons cut off by tide, gave help
	26	Canoe, saved craft
	July 4	Swimmers, saved 2
	15	Persons cut off by tide, saved 2
	29	Persons cut off by tide, gave help
	Oct 19	Sick person, gave help
1985	Mar 19	Thirty persons cut off by tide, landed 30
	June 1	Five persons cut off by the tide, gave help
	July 22	Cabin cruiser Tallisman, stood by

D-226 Relief inshore lifeboat

| 1986 | May 11 | Two persons cut off by the tide, g help |
| | 26 | Yacht Kabana, gave help |

D-260 Gwynaeth inshore lifeboat

	Aug 3	Cabin cruiser, gave help
	Sep 20	Two persons cut off by the tide, g help
	Oct 4	Two persons cut off by the tide, g help
1987	Apr 2	Body at foot of cliffs, gave help
	26	Boy cut off by tide, gave help
	May 25	Persons cut off by the tide, gave help
	28	Persons cut off by the tide, gave help
	29	Persons cut off by the tide, gave help
	Oct 23	Persons cut off by the tide, landed 1
	24	Persons cut off by the tide, landed 2
	31	Body in water, landed a body
1988	Apr 9	Yacht Cymba, landed a body
	May 28	Two persons cut off by tide, gave help
	June 15	Two persons cut off by tide, gave help
	19	Fishing coble Karen D, of Whitby, stood by
	July 10	Motor launch, gave help
	Aug 1	Motor boat Phil Macoy, gave help

D-369 inshore lifeboat

	Aug 15	Two men cut off by tide, gave help
	17	Rubber dinghy, saved boat
	28	Three persons cut off by tide, gave help
	29	Five persons cut off by tide, gave help
	Sep 9	Two men cut off by tide, gave help
	11	Motor boat Rose, gave help
	Oct 2	Two persons cut off by tide, gave help
1989	Mar 8	Man stranded on cliff, gave help
	26	Three persons cut off by tide, saved 3
	Apr 12	Motor boat Aruba, gave help
	May 9	Body in sea, landed a body
	12	Fishing vessel Golden Hope, g help
	June 4	Speedboat, saved boat
	18	Two persons cut off by tide, saved (and a dog) 2
	July 22	Skin diver, gave help
	Aug 18	Persons cut off by tide, landed 3 and gave help
	28	Two persons cut off by tide, saved 2
	Sep 17	Two persons cut off by tide, gave help
1990	May 7	Persons cut off by the tide, saved 2

	Aug 5	Persons cut off by the tide, landed 4
	9	Persons cut off by the tide, saved 2
	11	Persons cut off by the tide, saved 2
	29	Rubber dinghy, saved 3
1991	Mar 29	Persons cut off by tide, saved 3
	Apr 2	Persons cut off by tide, landed 3
	May 12	Persons cut off by tide, landed 2
	25	Persons cut off by tide, gave help
	26	Persons cut off by tide, saved 5
	July 13	Persons cut off by tide, gave help
	27	Bather drowning, gave help
	29	Fishing vessel Libby B, of Whitby, landed an injured man
	Aug 11	Motor boat, landed craft
		Yacht Vedra, stood by
	25	Persons cut off by tide, landed 3
	26	Persons cut off by tide, gave help
	Sep 18	Fishing vessel, escorted
1992	Feb 7	Persons cut off by tide, landed 2
	May 20	Motor boat, saved boat and 1
	June 12	Persons cut off by tide, saved 3
	July 19	Persons cut off by tide, saved 3
	27	Rowing gigs, saved 8
		Rowing boat, landed craft
		Cabin cruiser, saved craft and 2
	28	Canoe, saved craft and 1
	Aug 10	Persons cut off by tide, saved 2
	13	Persons cut off by tide, saved 4
	22	Sailboard, saved board
	24	Fishing vessel, landed craft
	29	Persons cut off by tide, gave help

D-428 St Vincent Amazon Relief ILB

	Oct 8	Dead body to be recovered, gave help
	11	Persons cut off by tide, gave help
	23	Persons cut off by tide, landed 2

D-369 inshore lifeboat

1993	Feb 20	Power boat, saved 1
	May 7	Person cut off by tide, gave help
	July 3	Person cut off by tide, gave help
		Yacht, escorted
	31	Diver, gave help
	Aug 25	Yacht, escorted
	Oct 26	Fishing vessel, gave help
1994	Apr 30	Two persons cut off by tide, gave help
	May 8	Person cut off by tide, saved 1
	27	Yacht Chenoa, gave help
	June 16	Missing diver, gave help
	16	Diver support craft Dive Action, gave help
	25	Two persons cut off by tide at Yellow Sands, saved 2
	26	Person cut off by tide at Gunny Hole, gave help
	July 3	Fishing coble Pamela Maud, escorted
	23	Eight persons stranded at Gunny Hole, eight brought in
	27	Mine in sea, gave help
	Aug 7	Ten persons cut off by tide, saved 10
	23	Four persons cut off by tide Gave help
		One person (and a dog) cut off by tide, landed 1 (and a dog)
	Nov 20	Injured woman at Hawsker Bottom, one person brought in
		Eight persons cut off by tide, eight persons brought in
1995	May 26	Dog fallen over cliffs, gave help
	July 3	Four persons cut off by tide, four persons brought in
	18	Missing man, gave help
	Aug 15	Rubber dinghy, landed 2 and craft brought in
	Sep 26	Man cut off by tide, saved 1
	Oct 1	Yacht Tsimshian, assisted to save boat and 3
	9	Man fallen from cliffs, assisted to save 1

D-459 Winifred & Cyril Thorpe Relief ILB

1996   Mar 24   Diver support craft C2 Diver, gave help

D-369 inshore lifeboat

	May 29	Two persons cut off by tide, landed 2
	June 15	Rubber dinghy, landed 2 and craft brought in
	July 2	Sixteen persons cut off by tide at Gunny Hole, gave help
	3	Man cut off by tide at Gunny Hole, saved 1
	12	Two persons cut off by tide at Saltwick Nab, saved 2
	21	Rubber dinghy, saved craft and 1
	30	Two persons cut off by tide, two persons brought in
	Aug 3	Two men cut off by tide, landed 2
	15	Two persons cut off by tide, saved 2
	18	Sailing dinghy, landed 1 and craft brought in
	20	Speedboat, escorted craft
	Oct 30	Surfboard, assisted to save 1

D-428 St Vincent Amazon Relief ILB

1997   Apr 2   Five persons cut off by the tide, assisted to save 5
      June 3   Man cut off by the tide, stood by
      10   Car over cliffs, recovered a body
         Car over cliffs, gave help
      July 14   Body in sea, landed a body

D-521 OEM Stone II inshore lifeboat

	July 29	Speedboat, landed 3 and craft brought in
	Aug 5	Two persons in sea, gave help
	22	Yacht Minx, landed 2
	29	Rubber dinghy, saved 2
	31	Diver support craft Ocean Moon, two persons and craft brought in
	Dec 13	Cabin cruiser Old Slapper, gave help

D-371 41 Club III Relief ILB

1998   Mar 19   Inflatable dinghy, five persons and craft brought in
      Apr 14   Motor boat, landed 2 and craft brought in
      June 4   Sailboard, landed 1 and board brought in
      9   Dog in sea, gave help

D-521 OEM Stone II inshore lifeboat

	July 5	Two persons cut off by the tide, two persons brought in
	Aug 5	Four persons cut off by the tide, saved 4
	14	Sailing dinghy, saved craft and 1
	18	Inflatable dinghy, escorted craft
	Nov 21	Two youths cut off by the tide, assisted to save 2
	Dec 19	Man cut off by the tide, saved 1
1999	Feb 17	Woman fallen from cliffs, stood by
	May 1	Speedboat, four persons and craft brought in
		Speedboat, saved craft
	11	Yacht Marantha in tow of fishing vessel Nord, escorted

D-408 City of Derby Relief ILB

	Aug 24	Five persons cut off by the tide, landed 5
	29	Three persons cut off by the tide, landed 3

D-521 OEM Stone II inshore lifeboat

	Nov 27	Human body, landed a body
2000	Mar 21	Two people stranded, saved 2
	May 1	Three persons cut off by the tide, landed 3
	June 29	Powerboat Cerfin, gave help
	30	Man fallen from cliff, gave help
	July 30	Speedboat Blue Moon, four persons and craft brought in
	Aug 28	Six persons cut off by the tide, landed 6
	Oct 30	Yacht, saved craft
	Nov 27	Fishing vessel Stephanie, two persons and craft brought in

2001   Jan 16   Tug Goliath towing dredger, stood by
      July 15   Dive support rigid-inflatable, five persons & craft brought in

D-465 Relief inshore lifeboat

	July 28	Inflatable dinghy, two persons brought in
	29	Sailing dinghy, two persons and craft brought in
	Aug 20	Two persons cut off by the tide, two persons brought in
	Oct 5	Motor cruiser Phoebe, two persons and craft brought in

D-521 OEM Stone II inshore lifeboat

2002   Feb 17   Cabin cruiser Kingfisher, two persons and craft brought in
      Mar 1   Dredger Esk, stood by
      27   Four persons cut off by the tide, saved 4

D-447 Relief inshore lifeboat

	May 25	Two persons cut off by the tide, landed 2
	29	Pleasure craft Awd Rope, gave help
	June 25	Fishing vessel Sea Wraith, two persons and craft brought in
	July 30	Ex tug, escorted craft
	Aug 2	Yachts endangered by flood water, gave help

D-521 OEM Stone II inshore lifeboat

	Sep 8	Fishing vessel, craft brought in
	17	Animal in trouble, gave help
	Oct 23	Motor boat, escorted
	Nov 18	Motor boat, landed 1 and saved 1

D-491 Relief inshore lifeboat

2003   Jan 23   Motor boat Amy Lou, saved 3

D-521 OEM Stone II inshore lifeboat

	Mar 23	Fishing vessel Fairweather, four persons and craft brought in
	Apr 16	Persons cut off by the tide, landed 3
	30	Fishing vessel Olivier Rose, stood by
	May 22	Persons in danger of drowning, one person brought in
	24	Animal in distress, gave help
	28	Fishing vessel Warlock, gave help
	Aug 10	Four persons cut off by the tide, landed 4
	Sep 28	Jet ski, craft brought in
	Nov 9	Person in danger of drowning, saved 1
2004	Mar 20	Canoes, three people landed
	21	Powered boat Codonger 2, stood by

D-470 Relief inshore lifeboat

	Apr 20	Fishing vessel Good Intent, gave help – transferred salvage pump
	May 30	Powered boat, three people and craft brought in
	July 22	Person cut off by tide, one person brought in
	28	Powered boat, escorted craft

D-521 OEM Stone II inshore lifeboat

	Aug 15	Powered boat, one person brought in
	Sep 15	Yacht Inspiration of Dartmouth, stood by
	25	Person in sea, assisted to save 1
	Oct 8	Powered boat, gave help – advised casualty
	19	Fishing vessel Good Intent, gave help – assisted lifeboat
2005	Feb 10	People cut off by tide on shoreline, four persons brought in
	Apr 24	Tender to tall ship Grand Turk, two and craft brought in
	May 6	Powered boat Vikingen, two people and craft brought in
	12	People cut off by the tide, two people landed and three dogs brought in
	25	Powered boat, five people and craft brought in
	28	Yacht Shuna, stood by
	June 4	Four people and dog cut off at Longsands, four people and dog brought in
	22	Persons cut off by tide, four people brought in

Inshore lifeboat D-521 OEM Stone II at the foot of cliffs at Sandsend Ness (left) helping a woman who had fallen 40ft down a cliff on 10 January 2006. The ILB took the woman back to harbour (above) and she was taken to hospital, but only suffered bruising and shock, but no broken bones. (By courtesy of Whitby Gazette)

	July 8	Fishing vessel Kristanjo under tow by fishing vessel Success, stood by
	13	Powered boat Super V, four people and craft brought in
	Aug 17	Yacht Vaylel, two people and craft brought in
	Sep 17	Yacht Ladybird, gave help – assisted to berth
	Oct 9	Sick diver on board dive support craft My Clivey, gave help – administered first aid then transferred survivor to ALB
	Nov 21	Person at risk in sea, two people landed
	29	Powered boat Brian Hartley, gave help
2006	Jan 10	Person in the sea, landed 1
	17	Dog, gave help – recovered dog
	Feb 3	Person at risk on Whitby West Pier, stood by
	Mar 30	Yacht Inca, gave help – established tow
	Apr 28	Sick man, landed 1
	May 28	People cut off by tide, two people brought in
	June 9	Powered boat Misty Blue, escorted craft
	11	Powered boat, gave help – advice given
	12	Fishing vessel Copius, gave help – pumped casualty out
	July 15	Powered boat Safari, gave help
	22	Yacht Trump, four people and craft brought in
	25	Inflatable dinghy, three people and craft brought in
	17 Aug	Jet ski, landed 1
	19 Sep	Person cut off by tide, gave help
	26 Sep	Person cut off by tide, one person brought in
2007	Feb 14	Powered boat Misty Blue, four persons and craft brought in
	22	Surfboard, landed 1
	Mar 7	Dog at risk, gave help – located body

D-674 OEM Stone III inshore lifeboat

	May 30	People stranded on rocks, landed 4

D-512 Jane Ann II Relief inshore lifeboat

	June 2	Human body, landed a body

D-674 OEM Stone III inshore lifeboat

	June 13	People cut off by tide, two persons and four dogs brought in
	July 14	People cut off by tide, two people brought in
	17	People on rocks, two people brought in
	Aug 19	Catamaran Catawumpus, gave help
	Oct 24	Powered boat, escorted craft
	25	People stranded on shoreline, landed 2 and two dogs
2008	Feb 10	People cut off by tide, gave assistance
	Apr 8	People stranded on shoreline, gave assistance
	10	Motor boat, two people and craft brought in
	26	Persons stranded on rocks, gave assistance and saved 1
	27	Injured person on rocks, gave assistance
	May 8	Persons in water, landed 1 and saved 1

Relief inshore lifeboat D-512 Jane Ann II is recovered after launching on a false alarm to reports of someone in difficulty near Robin Hood's Bay, September 2007. While the lifeboat station was under construction between 2005 and 2007 two ILBs were operated, one launched across the beach by Land Rover and kept in one half of the Lifeboat Museum. (Nicholas Leach)

With the completion of the lifeboat station at the Fish Pier in 2007, a davit launching system was introduced for the D class inflatable and pictured is D-674 OEM Stone III about to be lowered into the water alongside the pontoon. (Nicholas Leach)

Appendix 5: Personnel Summary

Honorary Secretaries

Francis Pickernell	1861
Edward W. Chapman	1862 – 3.1892
Gideon W. Smales	1864 – 1877
Captain Robert Gibson	1877 – 2.1904
John W. Foster	2.1904 – 9.1948
Eric Thomson	1948 – 1974
Captain David Stevenson	1974 – 1976
Captain Gordon Cook	1976 – 1977
Ben M. B. Dean	1978 – 1980
Leslie Heath	1980 – 1991
Arnold G. Harper	1991 – 1998
Leslie Heath	1998 – 11.2003
Roy Weatherill	11.2003 –

Coxswains (pulling lifeboats)

John Storr	? – 1861
J. Pickering	1861 – 1876
Samuel Lacey	1861 – 1874
Henry Freeman	1874 – 1899
Thomas Smith Langlands	1899 – 1919
Richard Eglon	1919 – 1920
Thomas McGarry Kelly	1920 – 1923
Jospeh O. Tomlinson	1923 – 1931
Thomas W. Welham	1931 – 1936
James Murfield	1936 – 1939
Wilfred Elder	1939 – 1940
Henry Richardson	1940 – 1946
Wilfred Elder	1946 – 1952
Edward Verril	1952 – 1958

Coxswains (motor lifeboats)

Thomas Smith Langlands	1919 – 1920
Richard Eglon	1920 – 9.1923
Thomas McGarry Kelly	1923 – 1931
Robert Harland	1931 – 1935
David Harland	1935 – 5.1938
James Murfield	5.1939 – 1940
Wilfred Elder	1940 – 1941
Harry Murfield	1941 – 1947
Robert William Richardson	1947 – 1953
Eric Charles Taylor	2.1953 – 1962
William Harland	11.1962 – 1974
Robert Allen	1974 – 3.1977
Peter Thomson (Cox/Mech)	17.3.1977 – 1993
Keith G. Stuart	18.9.1993 – 8.2002
Michael C. Russell	8.2002 –

Eric Thomson served as Honorary Secretary from 1948 to 1974 and was the prime mover behind the setting up of the Lifeboat Museum in the late 1950s. (By courtesy of Whitby RNLI)

Lifeboat Operations Manager Roy Weatherill is Whitby born and bred, and comes from a long line of lifeboatmen. His great grandfather was Coxswain David Harland, and Robert Harland was his great great grandfather. (Nicholas Leach)

Mike Russell was appointed Coxswain in August 2002 after being crew since 1986. Originally a fisherman, he became Emergency Coxswain in 1993, Second Coxswain in 1997 and was appointed as full-time Coxswain in 2007. (Nicholas Leach)

Second Coxswains (pulling lifeboats)

James Pounder	? – 1881
Richard Eglon	1899 – 1919
Edward Josh	10.1919 – 9.1921
Robert Harland	10.1921 – 1923
James Kelly	10.1923 – 9.1930
Thomas W. Welham	1930 – 1931
David Harland	1931 – 1936
Wilfred Elder	1937 – 1946
Edward Verrill	1946 – 1952
Alfred F. Noble	1952 – 1955
William Noble	1955 – 1957

Second Coxswains (motor lifeboats)

Joseph Tomlinson	10.1919 – 1923
Robert Harland	10.1923 – 9.1931
David Harland	10.1931 – 9.1936
Henry Murfield	10.1936 – 9.1939
John R. Dryden (Acting)	10.1939 – 6.1940
Wilfred Elder	6 – 10.1940
Christopher Wale	10.1940 – 12.1943
Elliott Duke	1.1945 – 1963
Robert H. L. Pennock	1963 – 1974
Peter Thomson (joint Cox/Mech)	1974 – 1977
Terence Hansell	1977 – 2.1979
Dennis Carrick	2.1979 – 7.1980
Michael R. Coates	7.1980 – 1989
Keith Stuart	1989 – 9.1993
Keith Elliott	1993 – 1997
Michael C. Russell	1997 – 8.2002
John Pearson	8.2002 – 8.2006
Nicholas Botham	8.2006 –

Mechanics

William G. Hudson	1920 – 1938
James Philpott	1938 – 1951
William Dryden	1951 – 1967
Peter Thomson (later joint C/M)	7.1967 – 9.1993
Glenn Edmund Goodberry	1.9.1993 –

William Dryden served as Mechanic for sixteen years on board Mary Ann Hepworth. (By courtesy of Whitby Lifeboat Museum)

Glenn Goodberry was appointed full-time Mechanic in September 1993 after more than ten years as a volunteer. He first joined the crew in 1982, and served on both the inshore and offshore boats. He has lived in Whitby almost all his life. (Nicholas Leach)

Nick Botham, appointed Second Coxswain in 2006, joined the crew in 1983. (By courtesy of Whitby RNLI)

Appendix 6: What became of the lifeboats?

Robert and Mary Ellis (on station 1909–1934)

Robert and Mary Ellis was sold out of service on 8 March 1934 for £60 to Captain W. Milburn, of Whitby. She was converted into a houseboat named Highlander, as pictured, and was normally kept at Mexborough, South Yorkshire. In the late 1990s, she was based on the river Ouse at York being used as a pleasure boat-cum-home by a couple who had owned her since the 1970s. By 2000, still named Highlander, she was kept at Landel Gate, York, but moved to Thorne for the winter. (By courtesy of Tony Denton)

Jacob and Rachel Vallentine (on station 1938–1947)

Jacob and Rachel Vallentine was sold out of service on 1 July 1947 for £250 to the Whitby Boatbuilding Company. She was converted into a yacht named Janderval with a tonnage of 7.53 gross under the ownership of T. H. Smails. Registered in Whitby, she was fitted with a single six-cylinder Morris petrol engine. She was kept in Whitby for a number of years, but by the 1990s had been moved to York, and in May 1993 was at the Naburn Marina in the city, where she was broken up and burnt some time later. (By courtesy of Tony Denton)

William Riley of Leamington and Birmingham (on station 1919–1931)

William Riley was sold out of service in November 1931 for £35 to B. Greenstreet, of Hoe Street, Walthamstow, and, with a cabin added, was converted into a yacht named Whitby II. She was later owned by Horace Redding, of Kidderminster, and from the early 1980s by Steve Smith, of Stourport Builders, Redstone Wharf, Sandy Lane, Stourport. He kept her on the river Severn at Stourport and had her restored and refurbished in 1982, when she was fitted with a 2.2-litre BMC diesel engine. By the late 1980s she had been moved to Barnstaple, in North Devon, and was berthed on the south side of the river Taw, at Rolle Quay, named William Riley. She was then used for a number of years as a pleasure boat. In 2001 she was acquired by Andrew Bailey, had a new cabin added and was fitted with a stern-mounted engine.

Her situation changed after she broke her moorings in the Taw and collided with a bridge at Barnstaple. This almost destroyed the wheelhouse and she settled on a mooring post which holed her below the waterline. She remained there, in a semi-derelict state, her condition worsening, and her then owner decided to dispose of her. Dave Charlton, a fund-raiser for the RNLI in the north-east, discovered her and, realising her historical importance to Whitby, organised her purchase. In August 2005, a group from Whitby, led by Charlton, managed to patch her up sufficiently to get her to float down to a quayside from where a crane could lift her out of the water and onto a lorry. She was brought back to Whitby by low-loader, provided free by Dowson and Robinson Ltd, for complete restoration.

She was moved to Cross Butts Farm after owner John Morley gave permission for her to be restored in one of his farm buildings on the outskirts of Whitby. Parts of the keel had disintegrated and there were numerous holes in the hull so the boat was stripped down and the rotten wood removed. Much of the keel was replaced with fresh oak, and the hull's damaged mahogany was rebuilt using mahogany laminate. Work was carried out by volunteers with donations from suppliers, craftsmen and a grant from the Heritage Lottery Fund. In April 2008 the boat was taken afloat for her maiden voyage on the Esk. She was officially unveiled at a special ceremony on 1 June 2008, and in July 2008 she was rowed from the Tyne to Whitby via Sunderland, Hartlepool and Staithes as part of a fund-raising event.

William Riley at Ilfracombe in August 2000. She was used for many years as a pleasure boat around harbours on the Bristol Channel, and could often be seen around the ports of the West Country. (Nicholas Leach)

William Riley at Whitby in August 2005 on the back of the low-loader used to transport her back to her home port. She had just arrived from the West Country, and plans were being made to restore her to her original condition, make her seaworthy and then use her for fund-raising for the RNLI. (Nicholas Leach)

William Riley at Cross Butts Farm on the outskirts of Whitby in October 2005 before restoration work began. She was kept here, under cover, throughout the extensive restoration process, which included rebuilding the keel and parts of the hull. The intention was to restore William Riley so that she could become the centrepiece of a project to illustrate Whitby's historic connections with the lifeboat service. (Nicholas Leach)

William Riley enters Whitby harbour on lifeboat day, 13 July 2008, after being rowed south from the Tyne over the course of several days. This was her first trip following the complete restoration, and involved calls at Sunderland, Hartlepool and Staithes before the final leg of the journey saw her arrive on lifeboat day and the Blessing of the Boats ceremony on the Fish Pier. She was escorted into Whitby harbour by former lifeboat Mary Ann Hepworth, current lifeboat George and Mary Webb, inshore lifeboat D-674, Staithes Atlantic 75 and Runswick private ILB. (Nicholas Leach)

Robert and Ellen Robson (on station 1947–57)

The last pulling and sailing lifeboat to serve at Whitby, and indeed the last in RNLI service, Robert and Ellen Robson was withdrawn from operational duties in November 1957. A decision was made to retain this historic lifeboat for display purposes, and from July 1958 she became the centrepiece at the newly-created Whitby Lifeboat Museum, utilising the double boathouse on Pier Road where she had been based during her life-saving career. She has remained on display there ever since apart from a few moves for different reasons. In 1974, she was taken down to Plymouth for display as part of the RNLI's 150th anniversary celebrations, alongside a number of other former lifeboats. During 2006-07, while the new lifeboat house was being built on the East Side, she was moved into storage so that half of the double boathouse could be used for operational purposes and house one of the two D class inflatables. She returned to her home in the boathouse towards the end of 2007, and remains the most significant exhibit at the Museum. (Nicholas Leach)

Robert and Ellen Robson launching across the West Beach for lifeboat day in the early 1980s. She has since become a static only display in the Lifeboat Museum and is no longer taken afloat. (By courtesy of Whitby Lifeboat Museum)

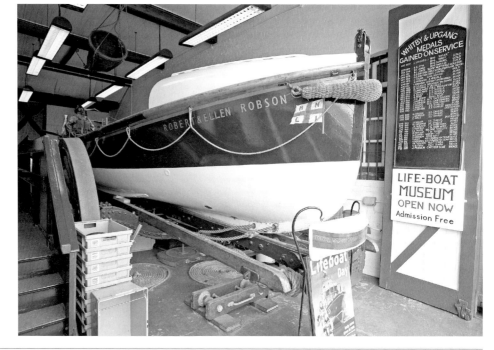

Robert and Ellen Robson on display inside the Lifeboat Museum, occupying one half of the historic 1895 former lifeboat house and forming the centrepiece of the displays. (Nicholas Leach)

Mary Ann Hepworth (on station 1938–1974)

Having become the longest-serving lifeboat at Whitby, Mary Ann Hepworth was sold out of service in July 1974 to W. J. Aldiss, of Sparrow Hill, Hindringham, Fakenham, Norfolk. She was later owned by Ronnie Blaymire, of Newark. Her hull was hollowed out forward of the forward cockpit to provide sleeping, cooking and toilet facilities and a glass hatch was built over the cockpit, but she remained essentially the same externally. In September 1980 she was taken via Great Yarmouth and inland at the Wash to a temporary berth in a boatyard on the Norfolk Broads, and was berthed at Newark during the early 1980s. She was subsequently sold and taken back to Whitby during the mid-1990s and was used as a trip boat, taking holiday-makers for trips out to sea, owned by former lifeboatman Barry Sneddon. Her season runs each year from about April to October and she is a regular sight in Whitby harbour. (Nicholas Leach)

Mary Ann Hepworth entering Whitby harbour having remained largely unaltered externally in private ownership. Her engine housing is painted white, but has subsequently been stripped back to the original. The boat has been used for the TV programme Heartbeat. (By courtesy of Whitby Lifeboat Museum)

Mary Ann Hepworth flying the RNLI flag as she leaves harbour with trippers, July 2008. (Nicholas Leach)

The White Rose of Yorkshire (on station 1974–1988)

Sold out of service on 15 March 1999 to the Canadian Lifeboat Institution for service at the Roberts Bank station, just south of Vancouver. Before being shipped to Canada via Sheerness, she took part in the parade of historic lifeboats organised for the RNLI's 175th anniversary celebrations at Poole. During 2007, her owners, the Roberts Bank Lifeboat Society, began an appeal to raise money for a faster boat to replace her. (Nicholas Leach)

City of Sheffield (on station 1988–1996)

After being replaced at Whitby, City of Sheffield served at a number of stations, including Ramsgate, Hartlepool and in the Relief Fleet. She was stationed at Poole in September 2001 and is one of two lifeboats to serve the station, one of the busiest in the UK. (Nicholas Leach)